The Stonehenge Landscape

The Stonehenge Landscape

Mark Bowden, Sharon Soutar, David Field and Martyn Barber

with contributions by
Neil Linford, Paul Linford and Andy Payne

Published by Historic England, The Engine House, Fire Fly Avenue, Swindon SN2 2EH
www.HistoricEngland.org.uk

Historic England is a Government service championing England's heritage and giving expert, constructive advice, and the English Heritage Trust is a charity caring for the National Heritage Collection of more than 400 historic properties and their collections.

First published 2015
Reprinted with corrections 2017

ISBN 978 1 84802 116 7

British Library Cataloguing in Publication data
A CIP catalogue record for this book is available from the British Library.

For more information about images from the Archive, contact Archives Services Team, The Engine House, Fire Fly Avenue, Swindon SN2 2EH; telephone (01793) 414600.

Brought to publication by Jess Ward, Publishing, Historic England.

Typeset in Charter 9.5/11.75 and 9.5/12.75

Graphics by Deborah Cunliffe and Sharon Soutar with guidance from Trevor Pearson
Reconstruction illustrations by Judith Dobie
Aerial photographs by Damian Grady
Photographs by James O Davies
Edited by Merle Read
Proofread by Kim Bishop
Indexed by Mark Bowden
Page layout by Hybert Design Ltd, UK
Printed in the UK by Gomer Press Ltd.

Front cover: In low winter sun and frost, on 10 January 2010, the earthworks to the north of Stonehenge (top right) are seen in exceptional detail. They include sink holes, barrows, the Avenue, the unfinished 18th-century road, old field boundaries, quarries, unexplained platforms and modern service trenches. (NMR 26554/021)

Frontispiece: Cursus Group barrows Amesbury 45, 46 and 47 in the foreground with the New King Barrows Amesbury 30 and 31 on the King Barrow Ridge behind. (DP101873)

P x: Extract from Philip Crocker's 'Map of Stonehenge and Its Environs'. (Taken from Hoare 1812 opp p 170)

CONTENTS

Stonehenge is arguably the greatest prehistoric monument in western Europe: as a World Heritage Site it ranks in significance with the Acropolis, the Pyramids of Giza or Great Zimbabwe. English Heritage is proud to have this dramatic and unique structure in its care.

Stonehenge sits at the heart of a landscape rich in other monuments and remains of the Neolithic period and Bronze Age that are also part of the World Heritage Site. English Heritage and Historic England promotes and conserves this landscape in partnership with other public bodies such as the National Trust, the Ministry of Defence, Amesbury Town Council, Wiltshire Council, the Royal Society for the Protection of Birds, and Natural England, and a number of private landowners. Together we are committed to preserving this landscape and also to enhancing the visitor experience. To this end we have worked hard to win back something of the former tranquillity of this area of downland, which has culminated in the closure and turfing over of part of the Amesbury–Shrewton road and the opening of a new visitor centre in December 2013.

Knowledge of Stonehenge and its surroundings has grown through the activities of antiquaries since at least the 17th century and major campaigns of archaeological excavation in the 20th, often sponsored by Historic England or its pre-decessors. Despite this effort over nearly 400 years, many aspects of Stonehenge itself and its surroundings remained poorly understood. However, the early years of the 21st century have seen an unprecedented level of research into this extraordinary place. This has involved a number of teams from academic institutions from Britain and abroad, as well as Historic England's own staff, who have brought to bear a suite of non-invasive survey techniques, both modern and traditional, to advance understanding of the prehistoric complex and to assess the impact of later developments in the landscape. This has resulted both in new discoveries and in reinterpretations of well-known sites, including Stonehenge itself, which are of interest in themselves and are also of value to those who manage the landscape. All of these discoveries have been presented in technical reports (see Appendix) but the most significant results of this work are presented here. It is hoped that readers will use this book, in conjunction with the recently published English Heritage map *Exploring the World Heritage Site: Stonehenge and Avebury*, as well as some of the other publications listed, to discover for themselves the wealth of archaeological treasures, both visible and hidden, within this most mysterious of landscapes.

Sir Laurie Magnus
Chairman
Historic England

ACKNOWLEDGEMENTS

The project was initiated by Pete Topping, then head of the Archaeological Survey and Investigation Team at English Heritage, who also took part in fieldwork. The project was completed and brought to publication by the newly formed Assessment Team assisted by colleagues in the Visualisation and Imaging Team and the Remote Sensing Team.

Fieldwork was undertaken by the authors with Elaine Jamieson (Normanton Down and Wilsford barrows), Nicky Smith (Stonehenge) and Trevor Pearson (Cursus, Stonehenge), assisted by Lynn Amadio (Cursus barrows), Andy Crispe (Cursus), Deborah Cunliffe (Stonehenge), Rachel Foster (Avenue and Stonehenge Bottom), Abby Hunt (Lake barrows), Sarah Newsome (Winterbourne Stoke), Matthew Reynolds (Avenue and Stonehenge Bottom) and Phil Sinton and John Vallender (Cursus). A number of people on the English Heritage Professional Placements In Conservation scheme – Kate Barrett, Sam Bax, Andrew Burns and Anna Komar – worked on the project at various times. One person on the Historic Environment Placement scheme, Zoe Edwards, also contributed to the project in the latter stages.

The surveys of earthworks at Lake and West Amesbury published here were undertaken for the Royal Commission on the Historical Monuments of England by Carenza Lewis, David McOmish and Paul Pattison in 1986.

Geophysical survey was undertaken by Neil Linford, Paul Linford and Andy Payne, and architectural assessment by Barry Jones, Rebecca Lane, Olivia Horsfall Turner and Nigel Fradgley. Aerial photographic transcription and interpretation was all done in advance of this project by Simon Crutchley, Fiona Small, Cathy Stoertz and Helen Winton.

Other EH colleagues (and former colleagues) who assisted with the project are: Paul Bryan (management of laser scanning); Judith Dobie (reconstruction paintings); Peter Marshall (information and discussion of scientific dating); Stonehenge site staff, especially Tim Daw and Simon Banton; and David Andrews, Justine Bayley, Isabelle Bedu, Allan Brodie, Graham Brown, Peter Carson, Emma Carver, Amanda Chadburn, Mick Clowes, Nicky Cryer, Andrew David, James Davies, Ursula Dugard-Craig, Felicity Gilmour, Damian Grady, Susan Greaney, Luke Griffin, Nicola Hembrey, Helen Jurga, Louise Martin, David McOmish, Diane Sims and Beth Thomas.

We are especially grateful to colleagues outside EH who made their expertise available: Andrew Dobson (Greenhatch Group); Caroline Hardie (Archaeo-Environment Ltd); Lorna Haycock (Wiltshire Heritage Library); Jacopo Sala (3d-Radar); Dorothy Treasure and Avis Lloyd (Wiltshire Buildings Record); and Joanna and David Bird, Henry Chapman, Ros Cleal, Ben Cooke, Jon Cotton, David Dawson, Jane Ellis-Schön, Stephen Fisher, Paul Garwood, Adrian Green, Roger Green, Martin Henig, David Jacques, Clare King, Clément Nicolas, Mike Parker Pearson, Mike Pitts, Josh Pollard, Lew Somers and Ron Yorston.

A special debt of gratitude is due to the landowners, tenants and occupants of the landscape and its buildings. At the National Trust we received help particularly from Lucy Evershed, Chris Gingell, Martin Papworth, Mike Dando and Nick Snashall, and at Defence Estates from Richard Osgood and Sgt John Clark. EH would particularly like to thank Peter Bailey (Springbottom Farm, Lake Estate), Ian Baxter (Durrington Down Farm), John Elliot (Druids Lodge Estate), Max Hosier (Boreland Farm), Carole Kent-Robinson (Wilsford Manor), Robert Turner and Tracé Williams (RSPB).

The Project Board was a fluid body consisting of, at various times, several of those mentioned above and Mike Allen, Paul Backhouse, Eamonn Baldwin, Tim Darvill, Renee Fok, Vince Gaffney, Jim Gunter, Pete Herring, David Hinton, Jonathan Last, Andrew Lawson, Ian Leonard, Stuart Maughan, Stuart Needham, Melanie Pomeroy-Kellinger and David Vaughan.

The authors are particularly grateful for comments on earlier drafts of the book from Susan Greaney, Pete Herring, Jonathan Last, Stuart Needham and Mike Parker Pearson.

SUMMARY

The Stonehenge World Heritage Site (WHS) Landscape Project, started in 2009 by the then English Heritage Archaeological Survey and Investigation Team, was set up to ensure that there is a full and up-to-date record and understanding of all upstanding archaeological monuments within the WHS. Neither the earthworks of Stonehenge itself nor many of the surrounding upstanding monuments had previously been surveyed by archaeologists to modern standards. With the opportunity to re-present this unique monument and its environs to a global audience through the new visitor centre, it was considered vital that this situation was rectified.

The project included surveys of Stonehenge itself, the Avenue, the Greater Cursus, all the principal barrow cemeteries and several sites of later date within the WHS, in detail; this amounts to just over 15 per cent of the total area of the WHS and includes nearly half of the known or suspected round barrows (that is, nearly all of those surviving as earthworks). A range of non-invasive techniques was employed – earthwork, aerial and geophysical surveys and documentary research. At the same time historic buildings within the WHS were assessed, a laser scan of the stones of Stonehenge was commissioned and new photography of the surrounding landscape was undertaken. The project involved colleagues from numerous teams within English Heritage (EH) and external contractors, and has provided training opportunities for a number of placements. This project has run alongside several university-based projects that have been studying aspects of Stonehenge and its landscape simultaneously – notably the Stonehenge Riverside Project, the Bournemouth University/Deutsches Archäologisches Institut Project and the Stonehenge Hidden Landscapes Project, as well as the recent chronological modelling programme.

A number of important discoveries have resulted from this project. At Stonehenge itself the possibility that the so-called 'North Barrow' may be a small henge enclosure and one of the earliest elements of the site has perhaps been one of the most significant observations, but there is also a slight, previously unrecorded mound beneath the south-eastern quadrant of the stone settings. It has been possible to demonstrate that this mound is unlikely to be the result of recent disturbance, but its significance remains a matter for debate. High-resolution magnetic and ground-penetrating radar (GPR) survey within the 'Stonehenge Triangle' complements the existing geophysical data and the new earthwork survey. It has added significant evidence for the existence of small henge-like monuments under the barrows immediately to the west of the stones, on Stonehenge Down, similar to those simultaneously recognised further away under Amesbury 50. Surveys of the barrow cemeteries have revealed details of chronological development, both of individual mounds and of the cemeteries. At the Wilsford barrow group, for instance, one of the least studied of the Stonehenge cemeteries, it has proved possible, using a combination of antiquarian, field and aerial photographic evidence, to construct a fairly detailed chronology, though many of the individual mounds have been extensively levelled by modern ploughing. Indeed, one of the more distressing (though not unexpected) discoveries has been the extent to which so much of the chalk downland, which had survived as pasture for centuries or millennia, was damaged by the plough in the mid-20th century, with scant respect shown for the ancient monuments. Happily, there have been significant improvements to the management regime in some of these areas over the last few decades. More land is being returned to grass through Environmental Stewardship agreements (agri-environment schemes), and other barrows surviving in woodland are being cleared of trees and scrub.

The later history of this landscape, so often neglected – understandably, given the pre-eminence of its Neolithic and Bronze Age remains – has been a particular focus. The medieval village remains at Lake and West Amesbury have been studied, and some unexpected survivals in the few standing buildings within the WHS have been discovered, including an 18th-century aisled barn concealed by its conversion into cottages in the 1930s. The impact of post-medieval emparkment, 'improved' farming practices and route ways – including the turnpike roads – have also been reviewed. The influence of the Arts and Crafts Movement of the early 20th century on the architecture of the Avon valley is also notable; it made an impact on rural life as well as on the architecture of the area, but also on Stonehenge itself, through the involvement of Detmar Blow. Blow's work initiated a period of 'restoration' of Stonehenge and its immediate environs that lasted for much of the 20th century. But one of the most interesting recent aspects of the Stonehenge landscape is its important role in early aviation history – from the 1909 flying experiments at Larkhill to the establishment of Stonehenge Aerodrome itself during the First World War. Slight earthworks from the buildings of the aerodrome are still traceable to the west of the stones.

The research reported here was undertaken by English Heritage between 2009 and 2012. In 2015 the organisation split into two separate bodies and the staff responsible for the research are now part of Historic England while Stonehenge continues to be cared for by English Heritage.

Stonehenge

There are many good recent descriptions of Stonehenge itself (for example Burl 2006; Darvill 2006; Lawson 2007, 177–97; J Richards 2007, 2013; Johnson 2008, 94–174; Field *et al* forthcoming a, b) and the detail of these will not be repeated here, except where recent work throws new light.

Chronology

Despite the recent refinements in scientific dating through Bayesian statistics (Bronk Ramsey 2009), the chronology of Stonehenge, and even more so of other monuments in the Stonehenge landscape, remains imprecise; while some events are relatively well dated, others remain uncertain.

For the purposes of this book we have adopted the current 'consensus' model for the chronology of the monument itself (Darvill *et al* 2012; Marshall *et al* 2012).

Radiocarbon dates are quoted as calibrated calendar date ranges at 95 per cent confidence (cal BC or cal AD expressed as BC or AD) according to the latest available analyses. Further scientific details can be found in the references cited.

Various types of prehistoric pottery are mentioned in the text: in each case a broad date range is indicated at the first occurrence, but for further details the reader is directed to Gibson (2002).

Barrow numbering system

Several different numbering systems have been applied to the barrows at various times in the past, beginning with early researchers such as Richard Colt Hoare (1812). The parish numbering system developed by the Revd E H Goddard (1914) and followed by L V Grinsell (1957) and the Royal Commission on the Historical Monuments of England (RCHME 1979) has been used here, as it is the most widely recognised system.

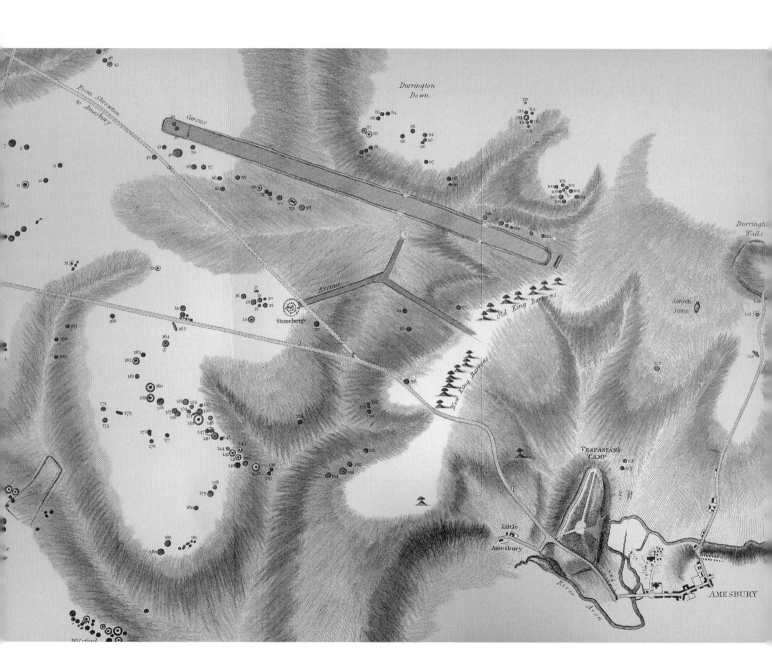

'Let me call the attention of my readers to the annexed map of STONEHENGE, and its environs, in which the hills, roads, antiquities, and barrows are accurately laid down, from actual measurement. In it you will find a striking picture of ancient times. You will see the spot selected by the earliest inhabitants of our island for their residence; you will behold that stupendous monument of antiquity, STONEHENGE, the building set apart for their civil or religious assemblies: you will perceive its connexion, by means of the AVENUE, with the cursus, a spot appropriated to their games, and races; you will recognise also in the camp vulgarly attributed to the Emperor Vespasian, the strong-hold of the Britons, or the asylum for their families and herds in times of danger: at Durrington, and on Winterbourn Stoke Downs, you will see the habitations of the Britons, with the lines of communication, from one village to another; and in the numerous barrows dispersed over this extensive plain, you will distinguish the simple memorials of the mighty dead. In short, you will have clearly traced to your imagination's eye a most impressive history of our ancient Britons.'

Sir Richard Colt Hoare (1812, 170–1), on Philip Crocker's 'Map of Stonehenge and Its Environs'

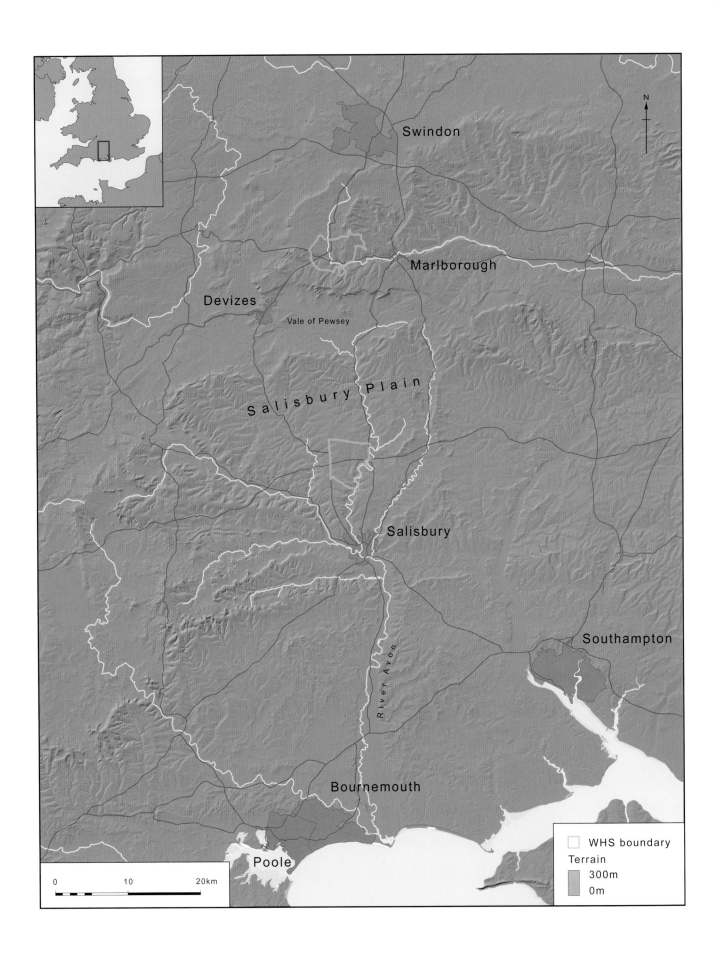

Swindon

Marlborough

Devizes

Vale of Pewsey

S a l i s b u r y   P l a i n

Salisbury

River Avon

Southampton

Bournemouth

Poole

WHS boundary

Terrain

300m

0m

0   10   20km

1

Introduction

Archaeology begins here. Stonehenge occupies a central position in one of the most heavily studied archaeological regions in Europe, with recorded research beginning in the 1620s. The Stonehenge World Heritage Site (WHS) lies on the chalk downs of southern England, on the southern edge of Salisbury Plain (Fig 1.1). The landscape today is one of undulating downland between the Rivers Avon and Till under grass or arable, with plantations and shelter belts of trees. Apart from the roads and military building along the northern edge there is apparently little obtrusive modern clutter (Fig 1.2), though when the area is studied in detail the reality is rather more complicated (*see* Chapter 7). High ground lies around the periphery. Stonehenge, therefore, though it is situated on the end of the spur of Stonehenge Down, is within a bowl; from many viewpoints the stones are inconspic-uous or invisible, but are dramatically skylined from others. The landscape is open and would have been so in prehistory: the latest research indicates that this downland never was heavily wooded but has remained since the last Ice Age broadly as we see it today; in detail, however, it was very different.

This chapter considers the underlying geology of the landscape. It then recounts briefly the history of previous antiquarian and archaeological research in the area before introducing the most recent phase of English Heritage research, the Stonehenge WHS Landscape Project.

Geology and topography

The underlying material is chalk, a soft rock that weathers easily, resulting in a characteris-tic landscape of undulating hills that is referred

Fig 1.1 (opposite)
The location of the Stonehenge, Avebury and Associated Sites World Heritage Site, central southern England. The WHS is in two parts: the Avebury part, which is not covered in this book, lies to the north, near Marlborough.

Fig 1.2
Aerial view of the Stonehenge landscape, looking west from the monument itself towards the new visitor centre and the Till valley, with the Greater Cursus and Cursus barrow group to the right; other barrows and the slight earthworks of field systems and the Stonehenge Aerodrome can be seen centre and left (10 December 2012).
(NMR 27659/028)

to as Salisbury Plain. It is part of a deposit, more than 200m thick, that rises steadily northwards to an escarpment overlooking the Vale of Pewsey and decreases in height southwards beyond Salisbury. It is generally considered to consist of three deposits, the Upper, Middle and Lower Chalk, within each of which is a series of members distinguished by the different nature of the chalk deposits.

For the most part the WHS area comprises Upper Chalk, the upper levels of which incorporate bands of grey flint nodules with thick white cortex. These occur close to the surface in places and outcrop on slopes such as Rox Hill and Oatlands Hill. These almost impenetrable layers provide perched water tables, and water can issue from outcropping seams during wet weather, but where on or close to the surface can affect ploughshares and may have discouraged cultivation. Except where a covering of Clay-with-Flints survives, the chalk is generally extremely porous and this has influenced land use, but seams of hard chalk and, to a degree, flint have also provided construction materials for farm buildings.

The chief components of the topography are the result of marine transgressions during the Eocene (55–38 million years ago) and Late Pliocene (5–1.6 million years ago) that cut benches at around 200m and 120m above Ordnance Datum (OD), leaving Sidbury Hill to the north-east and parts of Beacon Hill to the east as islands, both with deposits of Tertiary pebbles.

The slighter folds visible in the landscape today are the result of a series of episodes of glacial and periglacial conditions during the Quaternary period (1.6 million years ago to the present). Combes, such as that at Wilsford, are invariably the result of spring sapping (Sparks and Lewis 1958, 26–36), but this may be enhanced by soil movement induced by an annual cycle of freezing and thawing during cold periods. The west sides of valleys, such as Stonehenge Bottom, that faced the morning sun melted at a quicker rate and suffered greater solifluction, leaving asymmetrically profiled valleys. Even today winter frost on the east side of Stonehenge Bottom often does not melt until late afternoon.

Ice sheets did not reach the area during the later glaciations, but it would have been subject to permafrost. Following cold periods the annual process of thawing and freezing encouraged the widespread solifluction and gelifluction of old surfaces, and the material would have been carried far downstream by meltwaters. It is likely that Stonehenge Bottom and its dependent side valleys were formed by this process. Inspection by Mike Allen during fieldwork in the 1980s indicated that no colluvium existed in the Bottom, so any material has probably been swept away by flowing water (Richards 1990, 210–11).

Remnant high points within the WHS are largely around its periphery (Fig 1.3), at Rox Hill, at the western end of Stonehenge Down, on the Greenland Farm Ridge and on the King Barrow Ridge, where a capping of Clay-with-Flints over the chalk extends south towards Lake. Beyond the WHS boundary the land rises to Oatlands Hill south-west of the Winterbourne Stoke Crossroads and to the north, rising steadily to Knighton (147m OD) beyond Larkhill. Beacon Hill, to the east of the Avon, dominates all at 204m OD. The intervening landscape undulates – rather more than is obvious to the casual visitor – with rounded hills, ridges, dry valleys and re-entrant combes.

The process of freeze/thaw also left the surface of the ground cracked and pockmarked with involutions and striped areas where water had collected and frozen, forming patterns. Widespread evidence of this has been revealed by archaeological excavation at, for example, Greenland Farm (Evans 1968, 21), Stonehenge (Cleal et al 1995, 42) and the Stonehenge Avenue (Parker Pearson 2012, 244–5), and can sometimes be seen on the surface. Extensive spreads of soil stripes have been observed elsewhere on the chalk (McOmish et al 2002, 7). Sink holes, often referred to as swallow holes, occur in places – fissures in the chalk enlarged by acid rainwater suffer material collapses, leaving depressions at the surface. Surface drainage sometimes utilises these features. They are frequent on the Marlborough Downs and elsewhere, particularly at the boundaries of areas of Clay-with-Flints or remnant Tertiary covering, and seem to be present around Stonehenge (Geddes 2000, 167–8, 175–7; see Chapter 3).

The chalk topography reflects the southerly trending drainage. The major river, the Avon, rises in Pewsey Vale 18km to the north and discharges into the English Channel some 50km to the south. Just 8km to the west the River Till, now little more than a stream, similarly flows southwards, joining the Wylye before issuing into the Avon. Set between these rivers, Stonehenge is located on the lip of a currently dry and deeply incised intervening combe – Stonehenge Bottom – which joins the Avon 3km to the south at Lake. These all lie at much lower elevations, the main river valley of the Avon being around or below 60m OD and the Till at around 70m; Stonehenge Bottom is at about 85m OD at the Avenue and 80m OD to the south of the A303 (Fig 1.4).

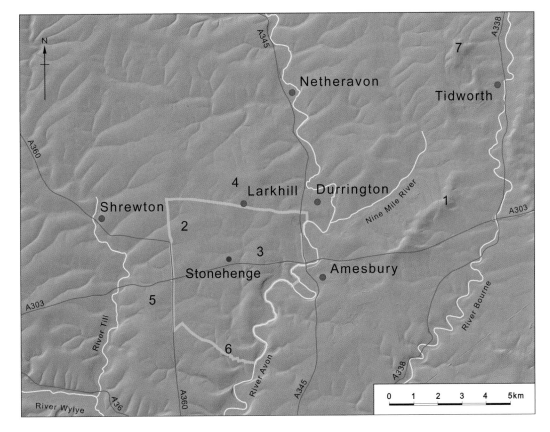

Fig 1.3
Topographic features mentioned in the text: 1 Beacon Hill; 2 Greenland Farm Ridge; 3 King Barrow Ridge; 4 Knighton Down; 5 Oatlands Hill; 6 Rox Hill; 7 Sidbury Hill.

Fig 1.4
Aerial view of the WHS looking north (10 January 2010). Stonehenge Bottom runs on a sinuous course down the right side of the picture, with the military establishment of Larkhill beyond in the distance. Stonehenge lies near centre in the middle distance and the Normanton Down barrows can be seen to the left. Springbottom Farm is in the foreground where another dry valley, dividing Normanton Down from Wilsford Down (out of shot to the left), joins Stonehenge Bottom.
(NMR 26555/033)

Both rivers have received considerable quantities of melt material from the chalk, and some of this is deposited in relatively narrow gravel terraces alongside. Much of this is now obscured by water meadows but will formerly have provided spreads of level, well-drained benches either side of the river, fed in some places – beneath Vespasian's Camp, for example – by fresh springs. However, it is considered that there is little gravel from earlier glaciations alongside the Avon (Wymer 1999, 112). The valley is relatively narrow, and Wymer supposes a long history of vertical downcutting with little horizontal erosion. The river in Palaeolithic times was perhaps 20m higher than at present.

An assessment of the Upper Chalk as part of the Land Classification Survey (1947) considered the thin soil and presence of flints comprised medium to poor land for agricultural purposes. Subsequently, Salisbury Plain was divided into three zones on the basis of height and the nature of the soils, and related to potential for settlement and subsistence: the Chalk Summit, the Higher Plain and the Lower Plain (Gifford 1957). Lying below 120m, the WHS falls within the Lower Plain, an area without the more dramatic combes of the north and altogether more hospitable.

Holocene environment – soils

The geology gives rise to a limited range of soil types. Most of Stonehenge Down and Stonehenge Bottom, and indeed much of the surrounding downs, are covered by light, humous soils of the Icknield series. However, there are also broad swathes of shallow, well-drained Andover series soils over the area, and interestingly these often show striped soil patterns (SSEW 1983, 7) perhaps reflecting periglacially patterned subsurfaces. As might be expected, soil depth increases on the valley floors. Towards the south, in the area of Lake Down and Rox Hill, the soils lie over Clay-with-Flints.

Drainage and water management

Retention of water on the Upper Chalk differs widely according to season. Filtration through the porous chalk is affected by lenses of chalk clay, seams of flint and occasionally fault lines. It was a fault that ensured a continual flow to the lowest three metres of the Wilsford Shaft

(see Chapter 4) and the water table was considered to be at about 66m OD, though a former water mark was noted at 72m OD (Ashbee et al 1989, 35). Early 20th-century well records indicate such perched water tables at 91m and 135m OD (Whitaker and Edmonds 1925), but there is much local variation. A well near Long Barrow Crossroads encountered water at 49.5m OD, but another on King Barrow Ridge at 80m OD. In Stonehenge Bottom a well at Springbottom Barn sometimes overflows in winter at 76m OD (Ashbee et al 1989, appendix E).

Bourne holes, which give rise to seasonal flows or winterbournes, occur at places along valley sides and floors, and can be utilised after the bournes have dried up. It is considered that the water table in the chalk has dropped considerably since prehistory (Aldsworth 1974; McOmish et al 2002, 10; Whitehead and Edmunds 2012) and today the water authorities take huge amounts from the aquifer. The possibility of former seasonal or permanent flow in Stonehenge Bottom can be entertained. To facilitate watering stock without recourse to the rivers, dew ponds and wells were widely constructed in the 19th century and earlier (see Chapter 6).

Current settlement and land use

Stonehenge itself lies within the parish of Amesbury, a historic small town on the Avon 4km to the east. A number of villages and hamlets based on medieval manorial cores are set at intervals every two or so kilometres alongside the rivers. Along the Avon are Durrington, Bulford, Amesbury, West Amesbury, Normanton, Wilsford and Lake. Along the Till are Shrewton, Rollestone, Winterbourne Stoke and Berwick St James. Each manor traditionally controlled strip-like units of land that stretched from the river meadows onto the higher downland with fields formerly situated on the slopes close to the village, and with the downland beyond used as common pasture.

To the north of the WHS is the extensive grassland of Salisbury Plain Training Area, the largest expanse of natural unimproved calcareous grassland in Europe (McOmish et al 2002). In contrast, the area to the south as far as the confluence of tributaries at Salisbury has been extensively cultivated, and evidence of former land use has therefore mostly been levelled by ploughing. To the west the land slopes down to the River Till, and most of this was enclosed and cultivated by the mid-19th century (WHC EA 104). Beyond the Avon to the east the fields of Durrington and Bulford give way to the prominent ridge of Beacon Hill and further south the lower but still undulating topography beyond Amesbury and Great Durnford. In the 19th and 20th centuries almost the whole area of the WHS, especially to the east and south, was cultivated (RCHME 1979, xv–xix, map 3). Increasingly the area immediately around Stonehenge and to the north, where land is owned by the National Trust, has been returned to grass since 1985. To the north the military ranges remain in grass, though a buffer zone, known as Schedule 1 land, is cultivated (Lawson 2007, 357–8).

Previous research at Stonehenge

Unfortunately we know little of the results of the trench dug at the centre of Stonehenge by the Duke of Buckingham at the behest of King James I in the 1620s, but we know more of the investigation by Inigo Jones, Surveyor of the King's Works, carried out soon after 1620. Jones was heavily influenced by Italian architecture and, though he surveyed the stones accurately enough for the period (Fig 1.5), it was his reconstruction drawings that endured and influenced other commentators. Having reasoned that only the Romans could design and build such a structure, using the Pantheon as his example he concluded, not unreasonably, that the stones formed a series of complete circles (Jones 1655).

With the template established, others followed, most merely refining the detail. John Aubrey (1626–97), who relied heavily on Jones but appears to have copied the latter's reconstruction drawing rather than his measured plan, checked off the stones that were missing, the same as Jones, and set his own plan alongside it. His 'bird's-eye view' is also thought to have been based on that of Jones (Piggott 1978, 13). While criticising Jones's view of the inner cell, he thought that it was 'neither a Hexagon, or heptagon: nor can all the angles be forced to touch a circle' (Aubrey 1626–97, 75). Unlike his astute observation and plane table survey at Avebury (Welfare 1989), here he simply sketched the sarsen setting. In turn William Stukeley took Aubrey's plan and annotated it. The architect John Wood chided Stukeley for not surveying Stonehenge accurately. In contrast, in 1747 Wood went to the extent of publishing his measurements and leaving survey markers in

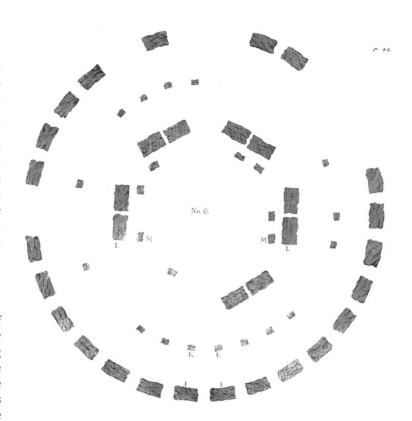

the ground so that others could check his work. Wood's plan (Fig 1.6) is the best and most reliable of the early antiquarian efforts and allows us a glimpse of the site before the south-west trilithon fell in 1797. Wood was the first to argue that the sarsen setting was never complete, as he felt that there were too many unexplained problems (Wood 1747, 61–2).

The extent to which successive landowners controlled digging is unclear. William Cunnington seems to have had free access and was able to dig where he wished in the first years of the 19th century. Unfortunately, no plans appear to have survived. Towards the end of the century William Flinders Petrie prepared a survey to match that of John Wood. While Wood claimed accuracy to half an inch, Petrie went to the extent of having a special surveyor's chain made, and claimed accuracy to a tenth (in some cases) or quarter of an inch. It was Petrie who provided the numbering system for the stones that we use today (Cleal *et al* 1995, fig 14). His survey gives us an accurate plan of the monument before the reconstructions of the 20th century. Like Wood and others, Petrie had difficulty reconciling the idea of a complete circle with the stones then visible on the ground (Petrie 1880).

The 20th century brought new forms of enquiry based on excavation, and three major

Fig 1.5
Inigo Jones's plan of Stonehenge, north to bottom; this is the plan of the monument as found, rather than the reconstruction plan which is more often reproduced. (Taken from Jones, I 1655 The Most Notable Antiquity of Great Britain, Vulgarly Called Stone-Heng, on Salisbury Plain, Restored London, p 42, plate 6)

Fig 1.6
John Wood's plan of
Stonehenge, 1747 (north
towards bottom right), is
the first accurate plan of the
monument. This copy has
been annotated by a later
surveyor.
(DP083197; Wiltshire
Museum, Devizes)

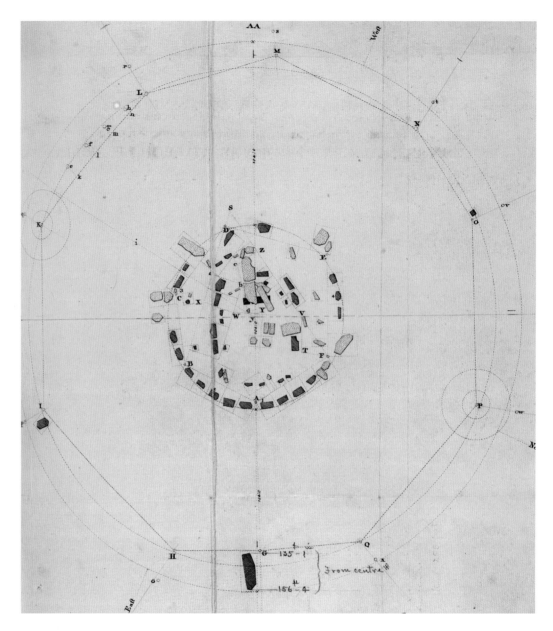

campaigns dug about half of Stonehenge (*see* Chapter 7). The available details on these excavations were finally brought together and published before the century closed (Cleal *et al* 1995), but the process of doing so merely served to emphasise that data on the earthworks was lacking and that a plan of the enclosure ditch had of necessity to be redrawn from a 1919 Ministry of Works survey.

Previous research in the surrounding landscape

In the early 17th century the 1st Duke of Buckingham examined some of the round barrows on King Barrow Ridge, and his men found a 'bugle horn tipt with silver' in one (Aubrey 1626–97, 100). In 1649 John Aubrey was told of another excavation of one of the Seven Barrows (ibid, 698) and later observed that 'round about Stonehenge one may count 43, or 45 barrows, some much bigger than others' (ibid, 83). It was William Stukeley who, fascinated by the concentration of barrows and other earthworks within the vicinity, provided the first description of the Avenue, the Greater Cursus, the hill fort known as Vespasian's Camp and barrow cemeteries on King Barrow Ridge, Normanton Down, and Lake and Wilsford Downs, and illustrated their relationship with both adjacent monuments and the natural topography. He was the first to describe the different types of barrow – 'archdruids', long; 'druids', disc; 'campaniform', bell (Figs 1.7 and 1.8). He noted that most were on high ground within sight of Stonehenge, 'For they all regard it', his comments thus presaging interpretations of recent years. He distinguished between old and new, the bowls of the 'Old' King Barrows being more ancient, he believed, than the bell shapes of the 'New' King Barrows (Stukeley 1740). The Earl of Pembroke opened a few barrows before funding Stukeley's excavations of the early 1720s (Atkinson 1985; Burl and Mortimer 2005, 97). Their first trenches were cut into the twin bell barrow (Wilsford 15/16) adjacent to the track from Wilton on Normanton Down (*see* Fig 1.7). This was followed by others in the same group, Amesbury 43 and 44 of the Cursus group, Amesbury 28 on King Barrow Ridge and others

on Stonehenge Down (probably Amesbury 1–3, 15 and 107–11). Subsequent antiquarian accounts imply that a number of barrows had been opened but without record. Two barrows within Vespasian's Camp were opened in 1770, during the landscaping of Amesbury Park (*see* Chapter 6).

The most important and relevant work is that of William Cunnington and Philip Crocker in the early 19th century, partly carried out with the financial support and encouragement of Sir Richard Hoare. Cunnington directed the excavations using his trusted labourers Stephen and John Parker to sink a shaft at the approximate centre of the barrow or cut a trench from the perimeter to the centre. This methodology preserved the outward form of the barrow and was usually successful in locating an interment,

Fig 1.7
Aerial view of the Normanton Down barrows from the north-west (10 December 2012). The group includes several disc barrows, including the well-preserved pair Wilsford 3 and 4 (bottom right); disc barrows are usually large and perfectly circular, enclosed by bank and ditch but with only a small tump in the centre. In the middle distance twin barrows 15 and 16 can be seen in the main linear group immediately beyond the track with the signs of Stukeley's excavations; antiquarian excavation shafts are also visible at the top of the Bush Barrow (right foreground) and others.
(NMR 27570/052)

Fig 1.8
Bell barrow Amesbury 11 from the west. This fine barrow lies close to Stonehenge, overlooking Stonehenge Bottom. Bell barrows have a more or less distinct berm between the ditch and the mound, but in many cases there are less obvious flat areas and breaks of slope which speak of different phases of construction or subsequent damage.
(DP148272)

often in a chalk-cut cist, but failed to locate satellite interments or record structural features (Simpson 1975, 14; Grinsell 1978, 11).

Frequently mounds display a shallow angular hollow on the summit, which is usually interpreted as the result of antiquarian excavations. Cunnington's backfilling seems often to have been very good and his trenches are not always clearly detectable as earthworks. Similarly, Stukeley's cruciform trench in Amesbury 43 is not visible on the surface. Many of the disturbances we see may be the result of other, unknown, plunderers – Hoare often comments that barrows had been opened before (1812, *passim*).

Philip Crocker was employed to survey the barrows and produce high-quality illustrations of the finds. He was a pioneer of archaeological cartography: he used shading to indicate the barrows and his maps are generally considered the first detailed archaeological mapping of the Stonehenge, or indeed any other, area (Chandler 1998, xxii; Darvill *et al* 2005, 8). This team not only produced the first map of the archaeological landscape (*see* p x), placing barrows, cursus monuments and other features in clear relation to the topography, but in addition recorded the presence of linear ditches and other features identified, and numbered all of the barrows. Hoare studied the finds and developed the descriptions and theories contained in Cunnington's letters and notebooks (WHM Devizes, MSS 2594–6), bringing everything together in published form, first as fascicules in 1810, and then as the first volume of *Ancient Wiltshire* in 1812. This was the first attempt at integrated 'total' archaeology and a key milestone in the development of British landscape archaeology. At around the same time the Revd Edward Duke opened about 16 of the barrows at Lake (Goddard 1908, 582).

Hoare and his team were frustrated by the absence of a suitable chronological framework against which to place their findings. Fifty years later, John Thurnam was able to propose that long barrows belonged to the Stone period and round barrows to the Bronze period (1868, 168). He 'successfully' excavated 40 round barrows in Wiltshire, in some instances finding burials where Hoare and Cunnington had found none (Thurnam 1871, 310). Thurnam combined the results from his own excavations with others, and presented statistical analyses of long and round barrows in the south of England. In contrast to the earlier investigators

Thurnam, who was medical superintendent of the Wiltshire County Asylum (now Roundway Hospital, Devizes), was interested in the skeletal remains.

Following Crocker's work for the One-inch Ordnance Survey (OS) map, the OS resurveyed many of the earthworks in preparation for the first edition 25-inch maps published in the 1870s and 1880s, which remain one of the most useful archaeological depictions available. Over time the shading was modified into standardised hachures, which has also led to a necessary simplification of the earthworks to allow depiction at different scales. Field observations made by the OS's Archaeology Division, particularly in the 1960s and 1970s, were used to amend the 'Antiquity Models', the field documents for map revision, but the barrows were never surveyed in any detail.

The wider landscape was largely ignored for much of the later 19th century, but Hoare's publications formed the starting point for the parish lists compiled by the Revd E H Goddard (1914) and expanded by Leslie Grinsell (1957). Goddard's list was accompanied by Maud Cunnington's invaluable comments on the barrows' condition, including whether they had been ploughed or quarried. Percy Farrer recorded the damage done to the Cursus by the military during the First World War (Pearson and Field 2011, 11), and later J F S Stone, a meteorologist based at Porton Down, placed trenches across its earthwork (1947) and also discovered a small henge within Fargo Plantation (Stone 1939). Changes to the agricultural regime in the early and mid-20th century resulted in many barrows suffering repeated damage (*see* Chapter 7). Increasing recognition and concern over their fate led the Ministry of Works to fund a series of excavations in the late 1950s and early 1960s (Christie 1963; Grimes 1964; Ashbee 1978; Gingell 1988). Other excavations responded to infrastructure and utility works (Vatcher and Vatcher 1969; Ashbee 1981; Pitts 1982) and examination of tree-throw holes left after winter storms (Cleal and Allen 1994). Additional sites were identified by the RCHME (1979). Meanwhile, early triumphs of aerial photography included the discovery of the Avenue extension and the elucidation of the character of Woodhenge, both of which were followed up by excavation (Crawford 1924a, 1924b, 13–15; Barber 2011, 136–40, 154–8); larger excavations, such as those at Woodhenge (Cunnington 1929) and Durrington

Walls (Wainwright and Longworth 1971), helped to fill in the picture of Stonehenge's hinterland, but landscape-based fieldwork was only carried out through the occasional intervention by the former Archaeological Division of the OS, until the RCHME (1979) and Wessex Archaeology (Richards 1990) undertook more systematic work.

The RCHME brought the available material together in a succinct volume on the Stonehenge environs (1979) and this provided a catalyst for targeted fieldwork and excavation in the 1980s. The RCHME survey was largely desk-based but utilised air photographs and introduced a new plan of the Avenue 'elbow', and for the first time considered the archaeology of later periods, incorporating historical documentation and discussing the effects of land use. The subsequent Stonehenge Environs Project (Richards 1990), based on surface artefact collection with targeted excavation, resolved many of the matters raised but, as is so often the case, served to highlight others.

The 21st century introduced a fresh appetite for enquiry, in part stimulated by the research framework published in 2005 (Darvill *et al* 2005). The Stonehenge Riverside Project investigated a number of sites across the area (Fig 1.9) – Durrington Walls, Woodhenge, the Cuckoo Stone, the 'Torstone' at Bulford, the Avenue and the Greater Cursus, and discovered a previously unknown henge adjacent to the river at the eastern end of the Avenue (Parker Pearson 2012). Small-scale and extremely well-targeted excavations at Stonehenge allowed fresh interpretations regarding the bluestones and the 'Aubrey Holes' (Parker Pearson *et al* 2008, 6–19: Darvill and Wainwright 2009). New ^{14}C dates provided greater clarity regarding the accepted chronology both of Stonehenge itself and of these other sites (Marshall *et al* 2012; Marshall *et al* forthcoming).

The Stonehenge WHS – history of protection

Protection of Stonehenge and access to it became a bone of contention even before it was fenced off in 1901 (*see* Chapter 7). Alongside Avebury, Stonehenge was inscribed as a WHS by UNESCO in 1986. The inscription recognised the outstanding universal value of its sophisticated prehistoric megalithic architecture, coupled with the presence of other near contemporary ceremonial and funerary monuments that help to reveal the nature of prehistoric ritual practices over some two millennia. The focal point of the WHS is of course Stonehenge itself, but the boundaries encompass an area of about 26 sq km. Aside from the River Avon, the boundary largely utilises modern features, which of course bear little or no relationship to the topography or prehistoric patterns of activity and habitation, though the boundary is currently under review.

During the first decade of the 21st century annual visitor numbers reached the million-per-year mark. Concern about the poor facilities at Stonehenge and the impact of the adjacent roads has been expressed for decades, and attempts by English Heritage to remedy the situation invariably foundered on the failure of other projects, lack of government funds or countless objections. However, the new visitor centre at Airman's Corner, built in 2012–13, along with the closure of the A344 and consequent opening up of the area, demanded fresh study and insight of the landscape in order to feed new state-of-the-art exhibition displays, guide books and other literature, as well as to inform future management. Additionally, thorough analytical surveys of archaeological sites across the WHS were required to support the work carried out by universities.

The Stonehenge WHS Landscape – the English Heritage research project

The Stonehenge WHS Landscape Project used a variety of non-intrusive techniques to analytically record and interpret the archaeology of the WHS between 2009 and 2012 (Fig 1.10). The project was set up to ensure that there is a full and up-to-date record and understanding of all upstanding archaeological monuments within the WHS. Neither the earthworks of Stonehenge itself nor many of the surrounding upstanding monuments had previously been surveyed by archaeologists to modern standards. With the opportunity to re-present this unique monument and its environs to a global audience through the new visitor centre, it was considered vital that this situation was rectified. A further aim was to provide a baseline record to inform future management initiatives by EH itself, the National Trust and other landowners.

Fig 1.9 (p 10)
Approximate areas covered by recent and ongoing archaeological research projects run by consortia of academic institutions, as at autumn 2013.

Fig 1.10 (p 11)
Areas surveyed by the EH Stonehenge WHS Landscape Project rapidly (level 1) and in detail (level 3). See Appendix for details.

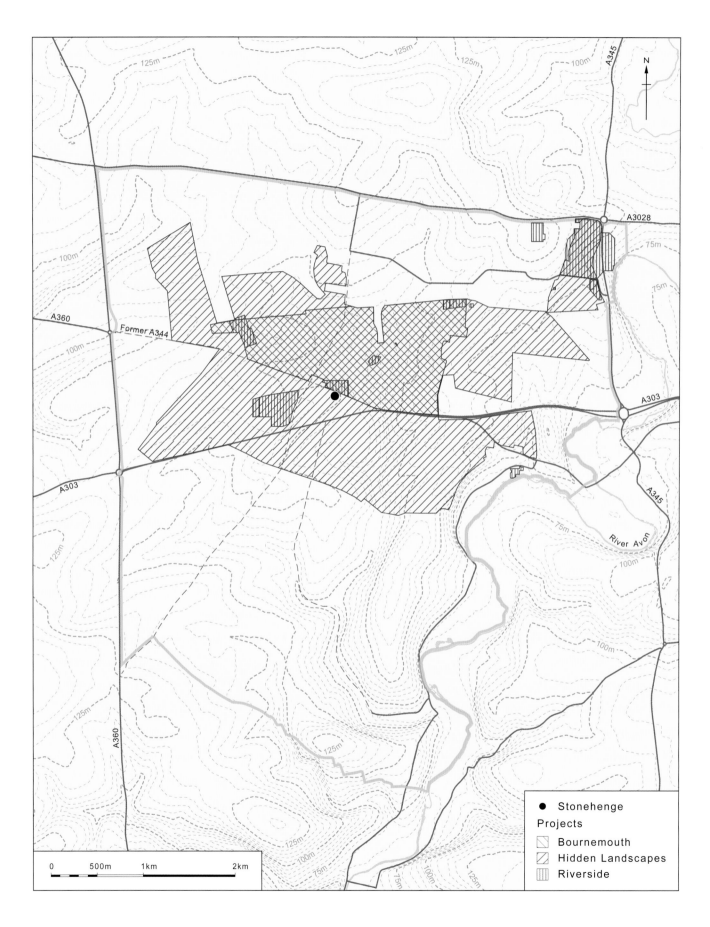

● Stonehenge
Projects
⬚ Bournemouth
⬚ Hidden Landscapes
⬚ Riverside

Durrington

Larkhill

A360

Former A344

Visitor
Centre

Countess

Amesbury

West Amesbury

River Avon

Normanton

Wilsford

Lake

Great Durnford

Upper Woodford

A360

A303

A345

A3028

A303

Survey Areas

Level 1

Level 3

0   500m   1km   2km

The extensive air photographic plot provided by the EH National Mapping Programme (Crutchley 2002), coupled with available lidar, provided the framework, while the earthworks of major monument complexes were surveyed in the traditional manner; the methodology is discussed further in Chapter 8. The detailed record of this work is contained in a series of EH Research Reports (*see* Appendix). All other monuments were inspected and features recorded. Certain features were targeted for geophysical survey by EH (Linford *et al* 2012). A new technique of laser scanning was employed on the ground surface within the Stonehenge Triangle, and the stones themselves were scanned to provide objective and thorough data of their surface that might provide details of construction, dressing, prehistoric art and modern graffiti (Abbott and Anderson-Whymark 2012). In addition, two academic groups set up major geophysical research programmes (*see* Fig 1.9), exploiting technological innovations, during the course of the project, revealing a wealth of subsurface features, many of them previously unknown (Gaffney *et al* 2012; Darvill *et al* 2013).

A landscape model

Analytical survey and investigation of the military area to the north during the 1990s revealed a palimpsest of earthworks, which when analysed allowed a model of chronological landscape change to be constructed (McOmish *et al* 2002, esp 18–20). The first component of this was a land of barrow cemeteries that was partly supplanted in *c* 1500 BC by extensive coaxial 'Celtic' field systems that imposed something of a template on the landscape. These in turn were widely cut through with effect from about 1000 BC by a system of linear ditches that carved up the landscape into units which might be considered similar to the parishes of later history. Subsequently in the Romano-British period, both 'Celtic' fields and linear ditches were brought back into use, the former for agriculture and the latter as trackways. Both were utilised during the medieval period, with the cross boundaries in the 'Celtic' field systems often being ploughed over to form longer strip fields, farmed from settlements in the valleys. The establishment of farms and field barns on the higher downs followed in the 19th century. It was noted that existing features in the landscape are often utilised rather than eradicated in subsequent periods (ibid, 20). There is every reason to believe that this model applies to the landscape immediately south of the military zone, including the Stonehenge WHS, and that the use of later periods will have had similar impact on the monuments of earlier periods.

2

Early prehistory

Evidence from the earliest prehistoric periods is, inevitably, scant. Nevertheless, it hints at the probability that the area around Stonehenge was used from the first periods of human occupation.

Evidence of early humans

While there is substantial evidence of early hominid activity at and around the confluence of the rivers Nadder, Wylye and Avon at Salisbury (eg Wymer 1999), only occasional chance finds occur further upstream. Rare finds of hand-axes have been reported from Pewsey and Wilcot in the Vale of Pewsey: there is therefore no reason to suppose that the Avon corridor, or indeed the higher downland, was not accessible to early human groups. A hand-axe was found on an allotment at Figheldean to the north-east of the WHS and another at an unknown location at Amesbury (Roe 1969, 11, 12). A few implements were found at Lake in 1865 and thereafter (Stevens 1870, 47). At least two ovate hand-axes were recovered along with two broad flakes (Roe 1969, 13). Evans depicts an ovate with typical notch on one side of the tip which he describes as being stained an ochreous colour and worn at the edges (Fig 2.1). He describes others of similar form but white, along with some large broad flakes (1897, 627–8, fig 468). He points out that the gravel was little worked at this point: it was only on the slope of the hill where the beds had been eroded by river downcutting that the finds were made.

The Mesolithic

The Mesolithic environment around Stonehenge (Fig 2.2) was one of mixed pine and hazel woodland with extensive open areas, a suitable habitat for large game animals and one providing an abundance of fruit and berries

Fig 2.1
Hand-axe found at Lake in the 19th century, bearing numerous collectors' and museum labels; length 98mm. This is the oldest artefact (possibly up to 350,000 years old) from the Stonehenge WHS yet discovered.
(DP159905; Courtesy of The Salisbury Museum)

(Allen 1995a, 471–2; French *et al* 2012). The latest evidence suggests that Salisbury Plain in the post-glacial period never was entirely covered by dense woodland (Mike Allen pers comm). However, numerous 'pockmarks' (of a type elsewhere shown to be tree holes) revealed by geophysical surveys across the Stonehenge landscape do suggest the removal of hundreds of trees at some time.

The best-known evidence for Mesolithic activity in the Stonehenge WHS is the group of monumental postholes (Fig 2.3) in the former car park (Allen 1995b). These have been extensively discussed, but there seems to be a degree of consensus that they have a significance that might be described as totemic (Allen 1995a, 472). Colin Richards and Julian Thomas have stated that: 'three of the posts form an alignment terminating on a tree-throw hole, and when this alignment is plotted onto the map its eastward extension points toward Beacon Hill … It follows that the post alignment … integrated two potentially significant elements of the local topography, a large tree and a pre-eminent hilltop' (2012, 30). But in fact these features are not in a straight line: the postholes

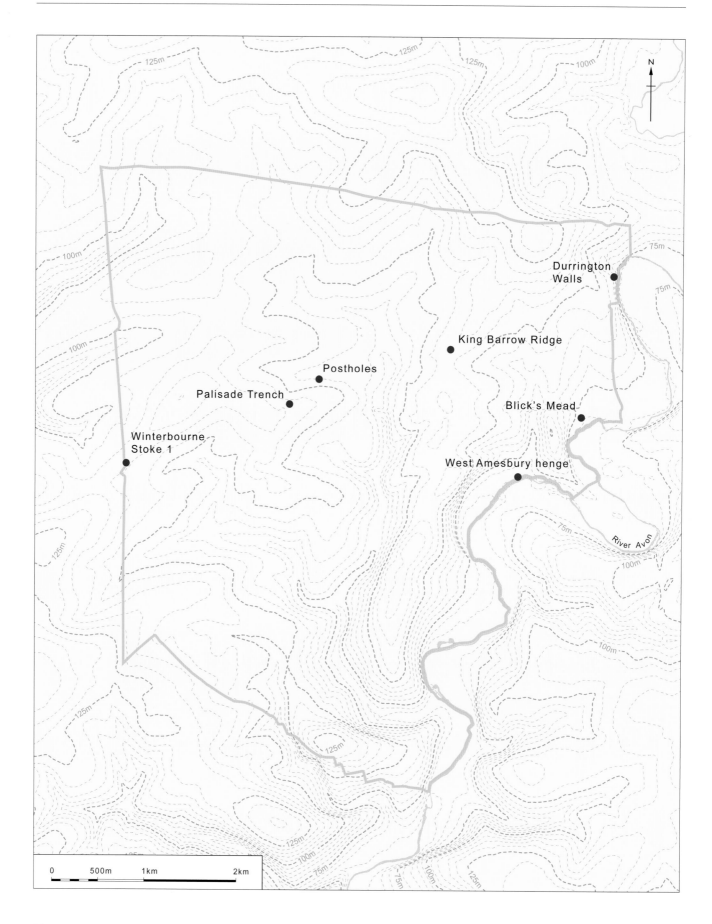

are on a gently curving arc and the tree hole lies just off any line drawn through two adjacent postholes.

The various bearings that can be drawn from posthole A (the westernmost) through any of the other three features vary between 84° and 92° east of Grid North. The total length of this array of features is just less than 50m; Beacon Hill is about 7.5km away, and the angular difference between the extremes (8°) subtends nearly a kilometre at that distance. The bearing of Beacon Hill from Stonehenge car park is about 87°: so the posts *could* be aligned on Beacon Hill but it seems a big leap to say that they definitely link the tree and the hilltop, especially as the tree hole is completely undated and could belong to any period – despite the suggestion that this feature might have been another posthole (Cleal *et al* 1995, 56). Even more significant than the undated tree, however, is the spread of radiocarbon dates which suggests that the posts could not all have been standing at the same time, as Allen and Gardiner have pointed out (2002, 143); posts A and B cannot have been contemporary with one another, and while a post in pit WA9580 could have been standing at the same time as either A or B, it was almost certainly not contemporary with both.

What may be more significant than any supposed alignment is the fact that these postholes stand along the lower slopes of a dry valley, the one that meets Stonehenge Bottom at the Avenue 'elbow', and that their 'alignment' parallels this valley. These posts are a very rare but possibly not unique discovery: Mesolithic pits that might have held posts have been found in other parts of Britain – at Boscombe Down, Wiltshire; Hambledon Hill and Thickthorn Down, Dorset; and Billown, Isle of Man (Allen and Gardiner 2002) and at Crathes, Aberdeen (Murray *et al* 2009), for instance. Parker Pearson has suggested that it would be a coincidence if the posts in the Stonehenge car park were the only ones in the vicinity (2012, 137); indeed, only 100m to the south of the 'car park' posts, GPR survey for the EH project revealed two large, deeply buried pits of similar proportions and spacing that could also be of Mesolithic date (Linford *et al* 2012, 9, fig 23). It has been suggested that three pits dug into the chalk beneath the later Winterbourne Stoke 1 long barrow might also be of Mesolithic origin (Bax *et al* 2010, 37), but they are perhaps more likely to be of early Neolithic date.

Despite their relatively low position in the valley, the Mesolithic posts at Stonehenge would have been clearly visible, especially from the north and east. It is probable that water would have flowed in this valley at some seasons and that it would therefore have been attractive to the large animals – aurochs, red deer and wild boar – that roamed this area and that were hunted by the human population. The posts might have marked the position in the valley where water was likely to issue.

The Stonehenge Environs Project recovered little evidence for Mesolithic activity, though it was acknowledged that the methodology employed was possibly unsuitable for the recovery of diagnostic Mesolithic artefacts (Richards 1990, 16, 263). Few Mesolithic

Fig 2.2 (opposite)
Mesolithic sites mentioned in this chapter.

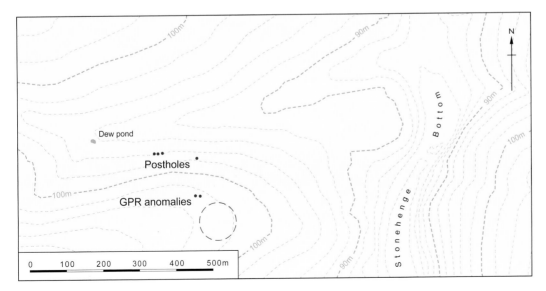

Fig 2.3
The Mesolithic postholes in the former Stonehenge car park and some possibly related features in their topographic context, along the side of the dry valley. The circle shows the area later occupied by Stonehenge. The dew pond was built, probably in the 18th century AD, to exploit the moisture in this valley.

artefacts had been recovered from the area generally (Wymer 1977, 332–46), though there is a cluster on the King Barrow Ridge (Darvill *et al* 2005, 38–40, map F). This situation was changed dramatically by the discovery of a rich Mesolithic assemblage around a spring at Blick's Mead, below the northern end of the hill subsequently occupied by Vespasian's Camp and close to the Avon. One of many interesting aspects that have been claimed for the assemblage is its inclusion of ideas from Sussex and material from Wales – a 'Horsham point' made of Welsh slate (Jacques *et al* 2012, 30–1); if correct this presages the wide contacts that are later evident in the Neolithic and Early Bronze Age around the monument at Stonehenge. The important discovery at Blick's Mead had been foreshadowed by Roy Entwistle's recovery of flints of blade form and microliths in a colluvial deposit a little further north on the western side of the Avon below Durrington Walls (Richards 1990, 263). Mesolithic flints were also recovered from beneath the bank of the newly discovered West Amesbury henge (Parker Pearson 2012, 230).

Taken together, these finds suggest considerable activity in the river valley during the Mesolithic period; downstream, Mesolithic settlements have been excavated at Downton (Higgs 1959) and Christchurch (Barton 1992). There is also now some further slight evidence of Mesolithic activity on the higher ground, with the recovery of diagnostic flints from the 'Palisade Trench' near Stonehenge (Parker Pearson 2012, 236), but the evidence remains sparse, suggesting that the uplands were reserved for hunting and gathering while other activities took place in the valleys. Preliminary reading of radiocarbon dates from Blick's Mead suggests that the beginnings of activity here were contemporary with the later post settings

at the Stonehenge car park, though they continued much longer, spanning the whole of the Mesolithic period (David Jacques pers comm). The spring below Vespasian's Camp also had significance in subsequent periods of prehistory, though there is no evidence of continuity. On the contrary, there is a gap of over 700 years between the ending of Mesolithic artefact deposition and the next recognisable activity in or around the WHS, at Coneybury.

The early Neolithic

The first indication of a new order is the presence of an exquisite axe made of jadeitite, found in a barrow 'near Stonehenge' (Grinsell 1957, 27), which was ground and highly polished into a characteristic form in use in Brittany during the latter part of the 5th millennium BC (Fig 2.4). Since there are other jadeitite axes from the region – one from further down the River Avon at Breamore and another 10km northeast of Salisbury at Winterslow – its presence in the area can be taken as indicating enduring contact with Brittany in the late 5th or early 4th millennium BC, and with it receipt of new ideas, technologies, beliefs and methods of subsistence. These influences can be seen in the construction of long barrows, particularly large examples such as the Knighton barrow at Larkhill.

The Coneybury 'anomaly'

The earliest known feature of the earlier Neolithic within the WHS is the so-called Coneybury 'anomaly', a term adopted from the technical language of geophysical survey, which discovered this feature: it is a large pit filled with the debris from feasting, dating to the early 4th millennium BC (Richards 1990, 40–60). Finds included eagle bones, a ground flint axe and grain, which provide an interesting social picture and the first indication of agriculture in the area. This is on a ridge top (like many of the later long barrows) and in a location that was later to be occupied by a henge monument. Like so many of the indicators of ritual or ceremonial activity in this landscape, it provides a link to other periods. Many ceremonial sites were revisited and reworked in later ages, which suggests that their original significance remained meaningful and perhaps that there were cultural threads that extended across archaeologically defined periods.

Fig 2.4
Axe in eclogite, a type of jadeitite; length 174mm. This type is now known throughout Europe as a 'Durrington style' axe, though the attribution of this find to Durrington was not made until relatively recently (Campbell Smith 1963, 164): previously it was always said only to be from 'a barrow near Stonehenge'. These axes exhibit an exquisite beauty and delicacy – it is inconceivable that they were used as practical tools. The material originated in the Italian Alps north of Turin and has been ground and highly polished into a characteristic 'tear drop' form.
(DP159902; Courtesy of The Salisbury Museum)

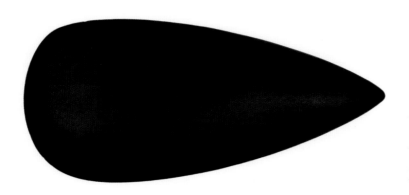

Long barrows and related structures

Earthen long barrows are among the earliest constructions in the British Isles: they all date broadly to the first half of the 4th millennium, most probably falling within the period from 3750 to 3400 BC (Bayliss and Whittle 2007). Traditionally thought of as 'burial mounds', they are in fact more various in their purpose; some, indeed, contain no burials at all, and discussion of their significance continues (Field 2006). There are nine long barrows and at least one mortuary enclosure within the current Stonehenge WHS boundary (Table 2.1; Fig 2.5). There are several more long barrows in the surrounding area, particularly beyond the northern boundary, including a group of four immediately to the east of Robin Hood's Ball. These include the largest in the area, the Knighton barrow (McOmish et al 2002, 24), positioned on a commanding height overlooking the WHS. The long barrows vary greatly in size and shape and, where details are known, in their construction and use. Several of them became the focus for later funerary monuments, including groups of round barrows (see Chapter 4); it may be significant that two of the largest long barrows, Winterbourne Stoke 1 and Wilsford 41, are both on ridge tops and both provided a catalyst for further ceremonial monument construction. Six long barrows (excluding the doubtful Winterbourne Stoke 71) and the mortuary enclosure are located in a small area encompassing the head of a dry valley in the south-western part of the WHS; this group coincides with a concentration of Neolithic artefacts (Richards 1990, 263–71; Smith 1991, 29, 34–8), indicating considerable activity in this area (Fig 2.6).

The surviving mounds (Fig 2.7) are from 20m to 80m long and up to 27m wide. The highest is Wilsford 41 in the Lake barrow group, standing at over 4m; this is arguably the best-preserved long barrow in the WHS. Others have suffered a greater or lesser degree of damage, some – such as Amesbury 140 – being ploughed completely flat. The side ditches often survive as earthworks: again Wilsford 41 is exceptional, its ditches being still over 1m deep. The most severely damaged barrows are known only from their ditches, which show up as cropmarks on aerial photographs.

Many of the long barrows were excavated in the 18th and 19th centuries, but only one, Amesbury 42 at the east end of the Greater Cursus, has been excavated recently (Richards 1990, 96–108; Parker Pearson et al 2008, 77–99). Though the mound of this barrow appears to have been severely flattened by the track running along it, a substantial amount of its body still survives (perhaps in part the result of its use as a plough headland in the post-medieval period). Excavations concentrated mainly on the eastern side ditch, which shows evidence of at least two phases of building, the first dated to about 3520–3350 BC (Peter Marshall pers comm).

The earlier excavators recorded no structural evidence but discovered a number of interments within long barrows. The first recorded excavation of a long barrow near Stonehenge was, strangely, in possibly the smallest of them all, the oval Wilsford 13 in the Normanton Down cemetery (see Fig 2.5, no 6); Stukeley dug into it in 1723 but found nothing (Burl and Mortimer 2005, 103).

Winterbourne Stoke 1, the substantial barrow which gave its name to the Long Barrow Crossroads (now Roundabout), was excavated by Thurnam. He found human remains at the north-east end. The primary interment was the crouched skeleton of a young man, dated 3630–3360 BC, born at least 100 miles from Stonehenge (Susan Greaney pers comm); he was accompanied by what Thurnam called a 'bludgeon-shaped' flint nodule but which has been more recently described as 'almost phallic-shaped' (Thurnam 1865, 142–3; 1868, 194, fig 2; Field 2006, 140–1, fig 65). A piece of animal bone, which Thurnam believed to be horse, was found near the feet of the skeleton: this awaits re-examination – it is unlikely to be horse, but if so it would be a very rare occurrence in a British Neolithic context (Lawson 2007, 39, 172–3; Worley 2013, 71). Of the three pits dug into the chalk beneath the barrow, mentioned above, one was close to the head of the skeleton.

Wilsford 34, situated on a spur 500m south-east of Winterbourne Stoke 1 and also orientated south-west to north-east, is one of the smaller long barrows in the area: the mound is about 25m long and 12m wide and survives up to about 1.5m high, and the accompanying side ditches are still about 0.3m deep. This barrow was excavated by Thurnam in 1866 in his relentless search for Neolithic skulls. Despite digging 16 holes in the mound and completely searching the eastern end 'down to the floor', he found only 5 secondary interments, of Beaker or later date (see Chapter 3). As Maud

Cunnington observed, 'This barrow is in excellent preservation, and shows little sign of the extensive excavations that have been made in it' (1914, 406).

The orientation of these long mounds also varies and seems to be related to the local topography rather than to any cosmological or astronomical alignment (see Ruggles 1997, 212–13); the mounds generally lie along the contours of ridge tops or flanks, though there are exceptions. In this respect they are like long barrows elsewhere on Salisbury Plain (McOmish et al 2002, 22). The massive Winterbourne Stoke 1 long barrow is aligned on midsummer sunrise or midwinter sunset, but the significant factor in its orientation is its alignment in accordance with the local topography, along a ridge (Field 2006, 69); in any group of monuments laid out in respect to the local topography some are likely by chance to share an alignment of apparent cosmological significance. Most of the long mounds, like Winterbourne Stoke 1, are in very prominent ridge-top positions, but some were placed on the sides of ridges in such a way that they were only clearly visible from one direction.

Mortuary enclosures are elongated, usually rectangular or trapezoidal, enclosures up to about 58m long and 24m wide, usually orientated approximately east to west and consisting of a slight ditch and internal bank, often with an entrance in the east end. They are often found buried beneath long barrow mounds and associated with burials, hence the name. Sometimes, however, they occur as distinct field monuments in their own right with no later elaboration or covering (Bradley 2007, 57). Close to long barrow Wilsford 30, the mortuary enclosure on Normanton Down survived as an earthwork until it was ploughed over in the later decades of the 20th century. It was first seen from the air by George Allen (Fig 2.8) and inspected on the ground by Richard Atkinson in 1949, when the bank was still visible. It was excavated by Faith Vatcher in 1959. Orientated east-south-east to west-north-west, it consisted of a causewayed ditch with internal turf bank enclosing an area of 36m by just over 16m, though slightly wider towards the east. There was an entrance at the east end, elaborated by internal post settings – possibly a 'mortuary house' which might have contained human remains. A sherd of Mortlake Ware, several animal bones and antler picks were found (Vatcher 1961). A radiocarbon determination from one of the antler picks yielded a date of 3512–2914 BC.

Robin Hood's Ball

Robin Hood's Ball (Fig 2.9), though lying outside the current northern boundary of the WHS, cannot be ignored. It is a causewayed enclosure, characteristic of the early Neolithic, and has been described most recently by McOmish et al (2002, 31–2, figs 2.14 and 2.15) and Oswald et al (2001, passim). Radiocarbon dates obtained from residues on pottery have been reassessed: the construction of the enclosure is dated to approximately 3640–3500 BC

Table 2.1 Long barrows in the Stonehenge WHS.

Amesbury 7 is an oval barrow and therefore probably considerably later than the others, though Wilsford 13 should perhaps also be reclassified as an oval barrow.

Fig 2.5 (opposite) Long barrows, numbered as in Table 2.1, and related earlier Neolithic monuments. Durrington 24 lies just outside the current northern boundary of the WHS on a southern spur of Knighton Down but may be included in the future – its dimensions are 43, 14 and 1.0m and its orientation is NW–SE. The Knighton barrow, further to the north on the crest of the down, measures 55, 21 and 3.0m and is orientated E–W.

	Site name/number	Note	Length (m)	Width (m)	Height (m)	Orientation
1	Amesbury 7	Oval	18	12	0.2	NNW–SSE
2	Amesbury 14		33	18	1.6	NNW–SSE
3	Amesbury 42		62	20	0.3	N–S
4	Amesbury 140	Levelled	20	12	–	NNW–SSE
5	Durrington (AMIE 1069293)	Cropmark	40	28	–	NE–SW
6	Wilsford 13		21	10	0.7	NNE–SSW
7	Wilsford 30		43	20	2.3	W–E
8	Wilsford 34		28	17	1.2	NE–SW
9	Wilsford 41		45	25	4.8	NW–SE
10	Winterbourne Stoke 1		84	27	3.0	NE–SW
11	Winterbourne Stoke 71	Doubtful	50	18	–	NE–SW

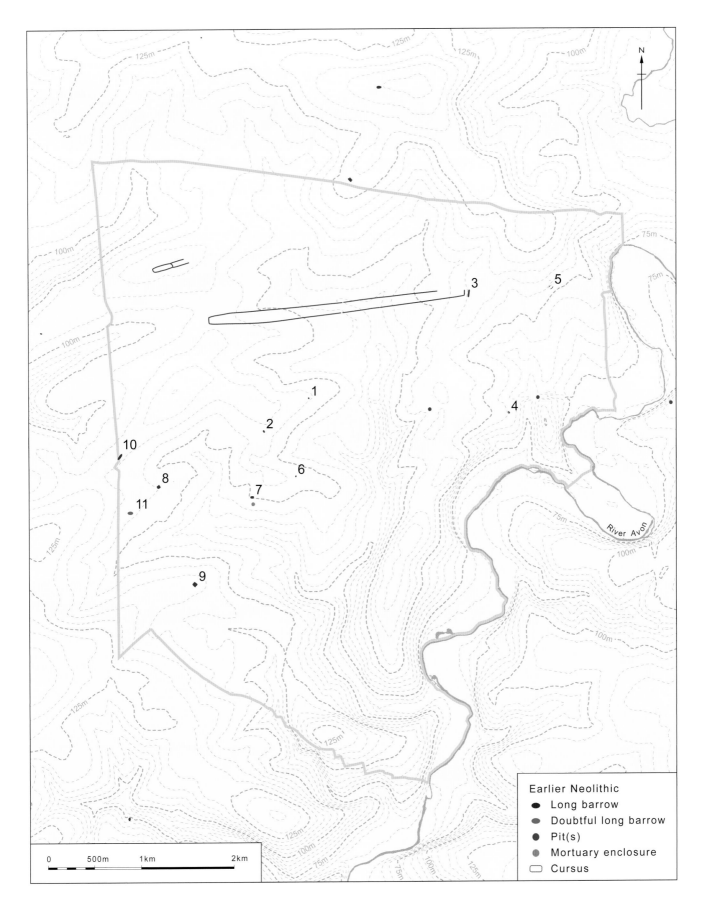

(Whittle *et al* 2011, 197). Its two circuits of interrupted ditches lie on a south-facing slope on the edge of the higher ground to the north-west of Stonehenge. It is the only site of its type for a considerable distance. Though cause-wayed enclosures are now generally thought of as multifunctional sites, with roles in set-tlement, seasonal gatherings, exchange and ceremonials, they are also closely associated with rituals of death and the near contempo-rary long barrows.

Early Neolithic pits

One element of the early Neolithic period is missing. In common with much of Britain no traces have yet been found of the dwellings,

settlement areas and agricultural structures of the builders of the visible early Neolithic monuments. Nevertheless, early Neolithic pits, perhaps indicative of occupation activity, have been discovered by chance (*see* Fig 2.5). One is on the ridge to the south of the King Barrows and another on the ridge immediately north of Vespasian's Camp (Richards 1990, 65–6).

The Greater and Lesser Cursus

The largest single monument in the WHS, and one of the largest prehistoric monuments in Britain, is the Greater Cursus (Fig 2.10; *see* Figs 1.2 and 2.5). This immensely elongated enclosure, surrounded by a substantial chalk-cut ditch and internal bank, is nearly 3km

Fig 2.6
Long barrows cluster around the head of a dry valley system in the south-western part of the WHS, shown with the densities of all worked flint found by the Stonehenge Environs Project.
(Information from Wiltshire Historic Environment Record; see Richards 1990, fig 10)

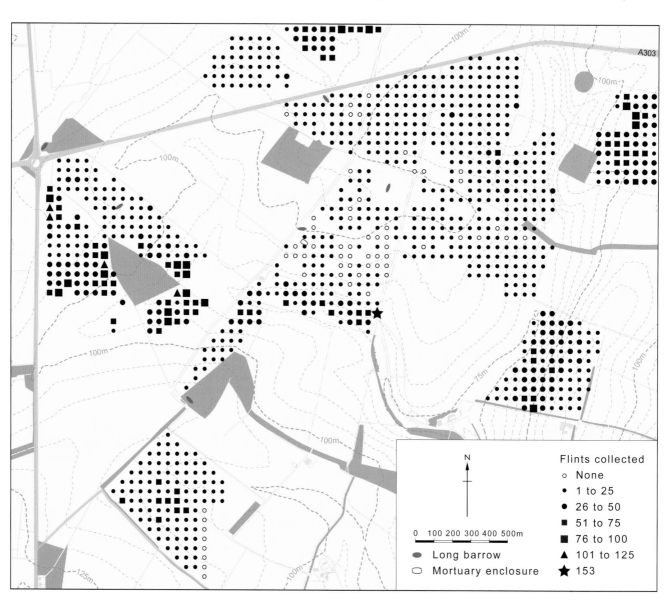

Flints collected

- o None
- • 1 to 25
- ● 26 to 50
- ■ 51 to 75
- ◼ 76 to 100
- ▲ 101 to 125
- ★ 153

⬭ Long barrow
▭ Mortuary enclosure

0 100 200 300 400 500m

long and up to 130m wide. The bank survives up to a maximum height of 0.5m and ditch depth of 0.5m; as originally dug the ditch was up to 1.6m deep. The south side is generally more massively built than the north side, and excavation evidence shows that the terminal earthworks were more massive still. The north side is more sinuous than the south side, an observation supported by geophysical evidence (Darvill *et al* 2013, fig 6). A considerable gap in the northern bank is evident in Stonehenge Bottom, and at least one clear terminal can be observed in the ditch. Other breaks through the bank are apparent along the best-preserved part of the southern side and may be the result of damage, though possibly they relate to the

original construction, which could have been in distinct sections, perhaps by separate groups. Geophysical survey has located several narrow gaps or causeways through the ditch, with one particularly clear example near the eastern end of the south ditch (Darvill *et al* 2013, fig 9) and possible broader gaps in Stonehenge Bottom (Gaffney *et al* 2012). A radiocarbon determination from an antler pick at the bottom of the ditch suggests that the Cursus was originally constructed about 3630–3375 BC (Thomas *et al* 2009, 49).

Both terminals of the Cursus lie at high points on the plateau-like interfluve between the Till and the Avon, but between these the Cursus drops into the locally significant hollow

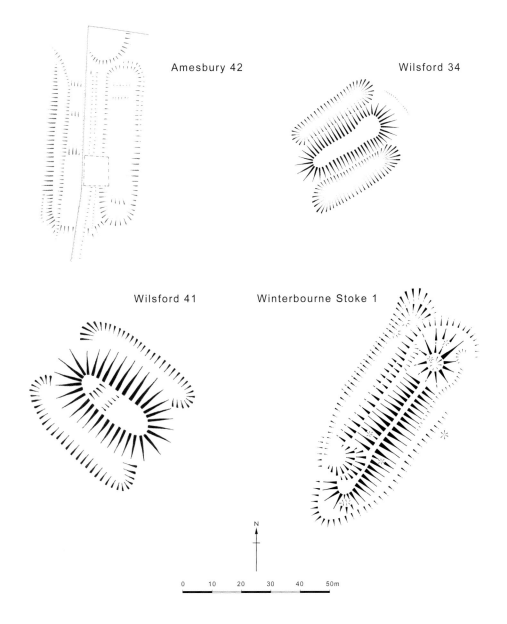

Amesbury 42

Wilsford 34

Wilsford 41

Winterbourne Stoke 1

N

0   10   20   30   40   50m

Fig 2.7
Comparative plans of long barrows: Amesbury 42, Wilsford 34, Wilsford 41 and Winterbourne Stoke 1.

of Stonehenge Bottom at the point where it is formed by two conjoining valleys. The orientation of the Cursus is approximately west-south-west to east-north-east; the earthworks are not straight, however, and it seems unlikely that the overall orientation is of any particular significance. (Other cursus monuments are aligned in various directions and celestial alignments have been claimed for some.) It has been pointed out (following Burl 2006, 90–1) that the westernmost section of the south side of the Cursus (about 500m long) aligns with the north side of Beacon Hill (Richards and Thomas 2012, 34); while this is true, its significance has been exaggerated. As with the Mesolithic postholes in the car park, it seems that conformity with the local topography is more important than distant alignments. The change of angle 500m from the western terminal places the Cursus earthwork on a break of slope for nearly 1km eastwards to the crest of the slope above Stonehenge Bottom; as a result, this side of the Cursus dominates the skyline and blocks all views to the south from the interior (Pearson and Field 2011, 21). It is also noticeable that while the Cursus ends at high points in the local topography these are linked with dry valleys that might have formed natural routeways. This is particularly clear to the west, where the Cursus terminal is situated at the top of a substantial dry valley that leads down to the Till below Fore Down, the dry

valley now occupied by the Stonehenge visitor centre. At the east end the topography is not so straightforward, but again broad dry valleys lead southwards and north-eastwards from close to the Cursus terminal to the Avon.

The Greater Cursus is named to distinguish it from the Lesser Cursus (*see* Fig 2.5), which lies 600m to the north-west of its western terminal. This smaller cursus, a monument of at least two phases, survived as a substantial earthwork until the middle of the 20th century, when it was ploughed over. Excavations in 1983 (Richards 1990, 72–93) demonstrated that it probably started as an insubstantial enclosure consisting of a ditch and internal bank measuring approximately 200m west-south-west to east-north-east by 60m transversely; subsequently the earthworks were enlarged and an open-ended extension of the same length – 200m – was added to the east. Though superficially the open end of this monument suggests that it was unfinished, geophysical survey and excavation demonstrated at least that the terminals were neatly finished off. Radiocarbon dates suggest the later 4th millennium for both phases, between approximately 3600 and 3050 BC, comparable with its much larger neighbour. However, there were indications that much of the ditch had been deliberately backfilled soon after construction. Later geophysical survey showed what seemed to be narrow entrances through the ditches (David and Payne 1997, 89, fig 8).

When William Stukeley first observed and described the Greater Stonehenge Cursus in 1723 he came to the conclusion that it was a race track for chariots or horses, and therefore named it the Cursus, after the Roman equivalent. Subsequently many more cursus monuments have been discovered (Loveday 2006), often through aerial photography, and argument as to their purpose or purposes has been lively (eg essays in Barclay and Harding 1999).

The Greater Cursus can be discussed in relation to some of the recent hypotheses – demarcation of alignments and events, linking earlier routes and monuments, processions (perhaps of spirits or the ancestors), enclosing a sacred space, providing a symbolic construction project (with the emphasis on process rather than product) or forming a boundary. It will be noted that these ideas are not mutually exclusive. One aspect of the alignment of the Greater Cursus has been briefly touched on

Fig 2.8
Normanton Down in the 1930s. Oblique aerial photograph taken by Major G W Allen showing barrows Wilsford 31 in the foreground and 30 top left; the mortuary enclosure is to the right, shortly before it was levelled by ploughing. (AA0053 Major Allen © Ashmolean Museum, University of Oxford)

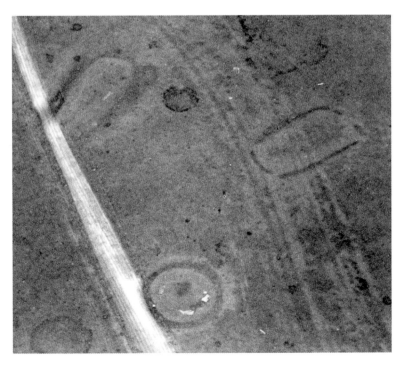

above; arguably, however, the Cursus is aligned between the long barrow on Winterbourne Stoke Down to the west (Winterbourne Stoke 53, outside the WHS) and that near its eastern terminal, Amesbury 42, since these may have been the only prominent constructions in this part of the landscape when the Cursus was constructed – this alignment, it has been claimed, is extended to the east by late Neolithic pits near the Cuckoo Stone and at Woodhenge (Thomas *et al* 2009, 42). It is possible that the Cursus formalised a route to Amesbury 42 from the west: its termination just short of this barrow suggests a relationship of respect for this monument (though radiocarbon dates suggest that the two are probably contemporary); the position of the western terminal, near the head of a dry valley linking it to the Till as mentioned above, may strengthen this idea.

The use of cursus monuments for processions has been much discussed (eg Exon *et al* 2000, 47–54; essays in Barclay and Harding 1999); accounts have drawn attention to the changing views experienced by anyone moving along the Greater Cursus, and the current investigation has shown that the way in which these different views emerge may not have been accidental but formed by deliberate choices in locating the monument, in the use of natural breaks of slope and possibly in the differing heights of the banks (Pearson and Field 2011, 15–21, 36). The idea that the Cursus earthworks enclose a sacred space is very plausible, but apparently untestable: earthwork survey, geophysical survey and excavations have all demonstrated that the interior of the Cursus is largely devoid of features except those of demonstrably recent date, with the possible exception of two large

Fig 2.9
The early Neolithic causewayed enclosure known as Robin Hood's Ball. (After McOmish et al 2002, fig 2.14; some modern features omitted)

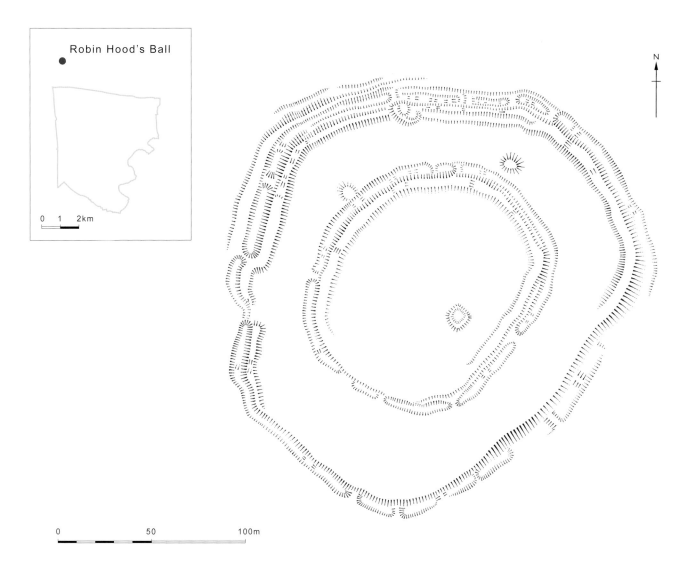

Robin Hood's Ball

0 1 2km

N

0   50   100m

Fig 2.10
Upper image: the Greater Cursus. Overall plan of the monument.
Lower image: the Cursus becoming fragmentary but still traceable as earthworks as it crosses Stonehenge Bottom. Some breaks in the banks may be original and the result of 'gang working', though some could have been caused by agricultural activity in the 19th or 20th century (parallel dashed lines).

pits near the east and west terminals respectively; it has been argued that these lie on the alignments of midsummer sunrise and sunset when viewed from the 'Heel Stone' (Gaffney *et al* 2012), but as they are undated and as the Cursus itself pre-dates the Heel Stone by several hundred years on the current understanding of Stonehenge chronology, this cannot be regarded as conclusive. The suggestion that the act of construction was itself a means of promoting social cohesion through communal endeavour might be supported by the observation that in the better-preserved sections of the monument the bank was apparently formed by a series of conjoined mounds (Pearson and Field 2011, 24), which possibly suggests construction periodically or by different groups.

The somewhat radical idea that cursus monuments might function as boundaries was explored in relation to the Rudston cursus complex on the Yorkshire Wolds (Harding 1999) and the Dorset Cursus (Mike Allen pers comm); certainly the Greater Cursus blocks what might have been north–south routes along Stonehenge Bottom and the high chalk-land on either side between the Till and the Avon. This idea can be further explored by considering the overall relationship of the Cursus to the network of valleys in the area: geographical information system (GIS) analysis shows how the Cursus, by extending to the watershed on either side, effectively blocks the drainage of the two valleys that unite to form Stonehenge Bottom; a similar relationship can be demonstrated for the much longer Dorset Cursus (Pearson and Field 2011, figs 16 and 17, 38–9). It is possible that the relationship with valley systems reflects the ritual significance attached to springs and watercourses, which has been discussed in relation to cursus monuments in recent studies (eg Brophy 2000; Loveday 2006, 133–6); the main problem with this idea in relation to the Greater Cursus, however, is that it has yet to be established whether or not springs were present in Stonehenge Bottom at the time when the monument was constructed.

Attention has been drawn back to Stukeley's original interpretation, that the Cursus may have formed an arena for competition, and thought has now turned to the idea of rites of passage, such as the transition from boyhood to manhood, which in many traditional societies involves strenuous activity related to the process of hunting; such an idea is supported by finds of arrowheads near the terminals of many cursus monuments (eg McOmish 2003, 12). It is also supported by the absence of entrances at many cursuses, or the presence of few, very narrow entrances, as here – rites of passage are often undertaken in liminal places, cut off from normal social activities (Fig 2.11).

The Lesser Cursus challenges many of the ideas discussed above. It is located, unusually for a cursus, on and along an almost flat ridge top; it is not aligned upon any other known monuments of earlier or similar date (or any particularly prominent natural features or celestial events); it cannot be said to link routes or monuments; it is not long enough, even in its extended form, to be a significant boundary; it has no relationship with valley systems or water in any form. It remains possible that it may have formed a processional route, though the large ditch and bank that remained across its line after it was extended would have formed an obstacle; it may have enclosed a sacred space – there is an irregular ovoid enclosure within its eastern end (David and Payne 1997, 89, fig 8) – and it may have been a communal construction

Fig 2.11
An imaginative reconstruction drawing of rites of passage taking place within the terminal of the Greater Cursus.

project. It may, too, have been an arena for the more strenuous ceremonies associated with rites of passage.

Later Neolithic pits

Pits found under the earthworks of Woodhenge contained deliberate deposits of Grooved Ware (2900–2200 BC), animal bone and worked flint (Pollard 1995a, 141–2). They are rather similar to others found just to the south along the ridge (again, like the earlier pits, in a ridge-top location) at Woodlands and Ratfyn (Stone and Young 1948). Two late Neolithic pits, dating to about 2900 BC, were found by the Cuckoo Stone and may relate to its erection (Parker Pearson *et al* 2008, 6).

An oval barrow

The diminutive barrow Amesbury 7, at the heart of the Stonehenge barrow group, was revealed by geophysical survey to contain a 'Cranborne Chase' style plan of a surrounding ditch with two causeways at the southern end (Fig 2.12). It is situated immediately to the west of Stonehenge and was once considered to be a round barrow. The narrow ditch surrounds an oblong area with rounded ends, orientated north-north-west to south-south-east (and therefore across the contours) and measuring

19m by 14m, with a partly blocked south-facing entrance; there is a suggestion that the ditch contains burnt material (Linford *et al* 2012, 11, 13, figs 24 and 25). Despite its small size and unusual orientation, this monument seems to share several of the characteristics of a mortuary enclosure. Intervisible to the south and at the heart of the Normanton Down cemetery, Wilsford 13 is just a little larger, its ditches obscured by cultivation; it also lies across the contours. Where dated, such diminutive oval long barrows are much later than the larger trapezoidal monuments.

Early henges

In 1937 the chance discovery of prehistoric sherds in Fargo Plantation led to the excavation of a small oval enclosure, only 7m across, formed of ditches with causeways to north and south, surrounding several burials (Stone 1939). Though the burials were dated to the Beaker period and Early Bronze Age, the surrounding ditch was undated except by a sherd of Peterborough Ware (3300–2900 BC) and a bluestone chip in its upper fill; there were hints that the ditch had been surrounded by an external bank. The excavator noted the similarity of this monument to the class of 'henges', which had only been recognised in 1932 and named after Stonehenge itself. Unlike causewayed enclosures and long mounds, cursus monuments and henges are distinctively British constructions and are associated with distinctively British styles of pottery. They mark a period when continental contacts were lost, or at least greatly diminished (Bradley 2007, 88–142).

There is a similar monument at Stonehenge itself. Just inside the enclosure bank on the north side is a feature which has long been known misleadingly as the 'North Barrow' (Fig 2.13). This feature has been largely levelled by later tracks but the remaining portion comprises a crescentic bank with an internal ditch that appears to butt up to or underlie the enclosure bank; it does not overlie the bank. It is not a barrow, for, despite the damage, its present form and antiquarian descriptions show that the interior was dished (and was levelled up in the late 18th century AD); with an external bank it might be better described as a small henge, perhaps similar to that at Fargo Plantation, or enclosed cremation cemetery. (The 'South Barrow', shown in Fig 3.9, is an entirely different

Fig 2.12
Interpretation of magnetometer anomalies and surviving earthworks of Amesbury 7, a small oval 'Cranborne Chase' type barrow on Stonehenge Down.

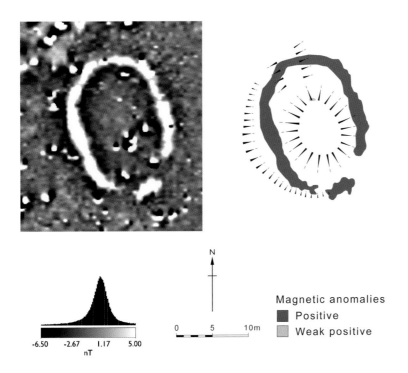

N

0   5   10m

Magnetic anomalies
■ Positive
▨ Weak positive

-6.50   -2.67   1.17   5.00
nT

feature which falls much later in the sequence.) The 'North Barrow' can be read as being earlier than the enclosure bank; this interpretation is supported by the observation that the Stonehenge enclosure bank changes direction at this point, conceivably to encompass a pre-existing feature. Some of the antiquaries who saw it before it was so disfigured by tracks certainly believed that it was earlier; most significantly Richard Colt Hoare, an acute observer of earthworks, believed that the 'North Barrow' was constructed before the enclosure ditch and bank were made (1812, 144–5), and Crocker's plan (ibid, opp 143) is not inconsistent with this interpretation. William Long concurred: 'The vallum cuts through the boundary ring of a low barrow on the NW side ... it is clear that it was in existence before the ditch was dug' (1876, 54). If this is accepted, then it is the earliest construction at Stonehenge itself so far identified.

Within the immediate vicinity some of the other similar small henges and pit circles, horseshoes and ovals (*see* Chapter 3) are likely to relate to an earlier 3rd millennium BC phase of activity, though some are undoubtedly later, while the 'Cranborne Chase' style oval barrow may well indicate that the sequence of ceremonial and funereal activity at the eastern end of Stonehenge Down commenced in the 4th millennium BC.

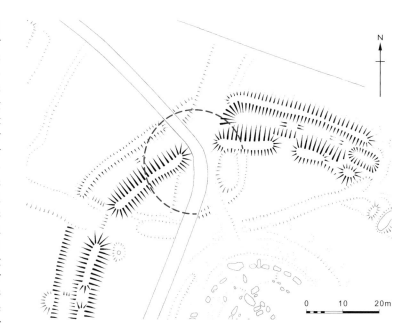

Fig 2.13
The fragmentary remains of the so-called 'North Barrow' at Stonehenge (the circle indicates its potential overall extent). Its relationship to the enclosure earthwork suggests that it may be an earlier feature. Later features are shown in grey.

3

Stonehenge in its landscape

For a long time it has been believed that the first phase of Stonehenge, the surrounding bank and ditch and the Aubrey Holes, was built in a more or less empty landscape populated only by defunct constructions of the much earlier Neolithic – the causewayed enclosure, the long barrows and a few pits. A pertinent question was why Stonehenge is located where it is, on the east-facing end of a not very striking ridge in a landscape that offered apparently more conspicuous locations for such a prestigious monument (Fig 3.1). The revised chronology, fuelled by fresh dates from recent research, has thrown up a number of surprises: the Greater Cursus is much earlier than previously thought, for instance, and pre-dates any activity at Stonehenge by several hundred years, though it had been redug in the 3rd millennium BC. The possibly late oval barrow Amesbury 7 suggests recent ritual activity on this part of Stonehenge Down. The proliferation of recently discovered small henge-like enclosures and pit circles also suggests that Stonehenge 1 was not alone; indeed it may have been built overlying one small henge, the so-called 'North Barrow'.

There are, however, other candidates for pre-existing features, even natural features, which might have influenced the precise location of the monument. Excavations by the Stonehenge Riverside Project have discovered that there are north-east to south-west trending periglacial stripes (lines of frost-shattered chalk) within the Stonehenge Avenue and, more controversially perhaps, have suggested that the Avenue banks themselves are, at least partly, natural chalk ridges. It is argued that it is these ridges – fortuitously aligned on midsummer sunrise/midwinter sunset – that determined the position of Stonehenge (Parker Pearson *et al* 2008, 20–33; Parker Pearson 2012, 243–5). The periglacial stripes were also found under the former course of the A344 (Heather Sebire pers comm). A further discovery, by the EH

project, may corroborate this idea: among the stone settings, just to the south of the centre of Stonehenge, is a low oval mound (Fig 3.2), no more than 0.3m high and underlying a number of fallen stones. On the west side there is a clear separation between this mound and the natural slope but on the other sides it merges imperceptibly, though it seems to extend to the east beyond stones 6 and 7 of the sarsen circle. While the date and purpose of this mound are quite uncertain, a modern origin has been discussed and found unlikely (Field and Pearson 2010, 59–61); the possibility that the mound is natural in origin is suggested by the profile of the natural chalk noted in various 20th-century excavations (ibid, 61–2). This mound, and possibly another under the 'South Barrow' (Hawley 1928, 174), coupled with the ridges noted under the Avenue banks, might explain why Stonehenge was located precisely at this point.

Such mounds might be explained by the presence of overlying deposits – large sarsen blocks, for instance – protecting the chalk from natural weathering. This is problematic, however: although Atkinson postulated a loss of as much as 0.3m of the chalk surface from weathering since the Neolithic period (1957) and one sarsen stone on the Marlborough Downs has been demonstrated to lie on a protected 'platform' of chalk (Bowen and Smith 1977, 193), more recent study has suggested that demonstrable lowering of the chalk surface elsewhere in southern England is the result of modern farming practices – especially deep ploughing and the application of nitrogenous fertilisers – and that natural weathering has a negligible effect on the chalk surface generally (Groube and Bowden 1982, 16–18). An alternative view is that solution hollows might have formed beneath recumbent sarsens, such as the Cuckoo Stone and the Heel Stone (*see* Pitts 2008, 14–15); this idea has much to recommend it

Fig 3.1 (opposite) Places mentioned in this chapter contemporary with the first three stages of Stonehenge (see also Fig 3.6 for henges and related sites).

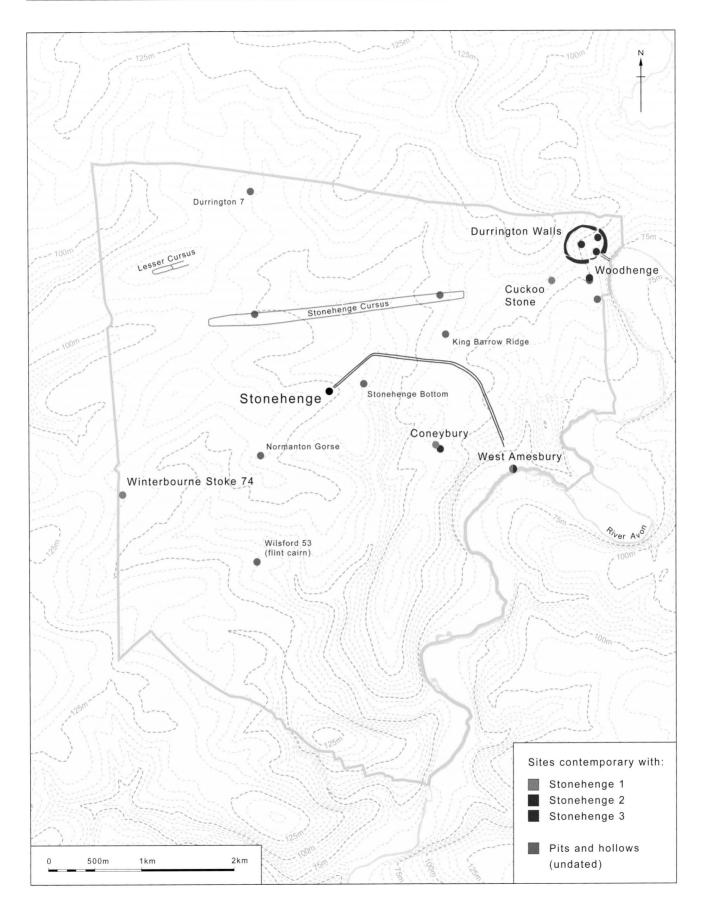

Durrington 7

Durrington Walls

Lesser Cursus

Woodhenge

Cuckoo
Stone

Stonehenge Cursus

King Barrow Ridge

Stonehenge

Stonehenge Bottom

Coneybury

Normanton Gorse

West Amesbury

Winterbourne Stoke 74

River Avon

Wilsford 53
(flint cairn)

N

Sites contemporary with:

Stonehenge 1
Stonehenge 2
Stonehenge 3

Pits and hollows
(undated)

0   500m   1km   2km

Fig 3.2
The newly recognised mound within the south-eastern quadrant of Stonehenge. In the upper image it is shown by hachures derived from conventional (subjective) survey; in the lower image, by colour tone from Differential Global Positioning System (objective) survey.

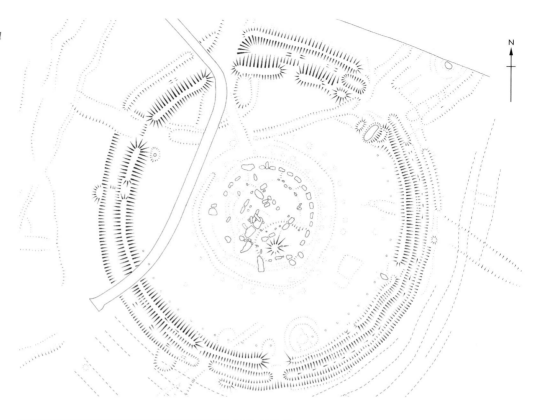

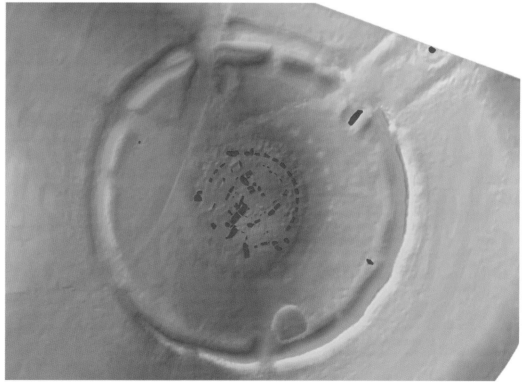

105m
100m

0   50   100m

and is discussed further below. Mounds and ridges are, at best, a rare occurrence in the surface of chalk but such rarity would enhance their significance. They would never have been more than a few centimetres high and would only have been visible in open, well-grazed ground. Soil stripes may be more common, though under-reported, and it is worth noting that GPR survey has noted a number of other deep, broadly north-east to south-west aligned features around Stonehenge and immediately to the west: these are thought to be geological features, such as seams of flint within the chalk, though it should also be noted that it is uncertain whether such underlying geological features ever had any surface expression (Linford *et al* 2012, 18). On the other hand a dry valley running down into Stonehenge Bottom

from Durrington to the north-east and heading directly towards Stonehenge is another potentially significant natural landscape feature.

Pastoral use of the downs will have kept the land clear of scrub and so enabled the monuments and their visual interrelationships to work across the landscape. This grazing was probably well organised and part of a wider pattern of agricultural and social practice.

Elements of uncertain date at Stonehenge

It is clear that several of the features that constitute the monument of Stonehenge (Fig 3.3) cannot certainly be attributed to any particular stage of its development: the many postholes, though William Hawley noted that most of

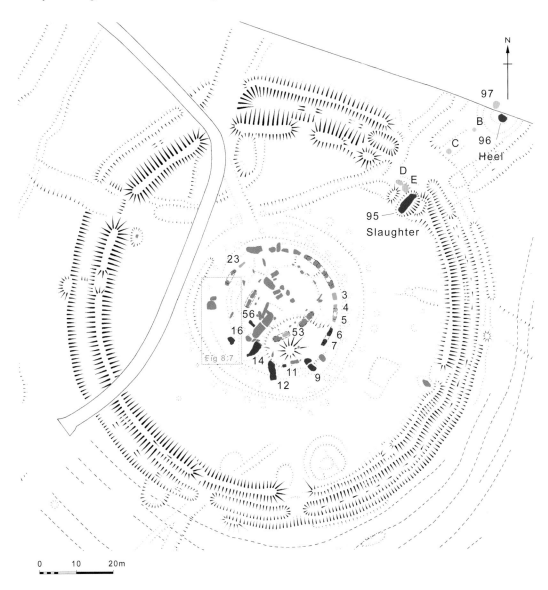

Fig 3.3
Analytical earthwork survey of Stonehenge at 1:1 000, reduced from original survey drawing at 1:500. Stones (dark red), stones with carvings (orange) and stoneholes (pink) mentioned in the text are numbered.

them were similar in form and fill, lacked finds, and were probably early (1926, 3); the Altar Stone, could be of any date before the collapse of the Great Trilithon, whenever that occurred; the Station Stones, apparently conform to the axis established in stage 2 but could be of later date; and, perhaps most tantalising of all, an inhumation burial from the centre of the site (Cleal *et al* 1995, 265–6; Pitts *et al* 2002, 132). Nevertheless, despite the continuing uncertainties, the chronology of Stonehenge is better understood now than at any time in the past. As noted above, we have adopted the current 'consensus' chronological model for Stonehenge (Darvill *et al* 2012; Marshall *et al* 2012); this divides Stonehenge into five stages.

Stonehenge 1: circular enclosures

The first stage of Stonehenge (Fig 3.4), dating to 3100–2920 BC, consists of the surrounding near circular earthwork enclosure and the X or Aubrey Holes (named after their discoverer, John Aubrey) immediately within the bank (Darvill *et al* 2012, 1028–30). The enclosure, approximately 102m in internal diameter, consists of a ditch, between 4m and 6m in width and surviving to 0.6m in depth, though excavation has shown that it was irregular, segmented and of uneven depth (and recut at a later date – *see below*); the sections on the east side excavated by Hawley remain relatively deep and of

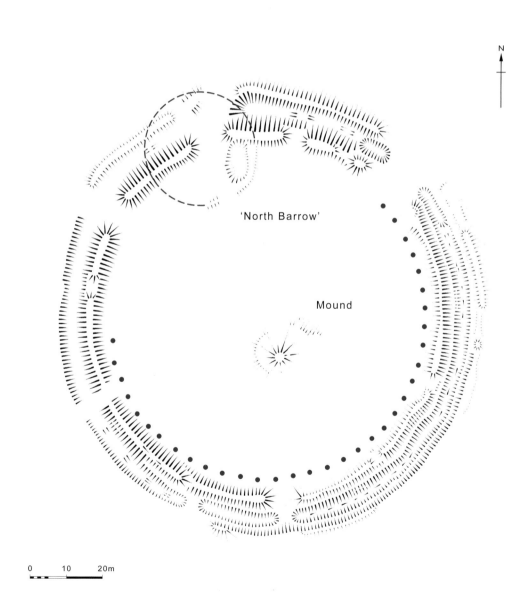

N

'North Barrow'

Mound

Fig 3.4
A simplified version of the currently accepted chronological model for Stonehenge 1, but with the 'North Barrow' and mound added. Some features, generally those not now visible – such as the postholes – are omitted for clarity.

0   10   20m

crisp profile. The ditch is flanked by inner and outer banks up to about 5m wide. The outer bank is poorly preserved and nowhere more than 0.4m high but it can be traced around much of the circuit. The inner bank is the same height but better preserved around almost the whole circuit. Wood referred to the enclosure as comprising a double bank separated by a ditch (1747, 43, 47) but Hawley referred to the outer bank as a 'counterscarp' (eg 1923, 14) and this term has prevailed, with the result that it is considered to be secondary. Geophysical survey has shown that it matched the inner bank in width and was clearly of some substance (Payne 1995, 501). Earthwork survey has confirmed that it is only differential treatment which has led to truncation of the outer bank – there is no compelling archaeological reason to consider it a secondary feature. There are some slight variations from a perfectly circular plan, notably in the north, where straight sections indicate that the earthwork may be influenced by the pre-existing 'North Barrow' (*see* Chapter 2), and in the south-east, where a sinuous indentation in the inner face of the ditch is followed by the inner bank, possibly respecting another pre-existing but long-gone feature (the straighter line of the outer face perhaps being due to later recutting). There are several breaks in the enclosure: those believed to be original are to the north-east, 11m or more wide, and to the south, 5m wide; a second, narrower southern entrance, 25m to the west, might also be original; the others are all certainly later breaches. The ditch is wider in the west than in the east, perhaps as a result of later – but still prehistoric – recutting. GPR survey also revealed considerable complexity in this, unexcavated, western sector (Linford *et al* 2012, 7–8, fig 23). The Aubrey Holes do not survive as earthworks, curiously (*see* Chapter 8), though several of them are visible because of the concrete slabs placed over them after excavation in the 1920s. They are dated very close to the digging of the ditch and could even pre-date it (Darvill *et al* 2012, 9).

This is a rare monument, with fewer than a dozen parallels in the rest of Britain (Fig 3.5) – including the Flagstones enclosure (Dorset), Llandegai A (Gwynedd) and Maxey and possibly Melbourn (both Cambridgeshire), though the last is undated. These monuments have been called 'formative' henges (Harding 2003, 13; Burrow 2010). Other commentators (eg Bradley 2007, 81–3) see them as late examples of causewayed enclosures. They can be seen as a transitional form between the two traditions of enclosure building – though there is at present a considerable chronological gap between the latest causewayed enclosures and the earliest classic henges – or as something entirely separate. While the outer earthworks enclosing these sites are similar and they seem to be of the same period, they are all different from each other in detail: for instance, their entrances are differently orientated. One thing that distinguishes Stonehenge from the others is the ring of Aubrey Holes just inside the bank, though there are smaller rings of cremation pits at other formative henges. The idea that there were 56 Aubrey Holes has been seen as astronomically significant by some commentators, but there is no such significance (Ruggles 1999, 47). There is, however, evidence of an alignment on the rising moon in the placement of cremations in the Aubrey Holes and in the enclosure bank and ditch, though this does not imply that the moon influenced the design of the monument (Pollard and Ruggles 2001). The packing material and secondary fills of the Aubrey Holes contained cremations, but Hawley's idea that they originally held standing stones (1921, 30–1; 1928, 158) has been revived, with the suggestion that these were some of the Welsh bluestones, already on site by this date (Parker Pearson *et al* 2009, 32–4).

There may have been other standing stones on the site in this first stage: stoneholes 97, B and C could all have had standing sarsens at this date; stone 97 stood in a backfilled depression (aligned approximately south-west to north-east) which might be the natural hollow in which it originally lay. A line of four postholes lay between stone 97 and stone B and perpendicular to the main axis of the site. Several pits, postholes and stakeholes within the enclosure must belong to this stage – some of them clearly pre-date stone settings at the centre – or even earlier (Cleal *et al* 1995, 107, 146–52), though none of them is otherwise dated. The interior postholes fall in five loose groups which have been named 'structures' (Darvill *et al* 2012, fig 3), though very little patterning is apparent; two lines of posts formed what have been described 'optimistically' (Johnson 2008, 105) as a passageway leading from the southern entrance; this passageway is blocked by further lines of posts, while a rectangular array of more than 50 posts filled the north-eastern entrance. The groups nearer the

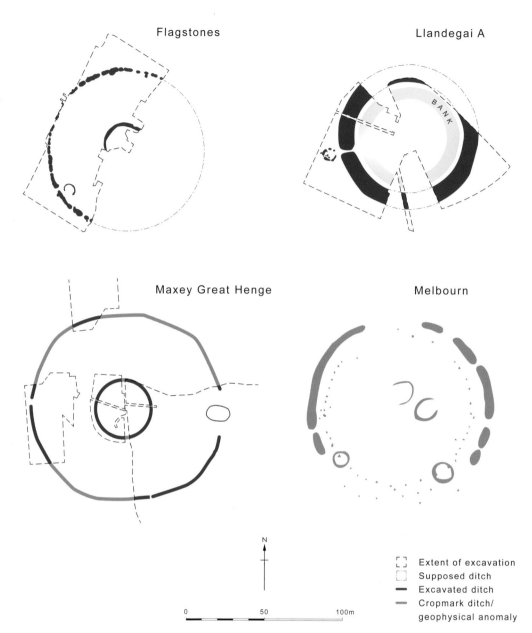

Fig 3.5
Comparative plans of sites
similar to Stonehenge 1 in
form and probable date.
(After Smith et al 1997, figs
17 and 22; Pryor et al 1985,
fig 168; Lynch and Musson
2001, fig 14; and Oswald
et al 2001, fig 8.1).

centre are amorphous clumps. Some of them possibly belong to later phases and could have been related to temporary timber structures connected with raising the stones; others might be much later still.

It is possible, as Piggott suggested (1951, 284), that there was a central timber structure, possibly a major circle, pre-dating the stone settings. This can only be speculation because any evidence for such a construction might have been totally destroyed in antiquity. Gibson's claim that there were at least six or seven rings

of posts within Stonehenge, based on the existing postholes (1998, 141, fig 37), is perhaps a little optimistic, though recent discoveries (*see* Chapter 8) might lend some support.

As well as the cremation burials in the Aubrey Holes there are many cremation burials in the interior and in various levels of the ditch fills and in the bank, some of them relating to this first stage of the monument, others to stage 2 (Parker Pearson *et al* 2009). Stonehenge has been called an 'enclosed cemetery' (Kinnes 1979, 18, 67–8).

Other early henges and pit circles

Potentially coeval with Stonehenge 1 in the landscape is the West Amesbury stone circle (*see* Fig 3.1), found by chance as the Stonehenge Riverside Project sought the end of the Stonehenge Avenue on the bank of the Avon. The West Amesbury stone circle, which is believed to have consisted of possibly 25 bluestones, was erected between about 3400 and 2600 BC and dismantled probably between about 2470 and 2270 BC, according to the excavator; the henge which replaced the stone circle dates to about 2460–2210 BC but must be later than the removal of the stones (Parker Pearson 2012, 219, 223; Marshall *et al* forthcoming).

The Coneybury henge is probably of slightly later date (3100–2450 BC). The post settings at Coneybury may be earlier than the henge (3254–2910 BC), though both elements are associated with Grooved Ware (Richards 1990, 138).

The Fargo henge (*see* p 26) remained an apparently unique monument in the Stonehenge landscape for some time after its discovery, then a close parallel, though orientated east-west, was seen on a 1993 geophysical plot (David and Payne 1997, fig 8) within the Lesser Cursus. Meanwhile, aerial and geophysical survey had revealed similarly unusual though larger monuments – a segmented ring ditch about 20m in diameter south-west of Longbarrow or Winterbourne Stoke Crossroads (outside the WHS), named Winterbourne Stoke 72, and a 'classic' henge with east-facing entrance, Winterbourne Stoke 74, 200m to the south-east (ibid, 98, fig 13A; RCHME 1979, 3). More significantly perhaps, geophysical survey in the Stonehenge Triangle found that some of the smaller barrows to the west of Stonehenge had interrupted ditches (David and Payne 1997, 83, fig 7).

There the matter rested until the present project and concurrent geophysical surveys and excavations resulted in an explosion of new discoveries (Table 3.1; Fig 3.6). These take a variety of forms, some conforming to the henge-like characteristics of the site in Fargo Plantation and often referred to as 'hengiform' enclosures, others more like miniature causewayed enclosures, but all considered together here. First, the Stonehenge Triangle was re-examined both by analytical earthwork survey and geophysical survey, which refined the view of what lay beneath the barrows: Amesbury 6

was raised over a small henge-like enclosure and a cluster of pits; Amesbury 7 has been discussed in Chapter 2; Amesbury 8 had a small segmented ditch with causeways to east and south-west, the latter subsequently cut through by a narrow ditch; most interesting of all, the ditch of Amesbury 9 was an irregular ovoid consisting of segments or distinct pits, partly recut by a narrow ditch, and surrounding a ring of 22 or 24 post pits, with a further arc of posts within that on the south-west side (Fig 3.7; Linford *et al* 2012, 10–11, 13–14, figs 24 and 25; Field *et al* forthcoming a).

More extensive geophysical surveys and excavations in the surrounding area by university teams revealed a number of small henge-like enclosures and pit circles, some of them beneath known monuments, others standing alone. One of the most spectacular is below barrow Amesbury 50 in the Cursus barrow group. The barrow side ditches, now visible as earthworks with causeways to south-west and north-east, enclose an oval area (*see* Fig 3.7), indicating that this is more than a 'normal' burial mound (Amadio and Bishop 2010, 8–9). The northern ditch has a distinct segment within it, adjacent to the causeway, and geophysical survey has shown that this is one of eight large pits within this ditch; they appear to be cut into the ditch and are therefore later. An oval setting of about 22 postholes was revealed under the barrow mound (SHL 2012, 15, fig 34); further work has suggested that the north-easternmost pit contains burnt material and points out that the long axis of the ring of post pits is not exactly aligned with the long axis of the outer pits or the visible earthworks (Linford *et al* 2012, 15, figs 26 and 27).

The features below Amesbury 50 are remarkably similar to those below Amesbury 9. Other similar features – oval segmented or causewayed ditches, oval or horseshoe-shaped arrangements of large pits – have been found by geophysical survey near the Winterbourne Stoke Crossroads barrow group, on Stonehenge Down, on King Barrow Ridge close to barrows Amesbury 31 and 32, at the locations recorded as barrows Amesbury 37 and 139, possibly below Amesbury 38a and to the north of Durrington Walls (SHL 2012; Vince Gaffney pers comm). The EH project has added further examples, with the recognition that the ring ditch known as Amesbury 115, south of the Cursus barrows, and the ditch of Wilsford

28 in the Normanton Down group both exhibit henge-like characteristics (Amadio and Bishop 2010, 29; Barrett and Bowden 2010, 8, 31). A segmented ring within a more conventional ring ditch, known as Amesbury 142 (RCHME 1979, 2), has recently been confirmed by aerial photography (Fig 3.8). All these features remain undated, though elsewhere a somewhat similar henge at Wyke Down (Dorset) has been dated to 2890–2480 BC (Green 2000, 154). The circular monument building tradition represented by these sites continued for centuries (Gibson 2012), and henges beneath later barrows have been found elsewhere (eg Parfitt and Needham 2012, 84–90).

No settlement sites of this period have been recovered, though finds of Peterborough Ware on the King Barrow Ridge hint at occupation in this area (Richards 1990, 109–23). Apart from continuing deposits of cremation burials, little change can be detected at Stonehenge between the creation of the enclosure and Aubrey Holes and the massive constructions of stage 2 some 300 or more years later.

Table 3.1 Henges and related sites in the Stonehenge WHS; *see* **Fig 3.6.**

Henges and henge-like structures				Causewayed ring ditches and related sites			
no.	name	description	source	no.	name	description	source
1	Amesbury 6	Small henge-like enclosure and pit cluster under barrow	EH	17	Amesbury 8	Segmented ring ditch	EH
2	Amesbury 9	Timber settings under barrow	EH	18	Amesbury 51	Causewayed ditch	Ashbee 1978
3	Amesbury 38A	Small henge (?) within later ring ditches	Stonehenge Hidden Landscapes (SHL)	19	Amesbury 115	Causewayed ditch	Aerial photography (AP)
4	Amesbury 50	Timber oval(s) under barrow	SHL/Bournemouth/EH	20	Amesbury 126	Causewayed ditch	EH
5	Coneybury	Henge with timber setting	Richards 1990	21	Amesbury 129	Horseshoe of pits	SHL/Bournemouth
6	Durrington Walls	Large henge succeeding timber settings, dwellings, etc	National Monuments Record (NMR), various	22	Amesbury 139	Causewayed ditch	SHL
7	Durrington Walls, north of	Small possible henge (?)	SHL	23	Amesbury 142	Segmented ring within ring ditch	AP
8	Fargo	Small henge	Stone 1939	24	Stonehenge Down W	Pit circle/causewayed ring ditch	SHL
9	King Barrow Ridge	Small henge (?) open to W	SHL				
10	Lesser Cursus	Small henge	David and Payne 1997				
11	Stonehenge	Henge	NMR, various				
12	Stonehenge Down, near aerodrome buildings	Small henge (?), open to E	SHL				
13	West Amesbury	Henge succeeding stone circle	Stonehenge Riverside Project				
14	Wilsford 28	Possible henge under barrow	EH				
15	Winterbourne Stoke 74	Henge	David and Payne 1997				
16	Woodhenge	Henge succeeding timber settings	NMR, various				

Fig 3.6 (opposite) Henges (black) and related sites (dark red) within the WHS; see Table 3.1. In 2009 a further possible pit circle was located by geophysical survey just outside the western boundary of the WHS, 200m north of Airman's Cross.

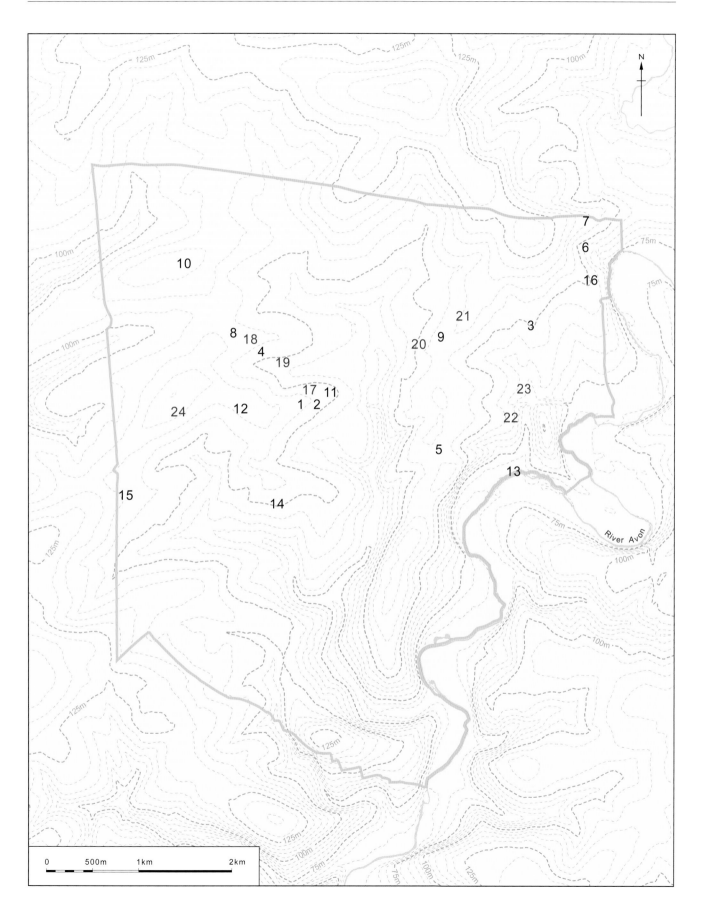

Amesbury 9

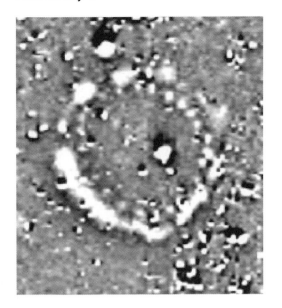

Amesbury 50

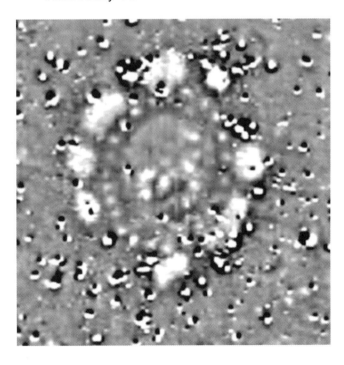

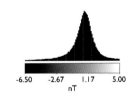

-6.50   -2.67   1.17   5.00
nT

N

0   5   10m

Magnetic anomalies
— Negative
■ Positive
▨ Weak positive

Fig 3.7
Analytical earthwork plans of barrows Amesbury 9 and 50, combined with an interpretation of
magnetometer anomalies from geophysical survey. Amesbury 50 shows the elongated mound
and the causeways in the ditch to south-west and north-east.

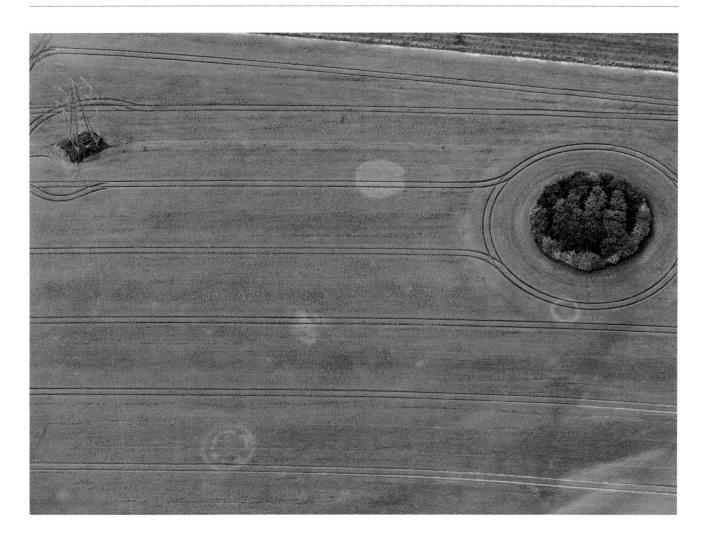

Stonehenge 2: stone and timber settings

This short-lived but significant stage (*c* 2620–2480 BC) witnessed reorientation of the north-eastern entrance towards the east and the erection of the main sarsen settings that can be seen today – the trilithon horseshoe and 'circle' – firmly establishing the midwinter sunset/midsummer sunrise axis of the site; a double bluestone setting, possibly a circle, in the Q and R holes shared this axis. The Altar Stone and Station Stones were possibly placed at this time, though this is uncertain; stones B and C were removed and stone 95 (Slaughter Stone) with stones D and E erected. Stone 96 (the Heel Stone) was also erected but whether it was added to stone 97 or whether it *is* stone 97 moved 4m to the south-east is uncertain (Fig 3.9). Cremations continued to be placed in the enclosure ditch (Darvill *et al* 2012, 1030–4).

The timber circles at Durrington Walls and

Woodhenge date to the middle centuries of the 3rd millennium BC and are therefore broadly contemporary with Stonehenge 2. The Southern Circle at Durrington began as a 'square in a circle' timber setting – of which there are at least three further examples along the ridge to the south of Woodhenge under later barrows (Parker Pearson *et al* 2007, 97–103) – and was linked to the Avon by an embanked track, an 'avenue' similar to the Stonehenge Avenue in form if not in dimensions, dating to 2500–2460 BC; the houses at Durrington Walls, the earliest domestic structures so far known in the WHS, also date to this period (Parker Pearson 2012, 110). Gatherings took place at Durrington Walls during the winter and possibly at the solstice. At about this time or earlier a series of pits was cut into the ditch of the Greater Cursus (perhaps to re-whiten or re-establish the significance of the monument), emphasising the degree to which connections with the past mattered at this time (Cleal and Pollard 2012, 326–7).

Fig 3.8
Amesbury 142 (left foreground), showing a causewayed ditch within the more 'standard' ring ditch. Above are: a solid blob which has been recorded as Amesbury 95 but which is probably not a barrow; and, to the right, below the tree clump, another small round barrow which was only recorded in the 1990s and does not yet have a parish number (SU 14 SW 617). Oblique aerial photograph, looking west (July 2013). (NMR 27746/026)

Fig 3.9
A simplified version of the currently accepted chronological model for Stonehenge 2. Bluestone settings (Q and R holes) are omitted for clarity. The 'South Barrow' is included here, just inside the south entrance to the enclosure, though its current distinctive earthwork form is due entirely to reconstruction after Hawley's excavations; in stage 2 it was a D-shaped rammed chalk surface.

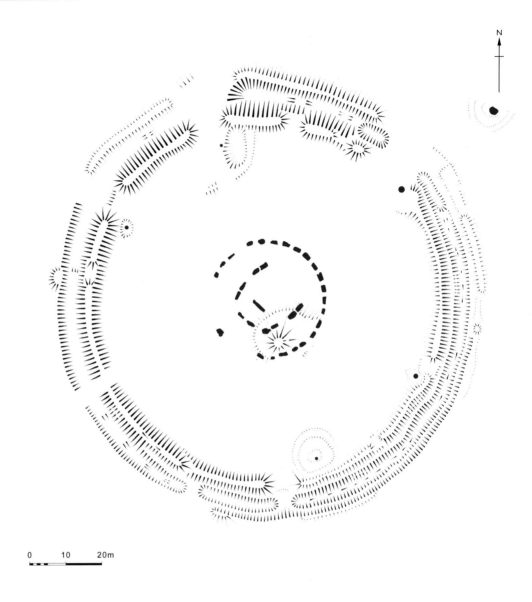

0   10   20m

Sarsens

Since Inigo Jones first proposed that the sarsens of Stonehenge had been brought from the Marlborough Downs the idea has often been challenged but has proved remarkably resilient. The evidence for the presence of large sarsen blocks closer to Stonehenge, slight though it is, should be considered.

Remnants of a Tertiary sand cover across Wiltshire and other southern counties, when weathered and eroded, left silicified remnants – sarsen slabs or masses – in many chalk areas. These broke up and drifted into valleys during periods of solifluction. They survive well on the Marlborough Downs and there are smaller scatters extending as far as the south coast (Bowen and Smith 1977). They are present across Salisbury Plain, probably formerly in greater numbers. They appear to have been gathered, broken up and utilised since antiquity and many may lie beneath 'Celtic' field boundaries here, as they do on the Marlborough Downs (Bowen and Smith 1977, 189, pl xxiv *b*). The Berril valley near Imber contains large numbers of small sarsen boulders, and there are concentrations of larger blocks around Warminster and in the Amesbury–Bulford area, including one in the Avon at Bulford and a group near Robin Hood's Ball (McOmish *et al* 2002, 151–2). Though Aubrey Burl has been at pains to point out that the long barrows of Salisbury Plain (with the exception of the one on Tidcombe Down near its north-eastern edge) do not contain megalithic chambers (eg 1991, 297–8), a number of long barrows on the plain do contain large sarsens. A standing stone within the Arn Hill long barrow near Warminster was described by Cunnington: 'The sarsen stone was irregular in form, and more than 5 feet [1.5m] in length, about 3 feet [0.9m] wide at the large end and terminating almost in a point, which stood in the ground' (WHM Devizes, MSS 2594–6; McOmish *et al* 2002, 29). At Knook the description that sarsens within the long barrow were 'man made' (WHM Devizes MSS, 2594–6, book 3) suggests perhaps that they had been broken from a larger piece, possibly a standing stone pre-dating the barrow (McOmish *et al* 2002, 29). Boles Barrow and Heytesbury North Field Barrow also contained sarsens (ibid, 14, 152). There was a massive sarsen boulder in the Corton long barrow in the Wylye valley, capping an earlier cairn of chalk and flints (Eagles and Field 2004, 56).

Some round barrows also contained sarsens. Famously there was a semicircle of large sarsen boulders under the Deverel Barrow (Dorset), covering cremations in globular and bucket urns (Miles 1826, 19–26) and therefore dating to the Middle Bronze Age. Broken sarsen boulders and flakes were present in the Late Bronze Age to Early Iron Age site at East Chisenbury, the larger examples evidently having been used for grinding (McOmish *et al* 2010, 82). The deliberate use of sarsen in building and monument construction in the Roman, medieval and later periods is also widespread (Bowen and Smith 1977, 191). William Cunnington commented that large sarsens were frequently found in valleys and on the downs in his day, and when first dug out were soft, but hardened on exposure to the air (WHM Devizes, MSS 2594–6).

Slight natural hollows have sometimes been noticed in the field (*see* Fig 3.1) and examined by excavation, such as the one next to Durrington barrow 7 (Richards 1990, 175) and, significantly, those adjacent to the Cuckoo Stone and the Bulford Stone (Parker Pearson 2012, 147, 152) and below stonehole 97. The EH project and extensive geophysical surveys have recorded numerous hollows, apparently of natural formation, in the landscape around Stonehenge. The smallest are less than 10m across and about 0.2m deep, the largest up to 30m across and up to 2m deep. There are several on the flanks of Stonehenge Bottom immediately to the north-east of the monument (Fig 3.10), at least one on the King Barrow

Ridge and a particularly large one on the northern edge of Normanton Gorse close to the 'Sun' Barrow (Amesbury 15). At the time of his visit Stukeley described the latter in romantic terms as 'a cavity … formd very regularly like a dish & perfectly circular … tis full of the pretty shrub calld Erica with a blew heath flower, which … exhald the sweetest smell' (Burl and Mortimer 2005, 102); it now lies on the edge of scrubby woodland with a barbed wire fence skirting its northern side and partly filled with large blocks of brick rubble from the Stonehenge Aerodrome buildings (Bowden *et al* 2012, 23–4). Stukeley dug a trench in it and found 'red garden mold with some flints in it' and a sherd of 'red earthen pot thin & crumbly'; he thought it had been dug to provide material for the adjacent 'Sun' Barrow (Burl and Mortimer 2005, 102), but it is probably, like the others, a natural swallow or solution hollow in the chalk. This is indicated by the regularity of the feature and the lack of spoil or other signs of extraction, and is possibly supported by the unexpected 'red garden mold' found by Stukeley. As noted above, such solution hollows might form beneath large sarsen blocks, or contain them; three sarsen boulders over 7m long were found in red Clay-with-Flints filling a solution hollow at Aston Rowant in Oxfordshire (Bowen and Smith 1977, 189). Sarsens from such hollows would be initially easy to work. As suggested above, stone 97 at Stonehenge itself was apparently raised to an upright position in the hollow in which it had lain; the possibility that some of the other sarsen stones at Stonehenge came from the immediate neighbourhood should not be discounted, though this is not to deny that some may also have been brought from further afield.

However, the ritual significance of deep holes in the chalk, whether natural or entirely artificial, is undoubted. A massive solution hollow at Down Farm, Gussage St Michael (Dorset), was used for deposits of material culture over a long time period (Green 2000, 80–4). At the other end of the scale and closer to Stonehenge, in the Early Bronze Age a cremation was carefully placed in a small solution pipe on Wilsford Down and covered by barrow Wilsford 53 (Smith 1991, 23, fig 9); solution hollows were found under other barrows in this group (ibid, 19, 23, figs 6, 10 and 11). Hawley's description implies that there were small solution holes under stone 29 of the sarsen circle at Stonehenge itself (1922, 45).

Stonehenge Café
and car park

Former A344

A303

0   50   100m

The pillar-like form of many of the bluestones indicates that they are unlikely to have been moved by glacial action, and it is now established beyond reasonable doubt that they were brought from south Wales by human agency (eg Parker Pearson 2012, 268–73). The methods by which this was done are still open to debate, so it is not unreasonable to accept that some of the sarsens too may not be of local origin. Much has been written about the moving and raising of the large blocks, and several large-scale experiments have been carried out (eg Richards and

Whitby 1997). The current project has added to this debate through the laser scanning of the stones, which has enabled a more accurate estimate of their weight to be made; this indicates that the stones are less heavy than previously thought (Abbott and Anderson-Whymark 2012, 59–60; Field *et al* forthcoming b).

This does not in any way diminish the awe that one feels in contemplating the monument, but it does turn that awe in the direction of the ideas behind the monument and the social impact of the work rather than the sheer physical effort involved. Attitudes to the builders of Stonehenge have changed over the years. To Richard Atkinson they were, strange though it may seem now, 'essentially barbarians' (1956, 163 – though the meaning of 'barbarian' may have altered subtly since 1956), but exaggerated expressions of wonder at their physical ability run the risk of going to the other extreme of being merely patronising. As Francis Pryor has said, 'I am not aware that we have ever over-estimated the abilities or sophistication of prehistoric people – we reserve that for ourselves' (1991, 124). It is now time to contemplate the ingenuity, engineering skills and intelligence of the architects of Stonehenge, rather than their brawn (Fig 3.11). In particular, attention has recently been drawn (J Wiltshire pers comm) to the engineering feat of ensuring that the lintels of the sarsen circle lie in a horizontal plane (within 10cm), though the ground on which the circle stands drops by more than 0.5m from west to east (see Fig 3.2); however, a caveat to this observation is that relatively few of the lintels remain *in situ* and it is therefore only conjecture that this 'horizon' was carried around the whole monument (see Chapter 7).

The sarsen circle: an unfinished arrangement?

This brings us to the question of the sarsen 'circle' and whether it was finished or whether, indeed, it was ever intended to be a complete circle. Recent reconstructions of the monument invariably show the sarsen circle as complete, though various scholars have questioned this over the past 250 years. What seems certain, on purely practical grounds, is that the circle was built after the trilithons. Whether these events, and the creation of the double bluestone circle, followed immediately upon each other or were separated by long periods has been subject to debate, but it has been argued that though the trilithons must, logically, have been *erected* before the 'circle', a similar logic suggests that the 'circle' was *laid out* before the trilithons were erected (Atkinson 1956, 126; Johnson 2008, 226–7); on this argument the whole process must therefore have taken place over a short period. However, none of this is certain – though it would have been slightly more laborious, the 'circle' could have been laid out after the trilithons were erected (*pace* Atkinson and Johnson). Another observation which has not been widely discussed is the remarkable fact

that these massive stones were brought into the enclosure, manoeuvred, dressed and erected without apparently damaging the pre-existing earthworks (see Richards and Whitby 1997, 252–3), though it is possible that the gap in the bank to the west could be of this antiquity.

John Wood (1747) was the first to suggest that the sarsen circle was never completed, and he was followed by William Flinders Petrie (1880, 15–16). Paul Ashbee also recognised the problem (1998), as have members of the Stonehenge Riverside Project (Tilley *et al* 2007, 199–201). Wood asked why lintels 103, 104 and 106 were not in position: the neatly mortised and grooved stones would have been locked in position and would have been very difficult to remove if they had ever been there (1747, 61–2). He also noted that several uprights in this part of the monument are irregular and were not dressed in the same way as others; stone 11 in particular is undersized in both width and depth (Cleal *et al* 1995, 205). Petrie added stones 21 and 23 that were also 'defective in size' (1880, 16). In addition stone 12 is irregular and stone 14 asymmetrical, such that it would be difficult to set them upright. Hawley's excavations seemed to show that the hole for stone 9 is askew to the otherwise regular circle. Stone 16, like stone 11, does not look as though it could have supported a lintel (Fig 3.12). Only 17 of a supposed 30 upright stones are in position: 8 are prone or in fragments and 5 are missing completely. Also, 22 lintels are

Fig 3.10 (opposite)
Hollows near Stonehenge Bottom. These, and other similar depressions, do not appear to be artificial and are likely to be solution hollows (blue), which may have contained sarsen blocks. Possible and known building platforms (purple) – including the site of the Stonehenge Café – and quarrying (orange) are also highlighted. Other earthworks include the Stonehenge Avenue, cultivation lynchets, the unfinished 18th-century road and hollow ways showing former alignments of the A303 across Stonehenge Bottom.

Fig 3.11
An imaginative reconstruction drawing of the preparation of the stones. The idea, expressed by Atkinson (1956), that Stonehenge was designed by a superior 'architect' is a modern construct and need not be accepted; we can think, rather, that the challenges involved in measuring, shaping, dressing and raising the stones were solved through trial-and-error, rule-of-thumb extemporisation, with the imperfect components patched together through exchanges (enlivened no doubt by anger and humour) between all those groups involved (Ingold 2013, 54–7).

Fig 3.12
Stone 16. Dave Field
demonstrates graphically
the apparent sequence of
working this stone which,
with its pointed top, has
long been questioned as a
bearer of lintels.
(Mark Bowden)

confront the possibility that some stones 'may have fallen during the use of the monument' (Cleal *et al* 1995, 205). This will be discussed further in Chapter 4.

Of crucial significance, however, has been the geophysical evidence: geophysical survey in 1994, though it did find an anomaly that would correspond to stonehole 20, did not detect stoneholes for stones 14, 15, 17 and 18 (Payne 1995, 505); this was not conclusive because the survey also failed to detect the known stoneholes 8 and 13. GPR survey has located an anomaly that, it has been suggested, is stonehole 18 (Linford *et al* 2012, 7, fig 23, gpr 32) but this lies outside the projected line of the circle. However, this leaves stones 14, 15 and 17 unaccounted for. Sudden drought in July 2013 after a prolonged wet period caused a number of parchmarks to form (Banton *et al* 2014); these showed the positions of some of Gowland's excavations, some of the Y and Z holes, and apparently stoneholes 19, 20 and – crucially – 17 and 18 (*see* Fig 8.7). Only stoneholes 14 and 15 are now unaccounted for, but the evidence for non-completion still needs to be addressed. (Though it has been argued from their position on the ground that stones 14 and 15 once stood – Abbott and Anderson-Whymark 2012, 39 – this is not conclusive.)

Various ingenious arguments have been woven around this problem (summarised in Field and Pearson 2010, 64–6), and the popular and enduring view of Stonehenge is of a neat and complete sarsen circle with equally neat internal arrangements. Other monuments of this period show less concern with symmetry and 'completeness'. Avebury, Barrett points out, is 'the physical remnant of a number of abandoned projects and not the culmination of a series of planned phases' (1994, 13). The 'Great Circle' of monoliths around Newgrange was never 'complete' (O'Kelly 1982, 66, 79); some Scottish recumbent stone circles were possibly never completed (Ruggles 1999, 99). Decorated menhirs in Brittany were broken up and reused within chambered tombs (Hornsey 1987, 189). Frequent change and development is demonstrated at many later Neolithic and Early Bronze Age sites – process may be as significant as product. Many henges have gaps or straight, asymmetrical segments. It may be that at Stonehenge the monoliths were erected in increments, or that the 'missing' part of the 'circle' was never intended and that it was designed to be an open arc or horseshoe, like

missing. It is possible that some of the 'inadequate' stones have been damaged and others removed, as Petrie acknowledged, but he did not believe that this accounted for the inconsistencies; he argued that if sarsen was in such short supply that full-sized stones could not be provided in the cases noted, there probably was not enough material for the circle to be completed.

None of the sarsens have been removed since Inigo Jones's survey of 1621. It has been argued that the process of damage and removal began in the medieval or Roman period or even in later prehistoric times (Ashbee 1998; Darvill and Wainwright 2009, 18), but Long argued that this explanation for missing stones had been exaggerated (1876, 76, 224). Certainly there is a large quantity of easily available stone that could have been taken without resorting to the difficulty of lifting down lintels or felling standing monoliths. Moreover, it is necessary to the trilithon horseshoe. Parker Pearson has recently pointed out that Woodhenge can be interpreted as two conjoined horseshoes (2012, 336), and horseshoe-shaped structures of similar date have been found elsewhere (eg Parfitt and Needham 2012, 87).

On the current evidence there seem to be two possible scenarios. Either the circle was intended to be completed but the supply of large sarsens, or the means to procure them, proved insufficient, or the setting was never intended to be a complete circle but was envisioned as an arc or horseshoe facing south-west, the direction of midwinter sunset, with other stones added later. It is, however, important not to assume that megalithic architecture was created according to a predetermined template represented by what we perceive as planned phases of construction; it may be rather that the builders were drawn on as they confronted the consequences of their actions, as they raised prone stones to the vertical and attempted to set other stones upon them, confronting the possibilities and limitations of the material as they progressed (Barrett and Ko 2009, 288) – abandoning, returning, altering, reworking and abandoning again. Maybe building the sarsen 'circle' involved an act of faith that a sufficient number of large enough stones would be found. The ideological need to build monuments in a certain way may have clashed with engineering possibility not only at Stonehenge; a similar tension has been noted at the Clava cairns (Bradley 2000, 166–7), for instance.

Astronomical orientation

Stonehenge 2 is aligned on midsummer sunrise; whether the alignment on midwinter sunset is equally or more significant is perhaps not capable of resolution. What is known is that many previously existing British and Irish monuments were constructed with reference to the midwinter sun. Long Meg and Her Daughters (Cumbria) is aligned on midwinter sunset and the same has been claimed for many other monuments. The entrance passage of the tomb at Newgrange (Boyne Valley) was famously aligned on midwinter sunrise. Lunar alignments have also been suggested at Stonehenge (Pollard and Ruggles 2001). These and an alignment on midsummer sunrise, which is implied by stone 96 (the Heel Stone) and its possible companion stone 97, as well as the later construction of the Avenue,

are aspects of Stonehenge which are unusual. As Bradley has pointed out (2007, 104), the convincing alignments of major late Neolithic monuments are all concerned with the movement of the sun, not the moon. (Possible lunar alignments are, nevertheless, evident at some minor, and almost certainly later, monuments.) Other monuments in the Stonehenge environs – Woodhenge, Amesbury 50 and Coneybury – arguably share the midsummer sunrise orientation, but it is not seen convincingly elsewhere in Britain. Even at Woodhenge and Amesbury 50 the orientations vary slightly in different phases, suggesting that precise orientation on the summer solstice sunrise was not always of prime importance.

This topic has been admirably covered by Ruggles (1997, 1999) and the details will not be pursued further here. However, if the alignment of these monuments is significant it must be explained. The answer is likely to be religious, political, economical, ideological or a combination of all, but the world view and belief system of the builders of Stonehenge are not our world view and belief system, and it is difficult for us to appreciate what their motivations may have been. Anthropology shows that the movements of celestial bodies are considered meaningful in most human societies but in ways that differ widely (Ruggles and Saunders 1993). Those differences may operate within societies, as well as between them. What may appear 'significant' to us might have no meaning in another cultural context. Nevertheless, the observation of certain patterns might suggest directions for future research: for instance, the apparent emphasis of major late Neolithic monuments on the midwinter sun, except around Stonehenge, where midsummer sunrise also seems to be referenced. The experience of, and presumably the ceremonies at, these opposite times of the year would have been profoundly different. Solar alignments can be marked by anything that will cast a shadow; what should perhaps be emphasised here is the monumentality of Stonehenge when the net result is that only a few people can witness the experience.

Timber rings

Broadly contemporary with Stonehenge 2 (and 3) are the West Amesbury henge, the main periods of activity at Durrington Walls, including the North and South Circles, and Woodhenge (Fig 3.13). Such circles of multiple rings of

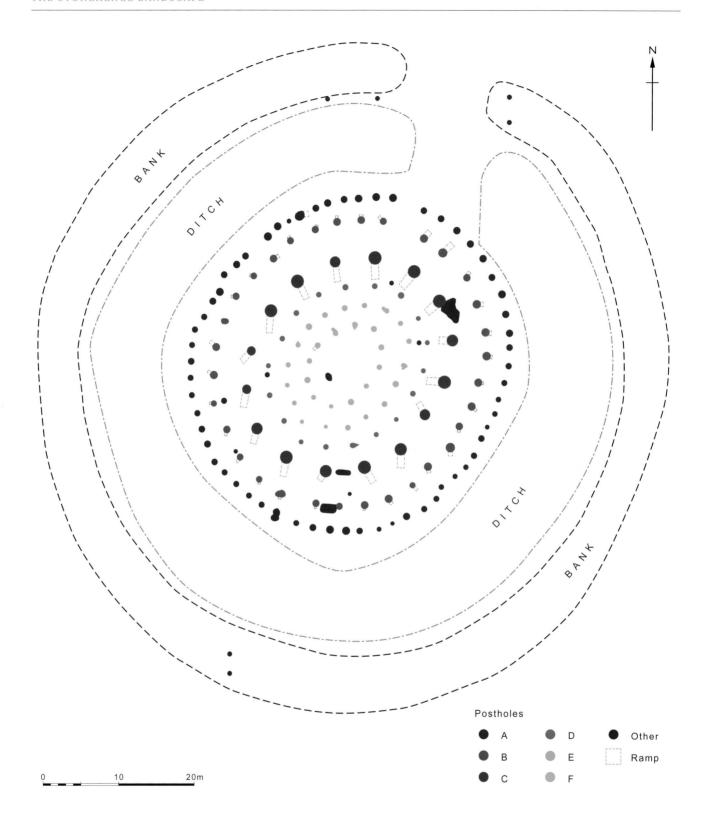

Fig 3.13
Plan of Woodhenge.
(After Cunnington 1929, plate 3)

Posarholes

● A   ● D   ● Other

● B   ● E   ▢ Ramp

● C   ● F

0   10   20m

posts are often thought of as being single-phase monuments, with posts standing in all the holes simultaneously. Reconstruction drawings nearly always show them in this way, as 'forests' of posts, sometimes even as rather unlikely complex roofed buildings. Yet it is equally likely that the different rings were occupied sequentially – in orders that may be for ever unrecoverable, unfortunately. Piggott pointed out long ago that this was the case at the Sanctuary (1939, 196–207; see also Pitts 2001), and the Southern Circle at Durrington Walls was recognised as having at least two phases from the outset (Wainwright and Longworth 1971, 23–38, 204–25, fig 9); this has been discussed more recently by Parker Pearson (2012, 90–1). Stonehenge itself provides us with a template in stone to suggest how these settings of wooden uprights would have changed over time, rings being removed and new ones created, sometimes perhaps the holes being dug but never occupied by uprights. However, as there are few clear cases of postholes intercutting, the phases may have overlapped. The activities that took place at these circles resulted in the placing of different classes of artefacts, and the bones of different types of animals, in different parts of the sites (eg Pollard 1995a).

Suggestions that the timber structures of Woodhenge are of more than one phase have been described as 'purely conjectural' (Pollard 1995a, 142), but they are no more conjectural than the assumption that they are all of one phase. It is difficult to see how the posts in the southern part of ring C could have been erected while ring B was standing, and equally difficult to see how the posts of the northern part of ring C could have been erected while ring D was standing. Ring C (if it is a ring and not two opposed horseshoes) could either pre- or post-date rings B and D (see Gibson 2012, 12, fig 10, for one possible scheme). The high levels of deposition of many objects in ring C might reflect the likelihood that this ring, with the most massive posts, was the longest-lived structure. This is not to deny that there is deliberate and meaningful spatial structuring of deposits at Woodhenge, though these deposits may post-date the timber rings (Pollard and Robinson 2007, 160).

The stone structures at Stonehenge have for some time been regarded as a skeuomorph for wooden constructions (Petrie 1880, 27), with the mortise-and-tenon and tongue-and-groove joints now thought of as a carpentry technique. This idea has been widely accepted, the only problem being that contemporary or earlier wooden structures of similar form survive only as arrays of postholes – the form and constructional details of their superstructure is unknown, though lintelled circles, arcs or pairs of upright posts seem likely. Evidence of carpentry from the Neolithic and Bronze Age is rare, but Coles and Coles have commented on ingenious Neolithic woodworking techniques (1986, 45–6, 50–2, 61–2). If Stonehenge is a stone imitation of a timber building it must imply that at least some of the contemporary timber rings were lintelled (but not roofed).

One thing is clear, however. As Mike Pitts has said, 'Stonehenge is engineered like wood not because its architects knew no other way but because that's how they chose to do it' (2000, 247).

It has been suggested, on ethnographic analogy, that the timber circles at Durrington Walls and Woodhenge represent monuments of the living, while the stone constructions at Stonehenge are a monument to the dead (Parker Pearson and Ramilisonina 1998). While this argument has not been universally accepted it does find considerable support in the different assemblage of objects recovered – portable artefacts and animal bones are prolific at the timber circles, while there is much human bone at Stonehenge (Bradley 2007, 126, 141). The pattern is not perfect, however: there are a few human bones at Woodhenge, for instance (Pollard 1995a). The dating of this material is not necessarily comparable.

Stonehenge 3: late henges and early Beakers

Between 2480 and 2280 BC some bluestones were re-erected in a circle within the sarsen trilithon horseshoe, and stones D and E were removed. A large pit was then dug to the west of the Great Trilithon, which implies disruption to the existing bluestone settings. The enclosure ditch, which had almost completely filled with silts and deliberately placed material, was partly or wholly recut. Subsequently a young man wearing an archer's bracer, who had been shot and killed by barbed-and-tanged arrows, was buried in a grave cut into the top of the ditch (Evans et al 1984). (Another inhumation in the centre of the site might be of this stage or later.) The Avenue was constructed late in this stage (Darvill et al 2012, 1034–6).

47

In the wider landscape, meanwhile, the stone circle at West Amesbury was dismantled, perhaps to provide the extra bluestones for the new circle at Stonehenge (Parker Pearson 2012, 224), and replaced by a henge; the henge ditches at Durrington Walls and Woodhenge were also dug at this period, at about 2480–2450 BC and 2480–2030 BC respectively. A megalithic cove was constructed within Woodhenge, replacing the timber settings which had now rotted. While there is a scatter (some 200 sherds) of largely unstratified Beaker pottery (2500–1700 BC) from Stonehenge itself, Beaker activity is very well attested in the surrounding landscape. This heralds a point of significant change – the introduction of metalwork, a distinctive new ceramic style and a new burial rite representing renewed contact with continental Europe.

Early Beaker burials

The Beaker evidence comes mainly in the form of burials (Figs 3.14 and 3.15). Apart from the 'Stonehenge Archer', mentioned above, there are famously the 'Amesbury Archer' (2440–2290 BC) and the 'Boscombe Bowmen' (2460–2280 BC) from east of the Avon (Fitzpatrick 2011), outside the WHS but within 5km of Stonehenge. Within the WHS there are about 30 Beaker burials (Table 3.2), some in 'flat graves' or inserted into earlier monuments,

but some under burial mounds. In some cases these burials became the focus for later ceremonials and further burials, so that some of them have been found under large and elaborate Early Bronze Age mounds.

One common feature of the Beaker burials in the Stonehenge area is a tendency towards burial in very deep pits or graves (*see* Table 3.2) not seen in the funerary rites of other prehistoric periods; this is notable within the WHS but also in the wider area, as in the case of barrow Shrewton 5K, just beyond the western boundary, which covered two Beaker inhumations in a deep shaft (Green and Rollo-Smith 1984, 275–9, fig 12). So noticeable is this pattern that it can be suggested with reasonable confidence that undated burials in deep graves, such as that under Wilsford 67, are of Beaker date (Bowden 2010, 16).

The earliest Beaker burials (from before about 2300 BC) are all located away from Stonehenge and out of sight of the monument, 'at a respectful distance' (Cleal and Pollard 2012, 328), whereas those from the following period (c 2300–2100 BC), coeval with Stonehenge 4, are closer and intervisible; these will be discussed further below.

The Avenue

The Avenue (Fig 3.16), which extends from the north-western entrance of the Stonehenge enclosure, has been convincingly dated to this phase. Its eastern bank kinks to avoid the ring ditch that surrounds the Heel Stone, showing that it is later than this feature (Field and Pearson 2010, 15).

Avenues forming part of later Neolithic ceremonial complexes are not common but where they do exist tend to be sinuous in plan. The Stonehenge Avenue, however, is straight in three sections, of approximately 500m, 700m and 900m, divided by a fairly sharp turn at the 'elbow' and a regular curve on the eastern slope of the King Barrow Ridge: it is unique in this respect and indeed unique in its overall form. Most Neolithic 'avenues' consist of rows of megaliths with little if any earthwork component; the Stonehenge Avenue resembles more nearly the form of the earlier cursus monuments, with its internal banks and external ditches. The Avenue itself is about 10m wide between banks that survive up to a maximum height of 0.2m; the ditches are now 0.2m deep, though excavation has shown that they were originally

Fig 3.14
Reconstructed Beaker from Wilsford barrow 54. Height 212mm, greatest width 155mm.
(DP158792; Wiltshire Museum, Devizes)

as much as 0.9m deep. The Avenue has been much disturbed by later roads and fields, but the survival of the section nearest to Stonehenge is remarkable (Field *et al* 2012, 19–23, 34–6). The first section, between Stonehenge and Stonehenge Bottom, is generally regarded as primary, and it has been supposed that the rest (across Stonehenge Bottom, over the King Barrow Ridge and down to the Avon at West Amesbury), which is a little wider overall, is a slightly later addition. Definite evidence for this is lacking, however.

There have been suggestions that the Stonehenge Avenue also included stones, beyond the Heel Stone and its neighbour stone 97. Stukeley did not mention this in his published account, but Roger Gale wrote to him to ask why he had omitted this detail; Gale clearly recalled having seen stoneholes as surface earthworks when inspecting the Avenue with Stukeley (Burl and Mortimer 2005, 16). Stukeley's response is not recorded (*see* Chapter 8). Certainly no stoneholes are now visible (and none have been uncovered by excavation), though the upper end of the Avenue has suffered two and a half centuries of traffic and other disturbance since Stukeley and Gale saw it. Geophysical evidence is inconclusive on this point: though there are anomalies along the line of the Avenue (Payne 1995, 506–7, fig 264) they cannot be interpreted as resulting from placed pairs of stones.

In terms of the Avenue's purpose, little evidence of use has been recovered and its road-like form has encouraged a view of processions of one kind or another. Stukeley considered that, 'We must suppose the intent of the avenue was to direct the religious procession to the temple … I suppose only the priests and chief personages came within the *area*, who made the procession with the sacrifices along the avenue. The multitude kept without' (1740, 34). Little has changed except perhaps on the emphasis: Atkinson believed that the route was a processional one but also one along which the bluestones were carried (1956, 57, 65–6), while – with better chronological evidence – Parker Pearson considers that the Avenue *commemorates* the route along which the bluestones had formerly been transported (2012, 225–6) and that it links Stonehenge with Durrington Walls via the Avon.

These arguments are predicated on the idea that the Avenue follows the easiest gradients from the river. This may be true for most of the route but at one crucial point, the 'elbow', it is not. A route 100m or so further west here, utilising the dry valley which runs down from the former car park, would have avoided the steepest part of the low bluff; this, however, would not bring Stonehenge into view on the solstice alignment. It could be argued that the extra effort of bringing the stones up the bluff on that crucial alignment was part of the purpose. Another curiosity of the Avenue's route up the bluff, however, is the lack of hollowing which we would expect at this point if it had been subjected to heavy traffic for any length of time (this lack of hollowing is clear both from surface observation for the EH project and from the excavations); it is precisely on shoulders such as this that hollow ways first develop. This argues somewhat against the 'elbow' either as a route for the stones or as a well-used processional route over any length of time. If processions did take place up this slope they either did not happen very often or did not involve many people, as Stukeley surmised. Another alternative, suggested by Josh Pollard and Mike Parker Pearson (pers comm), is that the Avenue was a route for the spirits of the dead, not for the living.

Stonehenge 4: late Beakers

The bluestones were rearranged between about 2270 and 1920 BC to form the bluestone oval of about 24 stones at the centre of the monument and a bluestone circle of 40 to 60 close-set pillars between the trilithons and the sarsen 'circle' (Darvill *et al* 2012, 1036–7). This arrangement would have made it difficult to see out of or into the centre.

Later Beaker burials

Whereas early Beaker pottery is very rare at the major monuments there is a notable change around 2200 BC, after which there is a diversification of Beaker burial practice and uptake of Beaker pottery in the domestic sphere (Cleal and Pollard 2012, 329). Several of the later Beaker burials near Stonehenge (*see* Table 3.2) are (more or less) in a straight line (Garwood 2012, 308). Here the argument for deliberate alignment is more compelling than it was in earlier periods, partly because similar alignments of Beaker burials can be cited elsewhere (ibid, 302–10); the alignment of Beaker burials in Amesbury 56, Amesbury 54, the Fargo henge, Amesbury 51 and the Stonehenge ditch does

Table 3.2 Beaker burials in the Stonehenge WHS (see Fig 3.15).
This includes some doubtful attributions (Amesbury 14 and 15; Wilsford 67). Lawson (2007, 154) and Garwood (2012, 308) include Winterbourne Stoke 30 but this seems to be an error. Burials are inhumations unless otherwise specified.

No.	Name	Burial(s)	Monument type	Finds	Date BC
1	Amesbury 14	2	Inserted into long barrow	–	–
2	Amesbury 15	1 (?)	Bell barrow	Possible beaker with later objects	–
3	Amesbury 18	2 cremations?	'Deep cist' under a bowl barrow	2 beakers; 2 incense cups; 2 bronze awls	–
4	Amesbury 22	1 primary; 1 secondary	Grave 1.2m deep under bowl barrow	Beaker with secondary	–
5	Amesbury 40	1	Shallow grave under later (?) barrow	Beaker; bone pin	–
6	Amesbury 51	1 primary; 2 secondary	Grave 1.8m deep under bowl barrow	3 beakers	c 2300–2000
7	Amesbury 54	1 primary; 2 (?) secondary	Under bowl barrow	2 beakers; flint dagger; beads etc	c 2300–2100
8	Amesbury 56	1 secondary	In bowl barrow	Beaker	c 2300–2100
9	Durrington 7	1; cremation	Grave 1.4m deep under flint cairn	Animal bone; antler	2275–1958
10	Durrington 8	1 skull	Bowl barrow	Beaker; large urn	–
11	Durrington 36	1	Under bowl barrow	Beaker	–
12	Durrington 65B	1	Under bowl barrow	Beaker	–
13	Durrington 67	1	'Large grave' under bowl barrow	Beaker; perforated stone axe	–
14	Durrington Down	1	Flat grave	2 beakers	–
15	Fargo henge	1; 2 cremations	Within earlier henge	Beaker	c 2300–2100
16	Stonehenge Archer	1	Grave in Stonehenge ditch	Bracer; arrowheads	2200–2000
17	Wilsford 1	8	In bowl barrow	7 beakers; antlers	pre-2300
18	Wilsford 2b	1 primary; 2 secondary	Grave 1.8m deep under undtiched bowl barrow	2 beakers	pre-2300
19	Wilsford 34	5	Inserted into long barrow	Beaker	–
20	Wilsford 40	1	Grave 1.5m deep under later bowl barrow	Beaker	–
21	Wilsford 51	2	Under bowl barrow	Beaker and fragments	–
22	Wilsford 52	2	Under bowl barrow	2 beakers	–
23	Wilsford 54	1	Under bowl barrow	3 beakers; barbed-and-tanged arrowheads; antler	2470–2200
24	Wilsford 62	1	Grave under later (?) bowl barrow	Long-necked beaker with lozenge decoration	–
25	Wilsford 67	1	Grave 3m deep under undtiched bowl barrow	–	–
26	Wilsford 70	1	Under later disc barrow	Beaker fragments	–
27	Wilsford Trench 15 A303	2	Flat graves	2 beakers	2460–2290
28	Winterbourne Stoke 10	2	Under later bowl barrow	Beaker	–
29	Winterbourne Stoke 20	1	Grave under a later bowl barrow	Beaker	–
30	Winterbourne Stoke 35c	1	In bowl barrow	Beaker	–

Fig 3.15 (opposite) Beaker burials within the WHS; for numbering see Table 3.2.

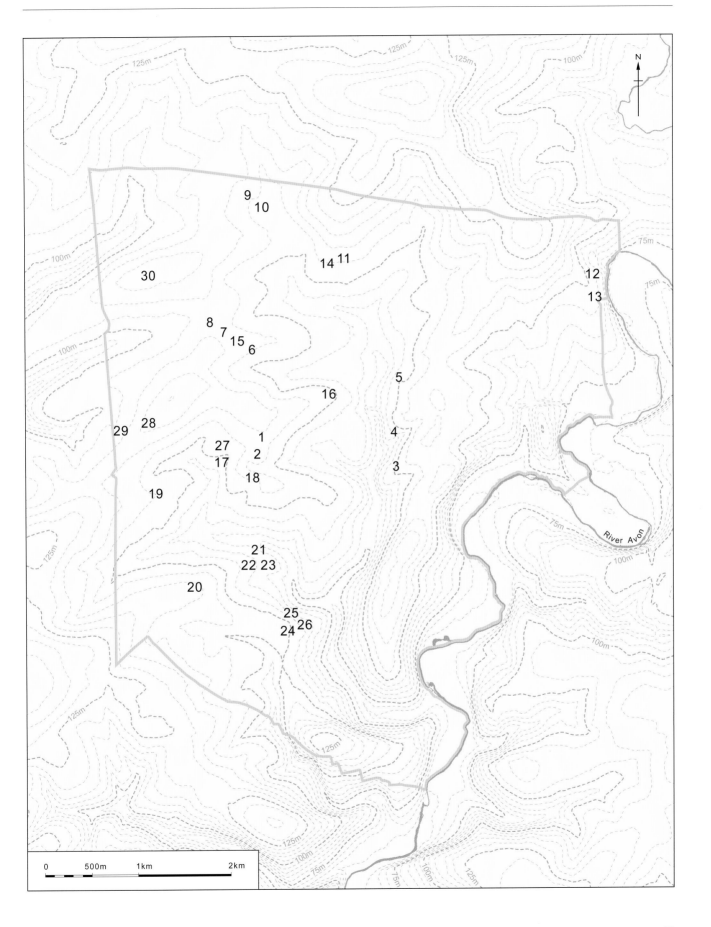

Fig 3.16
Plan of the Stonehenge
Avenue.

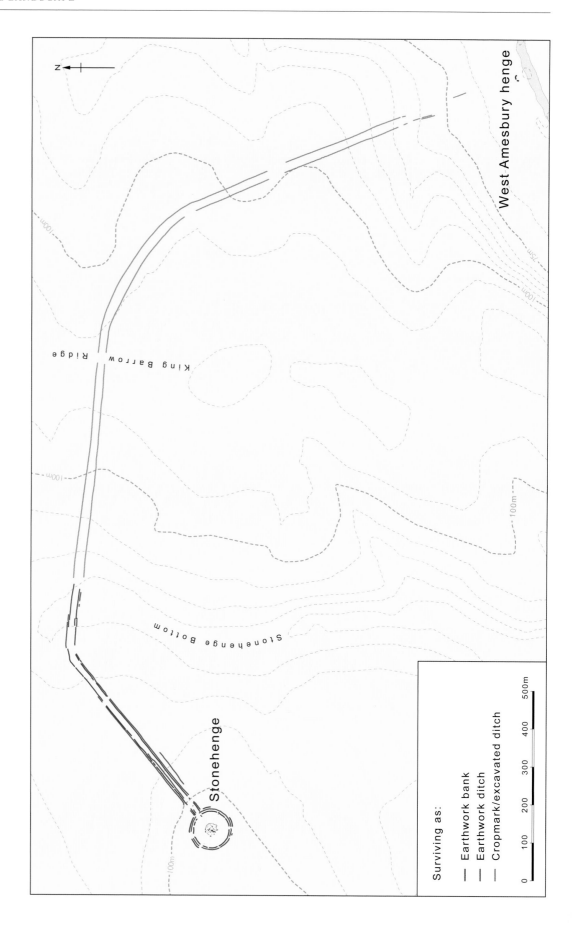

seem rather purposeful, even if its significance is hard to explain. However, the extension of this alignment to include (almost) the Coneybury and West Amesbury henges and the 'Amesbury Archer' is more difficult to sustain; it is divided by the high ridge on which Coneybury stands and a length of the Avon valley. This begins to look more like the wishful thinking of the ley hunter than anything that is likely to have had reality in prehistory. As Garwood himself notes (2012, 308–9), the alignment could be coincidental: the sites forming this 'corridor' belong to several different phases and it cuts across the Avenue, which was formalised by this time.

'North Kite'

There are many references in the literature to this large site on Wilsford Down (eg Crawford and Keiller 1928, 254–6, pl L), and despite the fact that its south side is open it is still referred to as an enclosure. It has been dated to the 'Beaker period' but as a result of our fieldwork we doubt that attribution, though there is undoubtedly strong evidence of activity in this area at the time. The 'North Kite' will be discussed in Chapter 4.

Stonehenge 5: Early Bronze Age art

This final phase of major prehistoric activity at Stonehenge (c 2010–1450 BC; Darvill et al 2012, 1037–8) is attested by finds of very late Beaker, Food Vessel (2200–1700 BC) and Collared Urn (1900–1500 BC) sherds and by the carvings on some of the sarsen uprights, which date to 1750–1500 BC; bluestones, and possibly sarsens, were being broken up at this time – debris has been found near the Heel Stone. The last structural alteration, which was apparently never completed, was the digging of the two concentric circles of pits known as the Y and Z holes.

Carvings

Prehistoric carvings of a dagger and axes (Figs 3.17 and 3.18) on the sarsen uprights were first noted in 1953. The laser scan of the stones has revealed further examples and the number known has now reached 118 (Abbott and Anderson-Whymark 2012, 26). The fact that they are restricted to a relatively small number of stones (3, 4, 5, 23 and 53) in particular

parts of the monument (see Fig 3.3) might be regarded as significant, even if the nature of that significance is unclear, or it could be that suitable flat surfaces were chosen.

Y and Z holes

There was apparently an intention to move the stones to new settings at this period but it was never carried beyond the digging of stone-holes in about 1630–1520 BC. The dating of these features, the Y and Z holes, is known from just four radiocarbon determinations but is currently accepted – in the absence of other evidence – as a reasonable indication of their chronology (Darvill et al 2012, 1038; Marshall et al 2012, 25). Hawley believed that they were the right size and shape to have accommodated the bluestones (1925, 34). These holes were dug in concentric rings around the existing sarsen 'circle'. The circles were slightly irregular, especially on the south-east side, and were not even completed, Y hole 7 being only partly dug and Z hole 8 being missing or seriously out of its expected position (Hawley 1925, 30). An intriguing possibility is that geophysical anomalies gpr 58 and 59 (Linford et al 2012, fig 23) could be Y holes containing stones. The only sign of ritual activity associated with these features is a bundle of antlers placed on the base of Y hole 30 (Cleal et al 1995, 257–8). Some of the Y and Z holes – and not just those excavated by Hawley – are still visible on the surface as depressions less than 0.1m deep (see Figs 3.2 and 3.3). Some others showed as parchmarks in the July 2013 drought. Within the circuit

Fig 3.17
Bronze axe head of a type similar to those depicted on the stones. Length 119mm. Unfortunately this splendid example is unprovenanced, though it was probably found in south Wiltshire. (DP158952; Courtesy of The Salisbury Museum, E T Stevens coll)

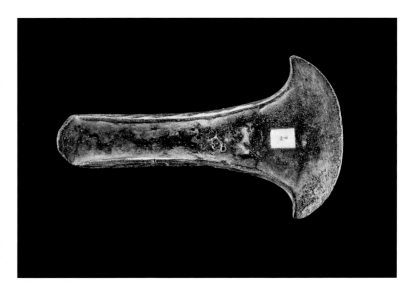

of Y holes is a shallow bank, and another lies between the Z holes and the standing sarsens. These might be traces of Hawley's spoil heaps, except that they appear to be visible on historic aerial photographs pre-dating Hawley's excavations and their origin is therefore uncertain (Field and Pearson 2010, 8–10, 56–8); they could be spoil from the original digging of the holes.

The focus of activity in this period was less at Stonehenge itself than the barrow cemeteries, and subsequently the fields, which were established in the landscape around it. These are the subject of the next chapter.

Fig 3.18
Axe carvings on the east face of stone 4. Laser scan image.

Example greyscale offset
image 7.5cm band

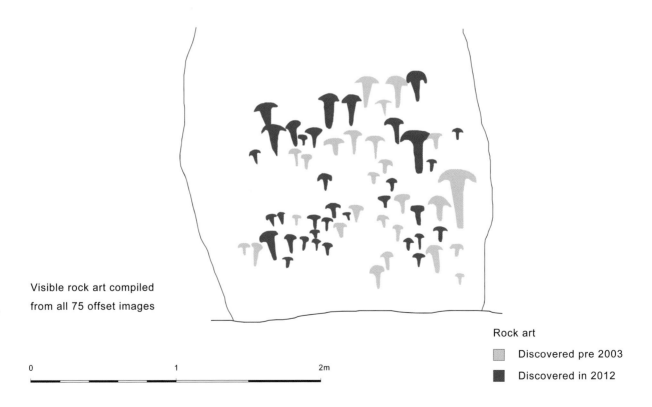

Visible rock art compiled
from all 75 offset images

Rock art

Discovered pre 2003

Discovered in 2012

0   1   2m

4

Later prehistory

Activity at Stonehenge continued well into the 2nd millennium BC, though perhaps intermittently, when it provided an ancestral focal point. In the surrounding landscape life was dominated by the development and use of extensive round barrow groups or cemeteries and subsequent field systems and linear boundaries (Fig 4.1). Many of the round barrows were opened by antiquaries in the early 19th century but modern excavation has been limited.

The round barrows

The WHS contains nearly half of the 1,000 round barrows estimated to occupy the area between the Till and Avon rivers (Lawson 2007, 202). Barrows have been classified according to their shape (*see* Chapter 1 and Richards 2007, 44–5; 2013, 25). Attempts have been made to define patterns in their distribution. Many of the barrows appear to have been deliberately clustered into groups that are usually described as 'linear', 'nucleated' or 'dispersed' (eg Darvill 2006, 166, fig 62). They have been discussed in terms of circular zones, sometimes described as sacred geographies, set around and having reference to Stonehenge (eg Woodward and Woodward 1996, 284, fig 6; Darvill 1997), despite Fleming's observation that their distribution extends towards Everleigh to the north-east and does not actually centre on Stonehenge (1971, 141). Indeed, their general ubiquity means that they could be regarded as a single extensive cemetery (Richards 1990, 273).

Closer study shows that such models do not adequately characterise these monuments. Elements of many groups can be said to be variously nucleated, dispersed or linear, and divisions are somewhat arbitrary and inconsistent, even in works involving the same authors (eg Darvill *et al* 2005, map I; Darvill 2006, 166, fig 62). Nor are the classifications of bar-row types always useful, since they often reflect only the cumulative physical manifestation of several events at each round barrow, aside from the effects of later land use.

Rather than seeking models that stress similarities, it may be more relevant to explore evidence of 'fluidity' and development within the landscape. As both excavation and survey increasingly demonstrate, these monuments were often the result of cumulative events, each constructed in several phases and over different timescales. Individual barrows were never conceived as a single plan and nor were the groups. Instead, they appear to have developed in a much more interleaved, piecemeal and organic way through the actions of individuals, groups and societies across the whole landscape and against a range of evolving ideologies (Garwood 2012, 303). The individuality of each round barrow can therefore be recognised, since each is the result of a complex series of interpretations and decisions that may be only partly reflected in their final form and topographical positioning.

The general lack of modern excavation means a corresponding absence of absolute dating. Only two radiocarbon dates have so far been obtained from the round barrows but they hint at their potentially earlier histories: carbonised planks from Amesbury 39 and 51 produced dates of 2459–1926 BC and 2270–1742 BC respectively (Ashbee 1981, 32; Ashbee 1978, 24). Although round barrows were being constructed as early as 2200 BC the main development of these monuments occurred between 2000 and 1520 BC (broadly coeval with Stonehenge stage 5; Darvill *et al* 2012, 1038). Typological dating of grave goods has been the only available method of phasing burials within this broad period (Fig 4.2).

Detailed analytical earthwork survey suggests the possibility of isolating phases of construction in the outward form of many of

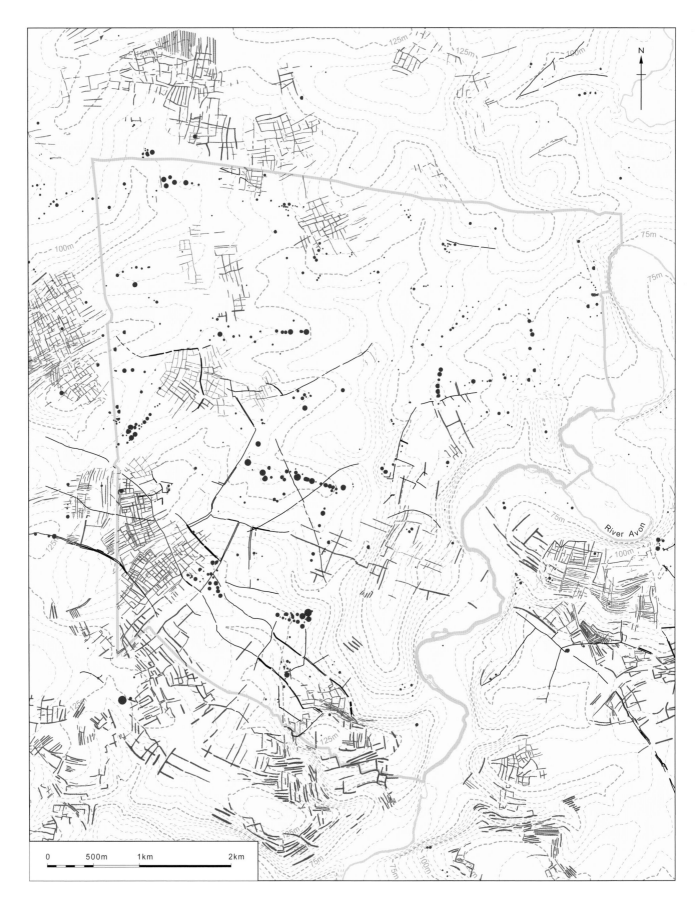

the barrows and, combined with other sources of information, can be used to indicate patterns of development within several of the barrow groups. It clarifies the stratigraphic relationships between the round barrows and other features, such as the linear boundaries. Survey highlights the ways in which the depiction of barrows on maps and their classification in lists has masked their true complexity.

The EH project has provided accurate spatial and interpretive data for almost half of the known or suspected round barrows within the WHS, effectively nearly all of those surviving as earthworks (Fig 4.3). The survey has more accurately located Amesbury 112 and Wilsford 92, both within woodland (Komar and Bishop 2010, 13; Bowden *et al* 2012, 17), and rediscovered the very subtle earthworks of part of Durrington 1, a disc barrow that was thought completely destroyed (Bishop 2011a, 27). Additional small mounds have been identified as possible round barrows. One is situated within the Wilsford group (Bowden 2010, 10) and another is located beyond the byway immediately east of the Cursus barrow group (Amadio and Bishop 2010, 13; Field *et al* 2012, 17). Neither is more than 0.3m high and the latter in particular is perhaps more likely to be the result of recent activity.

Multiple phases

Many of the barrows in the WHS marked significant places with long individual histories that stretched back into the Neolithic. Barrow groups at Normanton Down, Winterbourne Stoke Crossroads, Lake and Stonehenge developed around earlier monuments. The degree to which Neolithic round barrows are present is unknown because of the lack of modern excavation. Extant barrows have a wide variety of forms, within which a number of phases can often be identified; where excavation has taken place different combinations of burials contained on and within timber and stake structures have been identified, along with cists, causewayed and complete ring ditches, plinths, berms, outer banks and barrow mounds (Fig 4.4) – features increasingly common in round barrows found elsewhere (eg McOmish *et al* 2002, 41; Lewis and Mullin 2012, 199).

Although many mounds have been levelled or smoothed over by ploughing, or mutilated by burrowing animals and quarrying, the surviving earthworks still reveal some complexity, and a third of the surveyed barrows provide evidence for multiphase construction. In some instances up to four possible phases are visible (*see* Fig 4.3). Wilsford 17, for example, has a

Fig 4.1 (opposite)
Round barrows (red), field systems (green) and linear ditches (black).

Fig 4.2
Riveted bronze dagger blade from Wilsford barrow 54. Length 117mm, width 48mm. The dating of Bronze Age burials is largely dependent upon the typology of such distinctive artefacts.
(DP158896; Wiltshire Museum, Devizes)

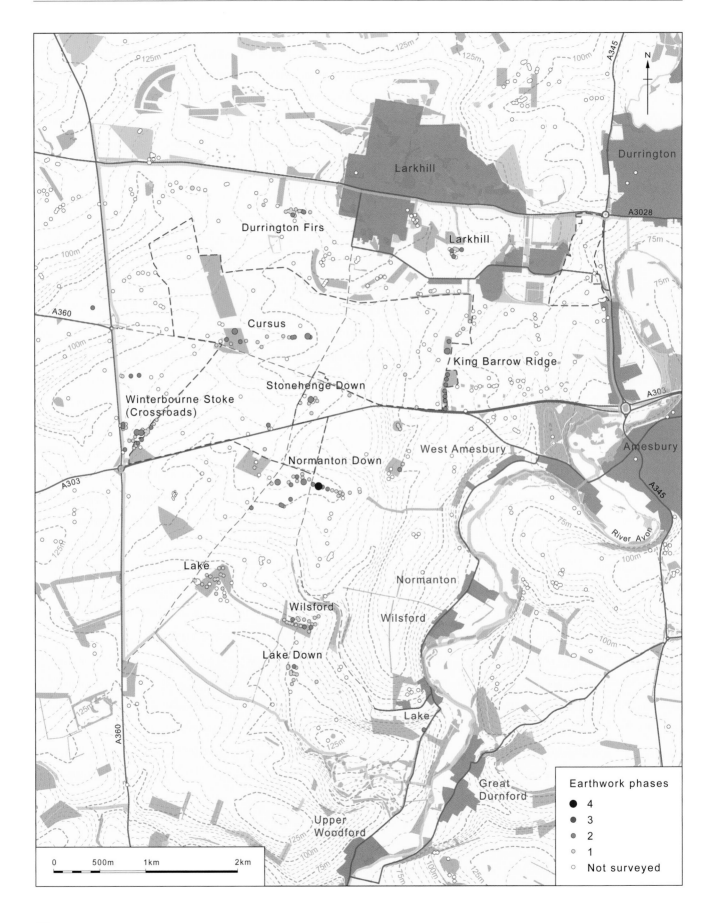

sequence of tiered breaks in slope which suggest three phases of construction (Barrett and Bowden 2010, 18).

Similarly, at Amesbury 44 it appears that the larger western mound was constructed, then the smaller mound added onto a plinth to its east and the ditch redug around both mounds. One of the clearest indications of multiple phase construction is the presence of plinths beneath the mounds of several bell barrows, notably of Amesbury 43 to 46 in the Cursus barrow group (Figs 4.5 and 4.6; Amadio and Bishop 2010, 10–11). Other examples include a kidney-shaped plinth observed beneath the twin mounds of Wilsford 15 and 16 (Barrett and Bowden 2010, 17). A number of barrows display a distinct change in gradient which may indicate phased construction. Over half of the

surveyed bell barrows show apparent multiple phases in their outward form.

Bush Barrow (Wilsford 5) has received a considerable amount of attention because of the remarkable gold assemblage found within it (Hoare 1812, 202; Needham *et al* 2009, 2010). The mound has three clear breaks in slope, which might be interpreted as three phases of development (Barrett and Bowden 2010, 10), though part of this may be due to post-medieval alterations to accommodate the sheep pen depicted by Stukeley (1740, tab XXXIII, 64; RCHME 1979, title page).

Sometimes material added to a mound is undoubtedly spoil from holes dug on the summit (for example Amesbury 37; Bishop 2011b, 16) but elsewhere there are more deliberate additions (Barrett and Bowden 2010, 32).

Fig 4.3 (opposite) Distribution of round barrows, showing those studied by this project and indicating where it has been possible to suggest the presence of a number of phases within the individual monuments from earthwork survey.

Fig 4.4 Reconstruction drawing of various stages in the construction and use of Amesbury 51, based on the results of excavation by Paul Ashbee in 1960 (1978) and survey. Digging the primary grave; the mortuary house; the body in the grave; building the mound; digging the ditch; digging a grave in the mound.

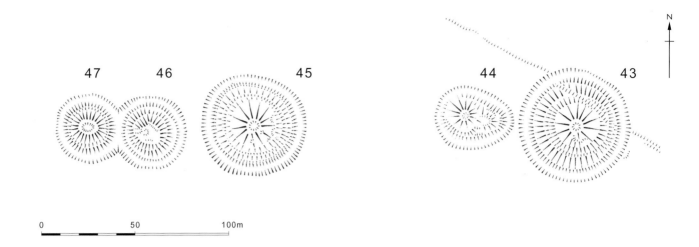

N

47   46   45   44   43

0   50   100m

*Fig 4.5 (above)
Amesbury barrows 43 to
47 in the Cursus barrow
group. It is not possible to
suggest a chronological
sequence on the basis of the
intercutting ditches of 46
and 47, but the decision to
join these barrows must
have been deliberate and
must have had meaning.
Barrow 43 has been
superficially damaged by the
abandoned construction of
the 18th-century road (see
Chapter 6).*

*Fig 4.6 (right)
Amesbury 45, Cursus
barrow group, showing the
plinth beneath the mound.
(DP159909)*

In the Lake group, a mound has apparently been added to the western end of the long barrow, Wilsford 41, effectively creating a round barrow on top of the earlier long barrow; Wilsford 44, previously classified as a bowl barrow, also appears to have been heightened (Bowden *et al* 2012, 25). Not all such alterations were made in antiquity. Wilsford 87 was enhanced as a prospect mount forming part of an aesthetic scheme associated with Lake House (*see* Chapter 6). Other changes represent recent damage: the disc barrow Durrington 20 once had two distinct tumps, which were refigured into one kidney-shaped mound at some point after 1943 (Bishop 2010, 13).

Causeways

The present survey adds significantly to the number of causewayed sites known through excavation (Ashbee 1978, 27) and henge-like structures identified from geophysical surveys (*see* Chapter 3). The two opposing causeways and the pitted nature of the ditches of Amesbury 50 are visible as very subtle earthworks despite ploughing in the 20th century (Amadio and Bishop 2010, 8). Possible causeways were observed in the south-western quadrant of the ditch around Amesbury 53 (Komar and Bishop 2010, 14), and a closer examination of historic aerial photographs suggests that Amesbury

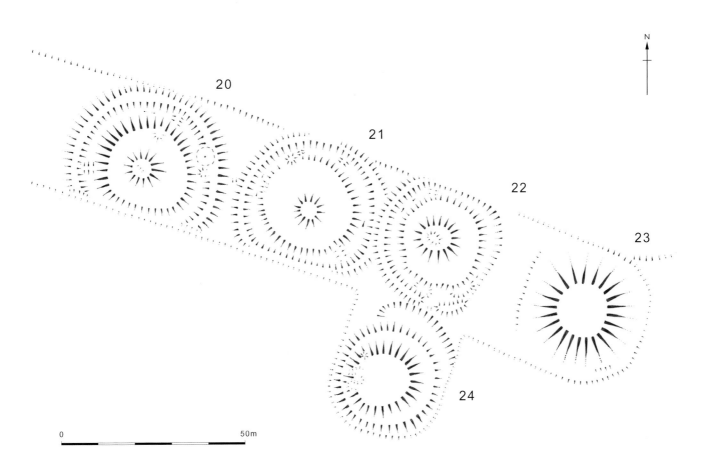

20

21

22

23

24

N

0   50m

115 comprises a causewayed ditch. There is the slightest suggestion of a causeway on the northern side of Amesbury 48 (Amadio and Bishop 2010, 24); ploughing in the 20th century has nearly destroyed the outer bank and ditch of this barrow, though it was formerly protected to some extent by fencing.

Examples of causeways have been identified elsewhere in the better-preserved round barrows across the northern part of the Stonehenge WHS landscape; those in the southern part are mostly too damaged by cultivation or tree cover. Several examples are located within the Normanton Down group (Barrett and Bowden 2010, 32). For example, the gap in the penannular ditch around Wilsford 28, another potential henge-like enclosure, appears to have been blocked by construction of Wilsford 28a immediately to its south-east. The three disc barrows of Wilsford 20 to Wilsford 22 all have irregularities in the bottom of their ditches, but 22 also has a possible causeway on its southeastern side (Fig 4.7).

Barrow group development

Relative chronological relationships can be established in certain cases where there are linked pairs or groups. Given the probably quite personal and small-scale activity at these sites, such phenomena are probably expressions of a desire or need to make a perceived relationship between barrows manifest. The stratigraphic sequences are particularly significant when considered against the general lack of finds or other dating material from these particular barrows, many of which Hoare considered had been opened before (1812, 211).

The main groups often appear to take an earlier, Neolithic, monument as a catalyst for their development; making use of long barrows, mortuary enclosures and cursuses, but also earlier occupation sites and Beaker graves. At Winterbourne Stoke Crossroads analysis of the earthworks implies that Winterbourne Stoke 5, 4 and 3a, which provide the clearest sequence within the main alignment, were developed

Fig 4.7 (above)
Wilsford barrows 20–24 on Normanton Down, showing irregularities in the ditches of disc barrows 20 and 21, and a possible causeway in the south-eastern side of 22. The outer bank of barrow 22 is clearly overlying that of barrow 21. The plough step surrounding the barrows shows how arable farming encroached on these monuments in the later 20th century.

from the north-east towards the south-west (Fig 4.8) – that is heading *towards* the long barrow (Bax *et al* 2010, 39). The alignment, although deliberate, is not precise and might result more from the direction and form of the ridge than the presence of the long barrow. Similar observations can be made elsewhere: at Lake the round barrows extend to the side of Wilsford 41, slightly downslope but again to the north-east. The distribution of the King Barrows pays more attention to the alignment of the ridge top than the nearby presence of long barrow Amesbury 42 or the Stonehenge Cursus, though the relationship of these and other barrows to the Stonehenge Avenue, flanking it but not impinging upon it, may be significant.

On Lake Down the bank around the pond barrow, Wilsford 77, overlies that around the evidently earlier pond of Wilsford 77a to its south (Komar 2010, 12), and in the Lake group the bank of disc barrow Wilsford 45b clearly overlies that defining Wilsford 45a, another disc barrow, to its north-west (Bowden *et al* 2012, 25). In both cases the later barrow is slightly larger in diameter.

At Durrington Firs, a remarkable group of diminutive barrows, overlapping earthworks indicate that the central arrangement of three similarly sized bowl barrows, Durrington 18,

19 and 22, developed east to west, towards the valley bottom (Bishop 2010, 22). Broad, low barrows were subsequently added, which abut them to the north (Durrington 13) and south (Durrington 20, a disc barrow); their edges are relatively flattened where they touch. A similar pattern has been observed outside the WHS, at Snail Down near Everleigh (Thomas 2005, 309), but this sequence by no means provides a rule. On Normanton Down a group of three disc barrows, of similar size, forms part of the main alignment (Barrett and Bowden 2010, 31). The western edge of Wilsford 22 overlies Wilsford 21 but the apparently later bell barrow of Wilsford 24 abuts the southern side of Wilsford 22 (*see* Fig 4.7). Several pairs of barrows share a causeway, hollow or step between their conjoined ditches, another feature that highlights how construction of the barrows was probably interleaved (Wilsford 17 and 15/16 for example; Barrett and Bowden 2010, 18). Prehistoric observers will also have been able to unpick these sequences: it is therefore probable that they were deliberately created and subsequently read as a narrative which had significant, but possibly changing, meanings regarding, for instance, lineage histories.

By combining such observations it is possible to revise the developmental sequence across several of the groups. It has been thought that the Normanton Down cemetery, for example, was constructed from west to east. The field evidence clearly shows that development was not that simple; instead elements combined and individual monuments were developed in a more fluid manner (Barrett and Bowden 2010, 31; Needham *et al* 2010, 4).

Using the earthwork plans together with other records it is possible to suggest slight refinements to the chronological narrative (Needham *et al* 2010, appendix 1) and demonstrate the fluidity prevalent in the development of the prehistoric landscape. The Wilsford barrow group has received less attention than most others in the Stonehenge WHS. There has been no modern excavation, geophysical survey or fieldwalking and the area was ploughed for much of the 20th century. Only 14 of the 19 known barrows survive as earthworks, in some cases barely. Nevertheless, antiquarian observations can be coupled with interpretation of aerial photographs and the new field survey to suggest a broad chronological narrative for the cemetery (Fig 4.9). This shows that the elaborate barrow structures are, in some cases

Fig 4.8
Barrows 3a, 4 and 5, Winterbourne Stoke Crossroads, showing their chronological relationship and the development of this part of the cemetery to the south-west, towards the earlier long barrow.

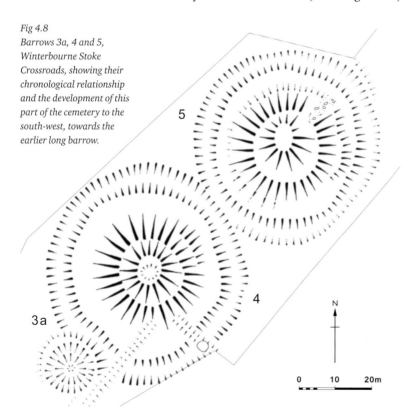

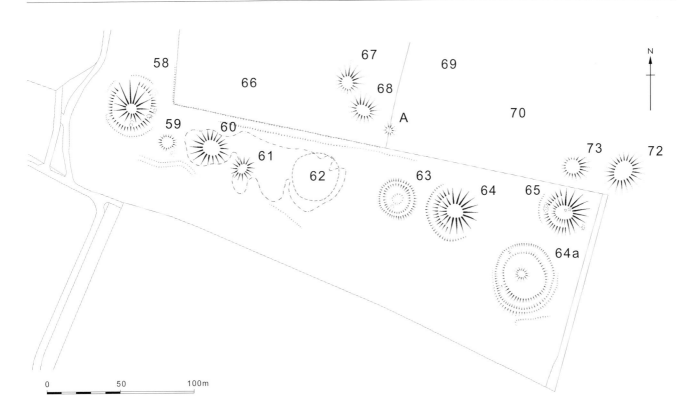

at least, much later in the sequence than the primary burials that they cover (Bowden 2010, 12–17; *see also* Woodward and Needham 2012).

In a few cases particularly rich bell barrows are located towards the western end of linear groups, such as Wilsford 8 (Fig 4.10) and 58 (Bowden 2010, 13; Bowden *et al* 2012, 27), but their arrangement is quite loose and not all large bell barrows in similar locations are apparently so richly furnished. In Amesbury 55, Hoare's 'Monarch of the Plain', only charred wood was found (1812, 164). Amesbury 43, the large bell barrow at the eastern end of the Cursus group, also disappointed its excavator, William Stukeley (Burl and Mortimer 2005, 96). Considered together, Amesbury 43 and 55 could be seen to 'bookend' the Cursus barrow group. Neither apparently contains a primary interment and, though such deposits could have been missed by the early excavations, this is far from unusual; many barrows could be used initially for ceremonies and functions other than burial. In this case these two barrows provided large focal points along the ridge, perhaps as cenotaphs (Jones 2005, 140; Thomas 2005, 297–9). Conversely, burials were not always marked by earthwork structures, such as the Early Bronze Age cremations placed adjacent to the Cuckoo Stone (Parker Pearson *et al* 2007, 118–20). Equally, burials could be inserted

into pre-existing Neolithic mounds in the Early Bronze Age, as happened at the Winterbourne Stoke Crossroads long barrow (Thurnam 1868, 197–8).

Fig 4.9 (above)
The Wilsford barrow group. Relationships between the levelled barrows in the northern part of the group can be teased out from aerial photographs. Bell barrow 58, marking the western end of the cemetery, contained a rich burial. Mound A is possibly a previously unrecorded barrow. Barrows 60–2 are currently under dense box planting and could not be fully surveyed.

Fig 4.10 (left)
Incense cup from the primary, richly furnished cremation under bell barrow Wilsford 8 at the western end of the Normanton Down group. The cup, height 44mm, diameter 104mm, is of a type known from the south coast and linked to a maritime network bringing influences and material from the continent (Needham et al 2010, 27–8).
(DP158911; Wiltshire Museum, Devizes)

Place in the landscape

Subtle interplays of position and tricks of perspective are evident within the barrow groups. Amesbury 55 is located on a slight ridge end which emphasised its size when Hoare observed it in open downland (1812, 164). Bush Barrow (Wilsford 5) is situated at a slightly higher elevation than its neighbours, which gives it the greatest intervisibility with Stonehenge even though it is not the tallest barrow in the group (Barrett and Bowden 2010, 11). At about 2.5m high, Winterbourne Stoke 25 is not as tall or broad as its neighbour Winterbourne Stoke 26 (3.2m high) but its location slightly higher up the slope makes it look the same size, if not slightly larger (Bishop 2011a, 43).

The strong visual relationship between Stonehenge and the linear groups of conspicuous barrows that define the visibility envelope around it has been described elsewhere (Exon *et al* 2000; Peters 2000). Given the environmental evidence for a largely open grassland landscape in the Early Bronze Age (Allen and Scaife 2007, 27) and the rolling downland topography, a high degree of visibility can be assumed. Indeed the creators of the round barrows appear to have favoured the gentler slopes and broad ridge tops (Fig 4.11). However, many barrows in the wider landscape, perhaps a majority, are not intervisible with Stonehenge; there are barrows, even bell barrows, on valley floors where they are not conspicuous. While there was clearly an awareness of visibility in the Early Bronze Age there were undoubtedly many other social and perhaps spiritual references invoked. In creating a round barrow, people were deliberately monumentalising those particular locations in the landscape, referencing a variety of ideas and things both near and far, temporally as well as spatially. Many barrows, such as the New King Barrows, had large quantities of turf in their mounds (Cleal and Allen 1994), implying the stripping of turf from a wide surrounding area, which might have left a visible expanse of chalk much larger than the barrows themselves.

One of the references invoked by barrow building was probably to water, an essential component for successful existence on the chalk. In the wider landscape of southern England round barrows and barrow groups are rarely located on the highest or most visible points but in valley slope locations associated with watercourses and springs (Field 1998,

320; 2008, 83–6; McOmish *et al* 2002, 46). Indeed, Hoare commented that he had 'found them in no part of our county so numerous, or large, as in the Vale of Wily' (1812, 98). Some 15 groups lie alongside or around the head of the Nine Mile River to the north-east of the WHS (McOmish *et al* 2002, 40), and recent aerial reconnaissance and mapping has identified numerous ring ditches along the River Avon, south-east of Marden henge in the Vale of Pewsey (Carpenter and Winton 2011, 29–32) and further down the valley in Hampshire (Field 2008, 110–11).

This connection with water may also have been seasonal, as suggested by the numerous 'winterbournes' in the wider area. Heywood Sumner's illustration of Oakley Down (Dorset) shows that although these barrows are perceived as 'up' on the downs there is still a seasonal accumulation of water, with an area marked 'In winter the springs rise here' (1913, pl XXX). In this context it is worth considering ancient hydrology and how it influenced use of the landscape. The Lake, Normanton Down, Wilsford, Lake Down and Winterbourne Stoke Crossroads groups focus on and bracket the dry valley between them, at the head of which lies the Wilsford Shaft (Bowden *et al* 2012, 28). Although the valley floors and dry valleys were probably much wetter in prehistory, when the water table was higher (McOmish *et al* 2002, 10), they appear to lack much alluvium or colluvium; this is attributed to the absence of arable agriculture in the intervening millennia, though it could also have been washed away by running water (Richards 1990, 210–11). On porous chalk with little overlying sediment valleys would have drained quickly, water perhaps disappearing almost as quickly as it appeared. If they were neither a barren dry valley nor a winterbourne stream, were they perhaps only occasionally, or even 'magically', wet? Water is known to have been flowing in Spring Bottom (the lower part of Stonehenge Bottom) in the 19th century (Richards 1990, 211).

Later chronology

Some barrows also display a stratigraphic relationship with later features. Wilsford 45b, a large disc barrow in the Lake group, is cut by the ditch of a linear boundary, and the accompanying linear bank overlies the ditch of Wilsford 46 to the south (Bowden *et al* 2012, 31). The linear boundary deviates very slightly around the

*Fig 4.11 (opposite)
The location of round barrows against relative steepness of slope, generated by GIS analysis. Much has been written about the apparent 'ring' of barrow cemeteries around Stonehenge but, as this image emphasises, the barrow groups relate to the local natural topography. The main barrow groups occupy broad ridge tops with gentle slopes and are laid out to conform to the topography of those ridges. This may help to explain the otherwise puzzling lack of barrows on the high ridge dividing Spring Bottom and Lake Bottom from the Avon (the southern extension of the King Barrow Bridge); the very narrow top of this steep ridge is unlike others in the area.*

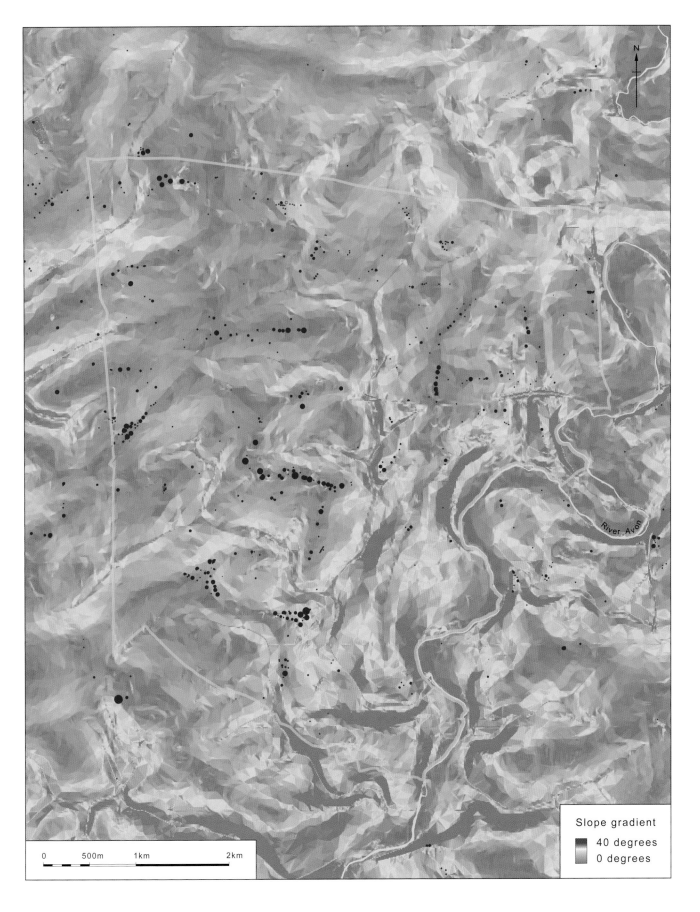

Slope gradient

40 degrees

0 degrees

River Avon

0   500m   1km   2km

N

*Fig 4.12 (opposite)
Field systems (green) and
contemporary settlements
(blue) against the strength
of solar absorption
throughout the year,
generated through GIS
analysis (20m resolution).
While many of the field
systems are laid out on
favourable slopes to
maximise the availability
of sunlight, there are
favourable areas that
apparently remained
uncultivated in the Bronze
Age; significantly, these
include areas around
Stonehenge itself and
Normanton Down, the zone
encircled by the 'Palisade
Ditch complex' (see p 72).
Some field systems also spill
into less favourable areas,
but these tend to be more
fragmentary, perhaps less
well-developed (and in some
cases probably much later)
elements. Recent discoveries
by the Stonehenge
Riverside Project (SRP)
and more tentative ones
by the Stonehenge Hidden
Landscapes Project (SHLP)
are shown.*

barrow in the expected sequence, which crucially differs from that interpreted in the past (RCHME 1979, 26). Excavations in 1958 and 1983 also uncovered late Neolithic and Early Bronze Age activity in the vicinity before the bank was constructed (Greenfield 1959, 229; Richards 1990, 184–6; Smith 1991, 11–39), and this was taken to demonstrate a Beaker date for the earthwork known as the 'North Kite'; doubts have been expressed (Needham *et al* 2010, appendix 3.8) and the field evidence contradicts this dating.

Many round barrows survived relatively undamaged in open downland for millennia. Medieval and later arable fields were concentrated in the eastern half of the Stonehenge WHS landscape (Bond 1991, fig H9; RCHME 1979, map 3), but this doesn't necessarily equate to fewer round barrows in these areas. In the parishes of Durrington and Wilsford cum Lake there are significantly fewer round barrows known in the 'field' areas; however, Amesbury's Middle, Hither, West and Parkland fields contain almost twice as many potential round barrows as the downs to their west. If this was their actual distribution, it is perhaps significant that this is the area between Stonehenge and Durrington Walls around which, according to Parker Pearson and Ramilisonina (1998), people in the Neolithic period had travelled from life to death using the Avenues and River Avon.

Across southern England the clustered distribution of round barrows implies that they may mark land units, dividing up the valleys in a system of social, economic, agricultural and symbolic units based on river frontage (Field 2008). However, the barrows should not be seen in isolation; the wider picture is of the two rivers – Avon and Till – with cemeteries at intervals along their valley sides (McOmish *et al* 2002, fig 2.28). At Stonehenge the river courses move closer together, forcing the occupation units closer to each other; the complexity of the prehistoric fields at Winterbourne Stoke testifies to the probable density of settlement there, but medieval cultivation has masked the picture on the Amesbury slopes. The linear trend of many cemetery groups also implies territoriality, with barrows placed along a boundary on land that is marginal to any settlement. These boundaries may have had a range of physical and spiritual meanings (Field 1998). The sheer number of round barrows around Stonehenge makes individual territories difficult to define,

and it is possible that the high downs were a vast no man's land shared by a number of communities (Fleming 1971, 159), until later earthworks were created to divide the landscape into fields.

Field systems

Major change came to the Stonehenge landscape in the middle of the 2nd millennium BC. Its sacred and ceremonial significance seems to have diminished sharply; a more mundane agricultural regime of farmsteads and fields took over, or at least intensified noticeably. Perhaps agriculture had been practised in the vicinity earlier – indeed it is very probable that it had – but the environmental evidence suggests that pastoralism had predominated and that arable was only a small component of the landscape until this time (French *et al* 2012), after which it rapidly became very significant. This is part of a widespread phenomenon which saw the establishment of extensive field systems across southern England – on downland, river valleys and coastal plains – at this period (Yates 2007).

Acres of small, rectangular fields were laid out, probably about 1500 BC, across the WHS and beyond (Fig 4.12). How these fields were used is not certain, but the fact that they can still be seen, at least on aerial photographs and in lidar data, and that they survived as earthworks until the mid-20th century, indicates that some cultivation took place – causing soil to move down from the upper to the lower boundary of each field, which resulted in the formation of lynchets. The soil on the chalk is relatively infertile, however. Though light and easily tilled it is rapidly exhausted, and, after a few good crops, yields fall dramatically unless the land is well manured and rested (Groube and Bowden 1982, 19; French *et al* 2012, 31). Presumably the Bronze Age farmers took one or two crops from each field and then grazed sheep and cattle for several years. There is no direct evidence as to whether they farmed well, badly or indifferently, but environmental evidence suggests that erosion in the Avon valley which can be ascribed to increased arable farming does not occur until 1000 BC or later (French *et al* 2012); this suggests that for the first few centuries these new fields were farmed with a relatively light touch.

What is certain is that the fields themselves were modified, the boundaries shifted. This is clear from the aerial photographs, which show

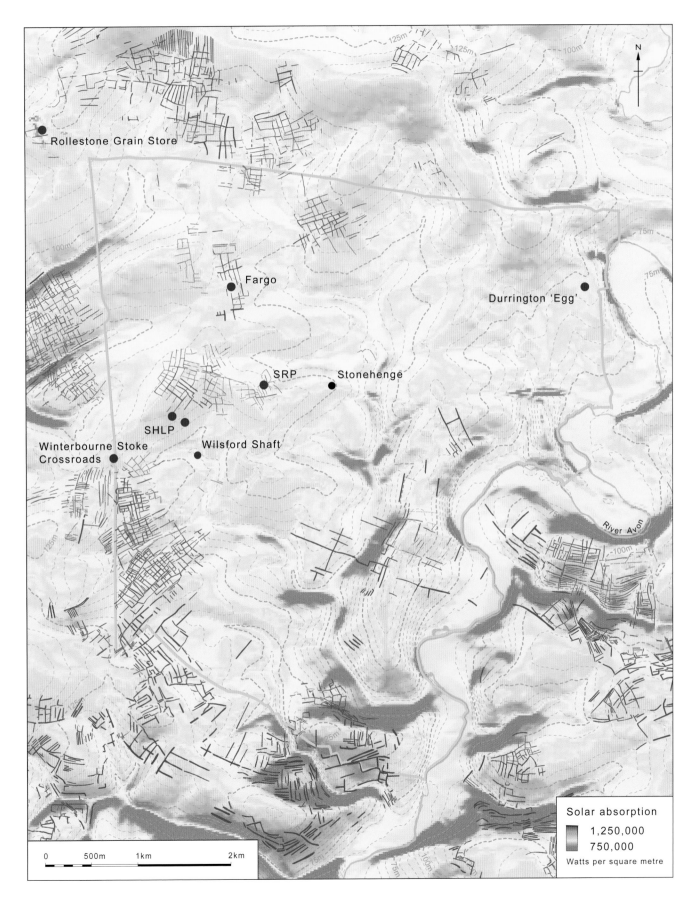

so many field banks in some areas that the plots within them are impossibly small: this is probably the result of reorganisation, and this is confirmed by the available lidar which (poor though its resolution is) shows that some lynchets still survive as low, spread earthworks, while most have been entirely flattened; the surviving lynchets must represent longer-lived, more substantial field boundaries within the system (Fig 4.13). Whether these modifications took place rapidly or over many generations is not known (though it is certain that some of the fields, those to the south and west of The Diamond, for instance, were brought back into cultivation much later, in the Roman period; *see* p 81). A possible practical explanation for the moving of field boundaries is that the precious soil accumulating in lynchets could be brought back into cultivation (Barrett 1994, 149; Kirkham 2012). There are several apparently discrete blocks of fields around Stonehenge (though none very close to the monument itself) but they do not conform to what might be the expected pattern of favouring south-facing slopes. Instead, as in other areas of the chalk-land, including the rest of Salisbury Plain (McOmish *et al* 2002, 53–4), those who laid out the fields ignored the topography – they run across the contours and include unfavourable

north-facing slopes (*see* Fig 4.12); by contrast many areas with an apparently inviting south-facing aspect have no fields.

Wilsford Shaft

An apparently unique monument, the Wilsford Shaft, at the head of the dry valley which divides Normanton Down from Lake Down, was discovered as the result of rescue excavation in 1960–2 (Ashbee *et al* 1989), after its slight standing earthwork had been cynically bull-dozed in 1954 on the patently absurd claim that it was a danger to livestock – in fact this part of the down was to be, perhaps for the first time ever, put under the plough. The monument proved to be not a pond barrow as had been supposed but a 30m deep vertical shaft cut into the chalk. The bottom of the shaft coincided with a water-bearing fault in the chalk. The infill contained pottery, flint, bone, charcoal, personal ornaments and, in the waterlogged bottom, parts of wooden containers, fragments of wickerwork or basketry, and cord. The objects from the lower part of the shaft were all of Middle Bronze Age or earlier date. Radiocarbon dating showed that the lower part of the shaft filled rapidly round about 1200 BC while the upper part was not filled until about 450 BC. (One anomalous date suggests the possibility that one of the wooden objects was 2,000 years older still.) The shaft was open and 'in use', whatever that use was, during the period when the field systems were flourishing. The environmental evidence, which was unusually rich, suggests that both pasture and arable were present in the area as the shaft began to fill, though there was also some scrub; the crops grown included wheat and barley but also flax. The authors agreed to differ over interpretation (Ashbee *et al* 1989, 128–37) as to whether the shaft was a well to water livestock at a distance from settlement or whether it had ritual significance; the debate continues, though the answer may be 'both'.

Despite the abundant evidence for arable agriculture, aerial photographic evidence suggests that the area around Stonehenge was less heavily cultivated in the Bronze Age than other parts of Salisbury Plain. Indeed some areas seem to have been deliberately avoided: the area immediately around Stonehenge itself, for instance (though there are some traces of fields within about 600m of the monument), and Normanton Down (*see* p 72).

Fig 4.13
The area around The Diamond, based on transcription from aerial photographs and lidar, showing alterations to the system and emphasising the larger, and therefore presumably longer-lasting, lynchets (red).

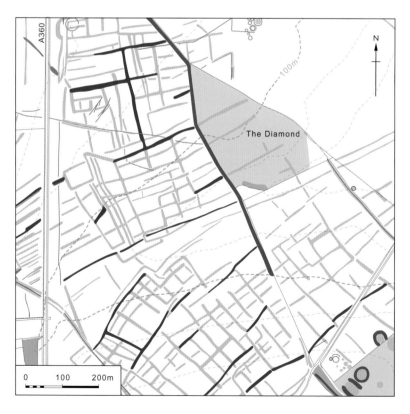

Settlement

The farmsteads or settlements where the later Bronze Age population lived have proved nearly as elusive as those of earlier periods, but one was discovered fortuitously at Winterbourne Stoke Crossroads, when the roundabout was being constructed in 1967, just to the south of the barrows (Richards 1990, 208–10; Leivers and Moore 2008, 37–9). The density of structural features suggests a lengthy sequence of occupation; certainly the largest roundhouse blocks the entrance of one of its neighbours and cannot therefore be of the same date. This settlement seems deliberately placed close to the barrows, which would have dominated it (Sharples 2010, 30). The three small buildings excavated there remain the only certain Bronze Age roundhouses known close to Stonehenge (Lawson 2007, 280), but recent geophysical survey has revealed several small circular features on the down just to the north-east of this location (Vince Gaffney pers comm) which might be further roundhouses. Fieldwalking and plough soil excavation revealed another area of later Bronze Age settlement on the eastern side of Fargo Plantation to the north of the Greater Cursus (Richards 1990, 194–208). Although no houses were found here (structural evidence was limited to one posthole, one possible pit,

one gully terminal, and possible hearths and ovens) there were considerable quantities of pottery, worked and burnt flint, querns and rubbing stones (suggesting the preparation of cereals), and animal bones, mainly of sheep/ goat and cattle. Appropriately, perhaps, this settlement sits within contemporary fields. The so-called Durrington 'Egg', an ovoid ditched enclosure discovered by aerial photography in the 1920s, is also part of an extensive later Bronze Age settlement (Fig 4.14; RCHME 1979, 23–4, pl 16; McOmish 2001, 78–9); postholes and pits within the enclosure represent a possible roundhouse and other structures (Piggott 1973, 398). Just outside the western boundary of the WHS a rectangular enclosure, previously known from aerial photographs, was discovered during extension of the Rollestone Grain Store to be a Middle Bronze Age settlement enclosure of a type associated with Deverel-Rimbury pottery (1500–1000 BC); this enclosure overlies some earlier field boundaries (*Wiltshire Archaeol Mag* 91, 1998, 163–4). Other settlements of this period might be represented by enclosures with curving ditches among the fields to the west of Stonehenge, for instance, but these are currently undated with the exception of one enclosure partly excavated in 2008 and dated to the period 1500–1100 BC (Parker Pearson *et al* 2008, 110–22).

Fig 4.14
*Cropmarks in the area around Woodhenge, including the Durrington 'Egg' (**a**) and other elements of Bronze Age and later occupation. Also visible are the side ditches of a long barrow (**b**) and three small rectangular enclosures (**c**, **d**, **e**) which are discussed in Chapter 5; **c** and **d** are shown enlarged, top left.*

The deposition of cremations in earlier barrows is a known practice of Middle Bronze Age (and later) populations. It is therefore unsurprising that the Winterbourne Stoke barrow group is the only barrow cemetery in the immediate Stonehenge area to have Deverel-Rimbury ceramics in significant quantity (Woodward and Woodward 1996, 288) and that the Shrewton barrows, immediately to the west of the Rollestone Grain Store settlement, also contain Middle Bronze Age secondary cremations (Green and Rollo-Smith 1984, 301–6 *et passim*). Four clusters of barrows with Deverel-Rimbury material lie around the western end of Normanton Down (Needham *et al* 2009, 17). It has been suggested that Deverel-Rimbury settlements and cemeteries are absent from the main zones of earlier monumental sites in Wiltshire and Dorset but concentrated on the periphery of these areas (Woodward and Woodward 1996, 287–8). This is reflected here to an extent, though the Winterbourne Stoke settlement sits beside the long barrow, the Durrington 'Egg' is close to Woodhenge and the Fargo Plantation settlement is close to the Greater Cursus.

Stonehenge: early dilapidation?

Stonehenge did not entirely lose its significance at this period. Two new circuits of stoneholes, now known as the Y and Z holes (Fig 4.15), were dug concentrically outside the sarsen 'circle' (*see* Chapter 3). Interestingly, one of these holes was found to have been filled with wind-blown agricultural soil, a further indication of

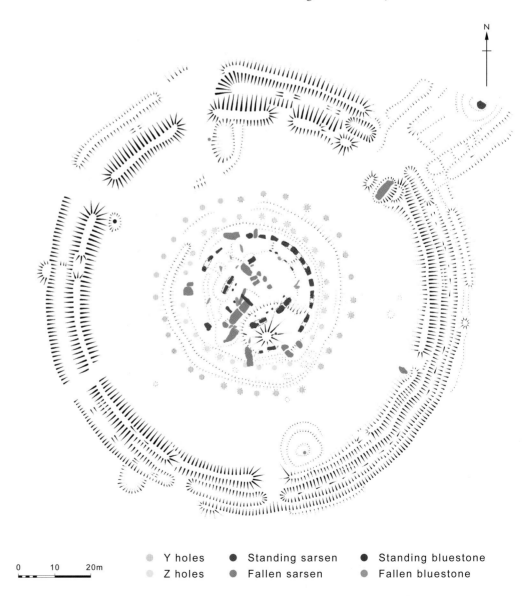

Fig 4.15
Plan of Stonehenge showing elements attributed to stage 4 (bluestone circle and horseshoe) and stage 5, emphasising the Y and Z holes and the stones which may have fallen early in the history of the monument. The positions of many of the Y and Z holes are based on ephemeral and conflicting evidence.

0   10   20m

⊙ Y holes	● Standing sarsen	● Standing bluestone
⊙ Z holes	● Fallen sarsen	● Fallen bluestone

the cultivation now going on not far from the stones (Darvill *et al* 2012, 17–18).

Looking at the Great Trilithon, with the slender and elegant stone 56 now upright again after centuries (or more) of leaning at an alarming angle, stone 55 lying smashed in two pieces over the Altar Stone, and their lintel, stone 156, beside it, it is possible to wonder whether this construction fell very soon after it was erected (Fig 4.16). Stone 56 is so narrow at the top that balancing the bulky 156 on it must always have been an act of faith; stone 55 was so poorly bedded in the ground that the instant

of resting 156 on it (assuming that 156 was ever raised) might seem the most likely moment in its history for it to have fallen, dragging 56 down with it before spilling 156 to the ground and smashing itself over the Altar Stone. (For a comparable suggestion that le Grand Menhir Brisé fell and broke at the moment of erection, *see* Hornsey 1987 and C Richards 2013, 9–12.) The problem with this scenario, however, is the relationship between the collapsed Great Trilithon and the bluestone circle, and the rearrangement of the bluestones. On current understanding of the chronology stone 68

Fig 4.16
The Great Trilithon.
Photograph taken by
J J Cole in 1881 with the
intention of proving that
stone 56 was not in danger
of falling. In the background
are the stones that collapsed
in 1900.
(AL0913/013/01, Historic
England Archive)

was erected after stone 56. However, it should be noted that the stratigraphic relationship between stones 56 and 68 is ambiguous (Cleal *et al* 1995, 203, 222–3). Also problematic is the large pit dug to the west of the Great Trilithon in stage 3 of the current chronological model, 2440–2100 BC (Parker Pearson *et al* 2007, 618–26), but this too could have been an occasion for the collapse of the Trilithon (Parker Pearson 2012, 130). A relatively early fall seems likely, and Hawley believed that stones 8 and 12 had also probably fallen 'at an early date' (1926, 6, 10). The Y and Z holes were perhaps a last half-hearted attempt to recreate something out of what was already, or was rapidly becoming, a ruinous site. The missing or misplaced Z hole 8 might reflect the fact that stone 8 of the sarsen circle had already fallen across its position. Despite any such early falls, however, the monument retained some significance.

If parts of the monument did collapse during construction or shortly thereafter, or if other lesser accidents occurred, it might have caused consternation. Apart from the immediate physical fear of being crushed by heavy stones, there would presumably have been superstitious dread concomitant with the belief systems that caused the construction of the monument in the first place. At the same time the limitations of what they could achieve would have been revealed to the builders. However, different people have different reactions. One fundamental aspect of human nature which rarely seems to be considered by prehistorians is humour. While the major or dominant sections of society might have found the collapse of the Great Trilithon – if it did happen when suggested here – terrifying, awesome and even mind-numbing, others may have found it hilariously funny, or at least a vindication of their alternative outlook (*see* C Richards 2013, 12–13). Such extreme architecture, at the limits of the possible, will have made the builders and witnesses aware of their relations with each other as well as with their material (*see* McFadyen 2007, 353–4).

Linear ditches

Linear ditches are a phenomenon of the latest phase of the Bronze Age (1000–800 BC) on the chalk-lands of southern England, striking across the field systems and signalling a new division of the land (Bradley *et al* 1994; McOmish *et al* 2002, 56–66). At Stonehenge, however, there is a hint of a slightly earlier phase of linear ditches, though here they perform a special function (Fig 4.17).

The main component here is the Palisade Ditch which runs very close to Stonehenge. Part of it was excavated when the visitor underpass was built in 1967. It consisted of a ditch, 2m wide and 1.4m deep, dug to hold timber posts 25–35cm in diameter, but it had a terminal close to Stonehenge, into which a burial had later been inserted (*see* Chapter 5). Another feature, excavated previously by Atkinson and known by him as the 'Gate Ditch', seemed to continue the line of the Palisade Ditch to the north-east. It ran close to the Avenue, and geophysical survey has recently shown that it continues further north, nearly to the line of the Greater Cursus (Gaffney *et al* 2012, fig 3; Darvill *et al* 2013, fig 4) and perhaps joining its southern side. However, though some aerial photographs appear to show the two as continuous (Cleal *et al* 1995, 155), geophysical surveys show a substantial gap between the southern terminal of the Gate Ditch (Gaffney *et al* 2012, fig 4) and the Palisade Ditch, so it is not at all certain that these two are part of the same feature, though their common alignment and similar proportions suggest that they are part of the same system. The Palisade Ditch continues to the south-west, surviving as a slight single scarp within the Stonehenge Triangle, where it can be traced across some 'Celtic' fields on Stonehenge Down. Here the system has been excavated more recently by the Stonehenge Riverside Project and dated to the Early or earliest part of the Middle Bronze Age; the palisade posts here were deliberately removed and a slightly larger ditch, the 'Main Ditch', dating to after 1500–1380 BC, replaced it (Parker Pearson *et al* 2008, 123–33; Josh Pollard pers comm).

A third, apparently similar, linear ditch, **g** (RCHME 1979, fig 14), seems to start close by on the summit of Stonehenge Down and runs near Amesbury 14 long barrow, where it changes direction to pass to the west of Amesbury 15, the 'Sun' Barrow. Part of this linear survives as an earthwork where it passes through Normanton Gorse. It is only a ditch 3.4m wide and 0.3m deep accompanied by a spread bank of similar dimensions (Bowden *et al* 2012, 21–2), much slighter than the majority of Late Bronze Age linear boundaries. To the south of the Gorse it can only be traced on aerial photographs, but excavation confirmed its diminutive nature (Richards 1990, 192–3). Near The Diamond it forms, with another ditch (**f**), part of a

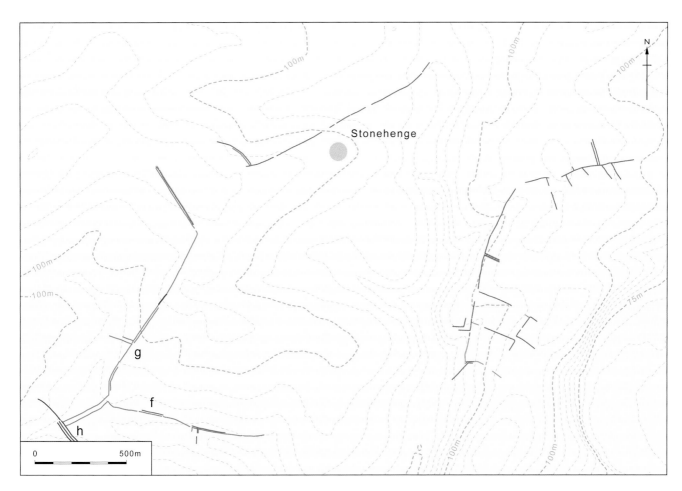

distinct trackway. This track opens up to form an enclosure around Normanton Down, which is distinctly free of fields, with ditches (**f** and **g**) following the contours of the dry valley on either side. A plough-levelled linear ditch runs north-north-east from Luxenborough Planta-tion towards the King Barrows (RCHME 1979, map 1); geophysical survey shows it extend-ing south and including two other elaborate entrances, similar to those previously known to the south-west (Vince Gaffney pers comm). This feature is possibly the eastern boundary of an enclosure formed with **f** and **g**. (A similar palisade ditch was discovered by Greenfield on Wilsford Down: Richards 1990, 184, fig 133.)

Arguably these relatively slight linear earth-works are defining a reserved space around Stonehenge and the Normanton Down bar-rows, an area also devoid of prehistoric artefacts (Cleal et al 1995, 490). Perhaps this was com-mon grazing, perhaps a sacred space around the significant monuments which may have developed a historical or genealogical impor-tance at this time (Parker Pearson et al 2008, 133). The relatively early date of the 'Palisade

Ditch complex', suggested by the excavation results, is confirmed by the more substantial Late Bronze Age linear ditch **h**, which cuts across them to the south-west and blocks one of the entrances to this space.

Linear **h** is part of an extensive system of lin-ear ditches which runs across the south-western part of the WHS and can be dated by analogy to the latest Bronze Age (Fig 4.18). These are more substantial features: **h** was found to be 2.4m wide and over 1m deep (Richards 1990, 192–3). Ditch **a** on the edge of The Diamond survives as an earthwork 5m wide and 1m deep with its accompanying bank, spread by ploughing, 6m wide and 0.5m high (Bowden et al 2012, 19). Further to the south-east, on Lake Down, the linear earthworks (**a** and **c**) are even larger, up to 12m wide and 1.1m deep with banks up to 5.2m wide and 1.1m high, though here they have probably been modified by later use (Komar 2010, 9, 21). Near the Long Barrow Crossroads, excavation showed that ditch **a** was V-shaped, about 4m wide and 1.5m deep (Leivers and Moore 2008, 39). The system runs from beyond the Long Barrow Crossroads to

Fig 4.17
The 'Palisade Ditch complex', almost entirely ploughed out. Only short sections within the Stonehenge Triangle and Normanton Gorse survive as slight earthworks: former banks (pink) and ditches (light green) have been revealed by a combination of aerial photography and geophysical survey. The out-turned entrances seem to be a common feature but whether the easternmost elements belong to the complex is uncertain.

Fig 4.18
The linear earthworks in the south-western part of the WHS. Banks (red) and ditches (green); elements surviving as earthworks are shown in darker tone. (Lettering follows RCHME 1979, fig 14.)

Rox Hill, and can be seen to cut through the earlier fields at several points (*see* Fig 4.1). These linear ditches can be related to those further north on Salisbury Plain (Bradley *et al* 1994; McOmish *et al* 2002, 56–66) and indeed those further afield on the chalk-lands of southern England, but they are a distinct group, only connected physically to other systems by a single linear running north-west up the Till valley from the Long Barrow Crossroads to join the east end of Old Ditch West, Tillshead. There are no linear ditches in the northern part of the WHS (with the possible exception of the ditch or pit alignment that cuts obliquely across the western end of the Greater Cursus and has been dated to the later Bronze Age; Parker Pearson

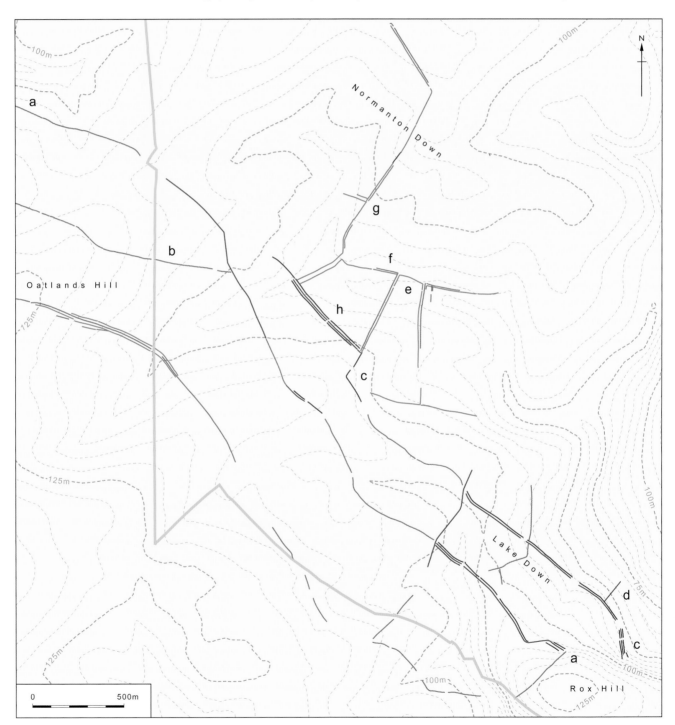

et al 2007, 136–9), and none, apart from the atypical Palisade Ditch, come close to Stonehenge itself.

One remarkable feature of the linears to the south of Stonehenge is the way in which **h** splits from **a** to bracket the Lake barrows, while **a** and **c** similarly bracket the Lake Down barrows (Fig 4.19), a pattern seen elsewhere, as at Snail Down for instance (Sharples 2010, 31–2). This perhaps marks a contrast with earlier practice: whereas Middle Bronze Age field systems sometimes impinged on earlier monuments, the Late Bronze Age linear ditches generally seem to respect them (ibid, 34). However, the reality is slightly more complex, as counter-examples can be found – fields at Orcheston Down respected the barrows (McOmish *et al* 2002, 18–20, fig 1.18) and a linear ditch at Lake cuts barrow Wilsford 45b (*see* p 64). It may be a matter of where the barrow is located with respect to later settlement – in heavily used areas the barrows will be flattened, whereas those that occur at the limits of the arable will be respected. Sharples has also noted that linear ditches never seem to be finished, starting and stopping apparently at random and frequently being realigned (2010, 308); this could certainly be true of the linear ditches to the south of Stonehenge. This non-completion perhaps marks another significant change, or series of changes, as the Late Bronze Age gives way to the Iron Age.

Fig 4.19
*Linear ditches **a** (foreground) and **c** bracketing the Lake Down barrows, which include a disc barrow and four rare pond barrows (Komar 2010). Beyond the hedge to the left the ditches have been ploughed flat in what was Lake's medieval West Field. The Wilsford barrows are in the small block of woodland beyond the Lake Down barrows; the Normanton Down barrows can be seen in the middle distance and Stonehenge in the far distance. Aerial photograph from the south (10 January 2010).*
(NMR 26556/01)

5

From the Iron Age to the medieval period

The Iron Age and medieval period are united by the apparent scarcity of evidence for activity around Stonehenge. However, when they are studied in detail the level of evidence fluctuates, indicating that there was at least one period when Stonehenge was apparently avoided and another – perhaps short-lived – when it was again the focus of attention.

The Iron Age

The evidence for Iron Age activity around Stonehenge (Fig 5.1) is sparse but not entirely lacking and has not been intensively studied. However, it is important to distinguish between the earlier parts of the Iron Age, from about 800 to 100 BC, and the Late Iron Age, from 100 BC onwards, as these periods are distinct from one another in the archaeological record (*see* Barrett *et al* 2011).

Earlier Iron Age

The only surviving, upstanding, Iron Age monument in the WHS is the hill fort known as Vespasian's Camp (*see below*). Otherwise contemporary settlements are known to have existed at Durrington Walls and at the Packway, where an enclosure has been excavated (Wainwright and Longworth 1971, 307–28; Graham and Newman 1993, 52–5; Darvill 2006, 196–7). Further Iron Age storage pits have been excavated within Durrington Walls more recently (Parker Pearson 2012, 101), and just beyond the WHS boundary there were enclosed settlements at Scotland Lodge (Leivers and Moore 2008), Ogbury, Salisbury Clumps, near Druid's Lodge (Barber *et al* 2003, 158–9) and by the Avon at Durrington (Clare King pers comm). Scattered finds of Iron Age pottery have come from excavations at Stonehenge itself (Morris 1995), the Wilsford Shaft (Ashbee *et al* 1989, 37–43), Winterbourne Stoke barrow 30

(Christie 1963, 378) and Stonehenge Bottom (Parker Pearson *et al* 2008, 103–4). The Iron Age deposit at the top of the Wilsford Shaft, which included some human and animal bone, yielded radiocarbon dates with a mean of 760–400 BC (Gardiner 1995, 342). The Stonehenge Environs Project, however, recovered very little Iron Age pottery – just a few sherds from the north-west part of the WHS (Richards 1990, 280, fig 20).

Lawson has concluded that much of the Stonehenge landscape was given over to pasture in the Iron Age (2007, 314) and this view has much to recommend it. Evidence from the wider landscape, at Netheravon and Durrington for instance, suggests that most activity was river based; the hill forts of this region, too, have a valley-side distribution. Nevertheless, there are some more intriguing and enigmatic Iron Age finds and possible monuments from the higher ground. At some time between the 8th and the 5th century BC the tightly flexed corpse of a young man was placed in the terminal of the Palisade Ditch, close to Stonehenge; there were no grave goods but the burial is dated by radiocarbon to 780–410 BC (Gardiner 1995, 337; Lawson 2007, 314). A human skull from the Stonehenge ditch dated to 520–390 BC, pottery from the Y and Z holes – including a substantial part of a pot found in the upper fill of Z hole 12 (Gardiner 1995, 337; Morris 1995, 435) – and a human tibia from Durrington Walls dated to 400–200 BC (Parker Pearson *et al* 2009, tables 2 and 3) have also been found. A bronze brooch dating to the middle of the 1st millennium BC was found allegedly 'near Bush Barrow' (Goddard 1914, 354; Grinsell 1957, 123). Finally, there are three small square enclosures south of Durrington Walls and Woodhenge (McOmish 2001, 78–9, fig 4.3; *see* Fig 4.14): they each measure approximately 5m by 5m and have central rectangular pits. One is also accompanied by a number of

Fig 5.1 (opposite) Iron Age sites (dark blue) and findspots (light blue) and Romano-British sites (dark red) and findspots (light red) mentioned in this chapter. Other morphologically similar but undated settlement enclosures, just south of the WHS, are known from aerial photographs but not shown here.

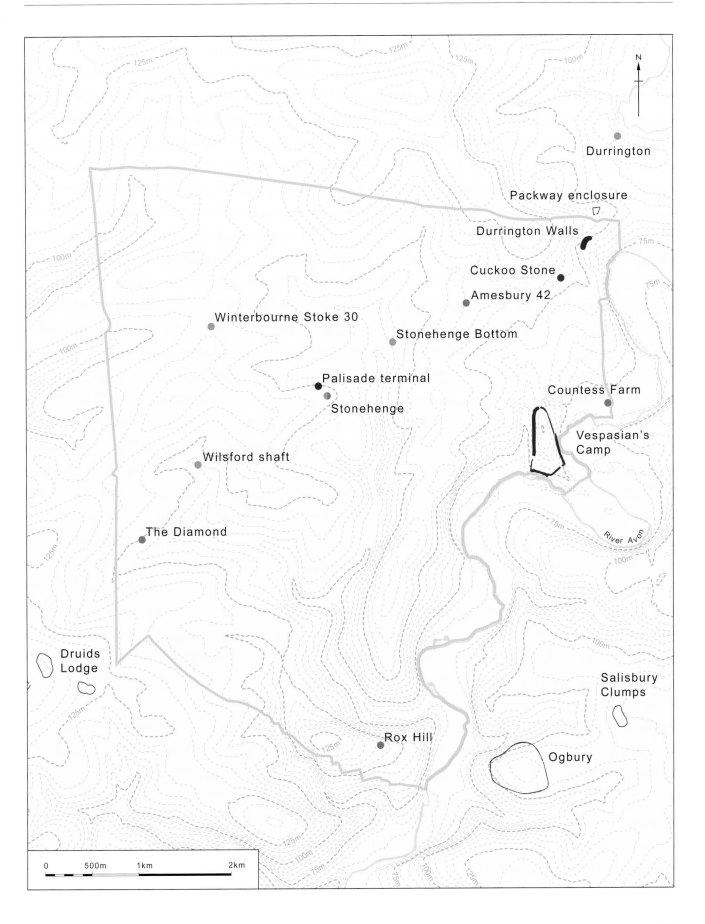

Durrington

Packway enclosure

Durrington Walls

Cuckoo Stone

Amesbury 42

Winterbourne Stoke 30

Stonehenge Bottom

Palisade terminal

Stonehenge

Countess Farm

Vespasian's Camp

Wilsford shaft

River Avon

The Diamond

Druids Lodge

Salisbury Clumps

Rox Hill

Ogbury

N

0   500m   1km   2km

similar external pits. These enclosures resemble Iron Age square barrows (Stead 1991, 5–28), though they are at the smaller end of the size-range for such monuments. If they are square barrows they would be a rare occurrence indeed in this region.

So there is some evidence of Iron Age activity within the WHS down to about the middle of the 1st millennium BC or a little later. Some of it indeed is very close to the stones. But generally the settlements and the meagre evidence for arable activity were kept at a distance – as at other major Neolithic ceremonial complexes with standing stones, the Iron Age population was avoiding or respecting Stonehenge. At Avebury not a single Iron Age sherd has been found in all the excavations at the site (Burl 1979, 264, n37) and there is little indisputable evidence of an Iron Age presence anywhere close to the wider complex (Bowden 2005, 156; Sharples 2010, 15, 27), though caution is necessary on this topic and further research

is needed. Certainly the avoidance or respect does seem restricted to the sites with standing stones. This is even possibly seen on a small scale at the Devil's Quoits (Oxfordshire), where Lambrick and Allen tentatively suggest that the area around the stone circle and henge was permanent pasture within a ring of settlements and more intensively used land in the Iron Age (2004, 479–83). However, it is not always the case: there was a Middle Iron Age settlement very close to the Rollright Stones, Oxfordshire (Lambrick 1988, 80–4, 125–9). Durrington Walls, without standing stones, like the large henge at Mount Pleasant (Dorset), has evidence for settlement activity in the 1st millennium BC (Sharples 2010, 27).

The single most impressive Iron Age site within the Stonehenge WHS, Vespasian's Camp (Fig 5.2), on analogy with similar sites belongs within the period *c* 700–400 BC; evidence for occupation and rampart building in the 5th century BC has been found (Hunter Mann 1999, 50). The name was given as the result of an association made by William Camden, who boldly and incorrectly stated that 'by the forme and manner of making, a man may easily know it was a Romane Campe' (1610, Wiltshire 10). Vespasian's Camp is a univallate hill fort of 15ha. The main rampart is a substantial bank to the north, west and south but elsewhere survives only as a scarp; it is up to 6.5m high above the ditch bottom and 2m high to the interior. This bank was built in two phases separated by an interval long enough for a soil horizon up to 0.3m deep to have developed on the rear face of the first phase bank. A counterscarp bank survives on the west side. There are entrances to the north and south-east (RCHME 1979, 20–1). It is sited on a locally prominent but low-lying ridge alongside the river. The north-facing entrance is a very unusual feature, as the entrances of southern British hill forts almost invariably face east or west; here the northern entrance gives access to the higher Ratfyn ridge. At Avebury the nearest hill fort, Oldbury, presents its bold and symmetrical eastward-facing façade of ramparts towards the constellation of Neolithic monuments around the great henge (Bowden 2004, 16), and in a similar way Vespasian's Camp presents its massive, straight array of westward-facing ramparts towards Stonehenge, though Stonehenge is not visible from any part of the hill fort because of the intervening King Barrow Ridge and Coneybury Hill. There is a palpable sense that the Iron Age

Fig 5.2
Ordnance Survey 'Antiquity Model', or field survey document, of Vespasian's Camp, for map revision in 1969, with profiles of the ramparts, notes and instructions by the field investigator for the fair draughtsman. Reduced from original scale of 1:2500. (1081026 © Crown copyright. HE)

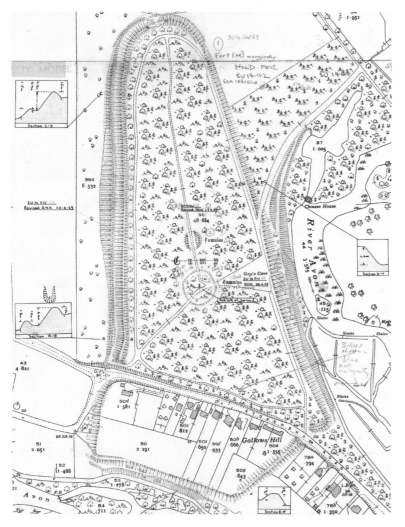

people were concerned to keep the spirits of the Neolithic megalithic ceremonial sites out of their lives (though elsewhere, of course, Iron Age hill forts frequently incorporated the remains of Neolithic earthwork enclosures).

Late Iron Age

In the subsequent period, the Late Iron Age, the evidence around Stonehenge is even more sparse, and all the more interesting for that. With the first glimmerings of historical evidence available, it is possible to see Stonehenge at this time on the borders between different tribal groups – the Durotriges, Dobunni, Atrebates and Belgae – and therefore on the boundary between the 'romanising' tribes of the south-east and the more 'conservative' groups to the north and west (Darvill *et al* 2005, 73–4; Darvill 2006, 200–1). With the exception of the Iron Age occupation near Durrington Walls and the Packway, which may have continued to the very end of the Iron Age (Wainwright and Longworth 1971, 326), and just two sherds of Late Iron Age pot from excavations at Stonehenge (Morris 1995, 434), there is not a single sherd, burial or settlement attributable to this period within the WHS or immediately around it. There is a scatter of Late Iron Age coins allegedly from the wider area. These include Greek and Carthaginian issues. Although there is no reason to doubt that such exotic coins were in Britain in the Late Iron Age, these are all antiquarian finds and poorly provenanced; the findspots are recorded by phrases such as 'near Amesbury', 'near Stonehenge', 'said to have been found at Amesbury' (Grinsell 1957, 29; Robinson 1991, 119; Darvill 2006, 201). These descriptions are part of the all too prevalent practice of making an object seem more interesting or valuable by giving it a significant provenance – 'near Amesbury' would ring bells with the cognoscenti; 'near Stonehenge' is more blatant. Unfortunately we can place no reliance on these claims. It does seem on current evidence that the major Neolithic megalithic monuments, at Stonehenge as at Avebury and other stone circles, were avoided in the Late Iron Age (Burl 2006, 21). If this is the case, what does it mean? It could reflect reverence, fear, a lack of interest or a combination of factors (Sharples 2010, 24). This lack of evidence from around Stonehenge is all the more remarkable given that the Late Iron Age is regarded as a dynamic period on Salisbury Plain generally (McOmish *et al* 2002, 82–6; Fulford *et al* 2006, 199–201), typified by the settlement enclosure at Figheldean (Graham and Newman 1993, 10–52; McKinley 1999), just north of the WHS.

The evidence from Stonehenge, negative though it is, seems clear. Whatever the historic druids attested by classical writers (Piggott 1968, ch 3; Hutton 2009, 2–23) were doing – and they were apparently judges rather than priests – they do not seem to have been doing it at Stonehenge. Absence of evidence is not necessarily evidence of absence, but when the absence is persistent it becomes possible to read it in that way.

The Roman period

Evidence for activity at and around Stonehenge in the Roman period (1st–4th centuries AD) has been almost ignored until recently; Darvill and Wainwright, however, in 2008 found evidence for 'structural' Roman activity within Stonehenge – the digging of substantial holes, certainly (2009, 14–15). A considerable volume of Romano-British material (Fig 5.3) has been found on the site, much of it clustering near stone 7 (Hawley 1921, 29; Gardiner 1995, 337; Montague 1995, 433–4; Seager Smith 1995, 435), and therefore close to the location of the 2008 trench, and dating predominantly to the 4th century AD; 12 of the 20 identified Roman coins from Stonehenge are from the period AD 330–95 (Davies 1995, 431–2). Darvill and Wainwright argue convincingly that this points to the use of Stonehenge for ritual and ceremony at this time – the holes were dated to the late Roman period (2009, 14–15). A shallow grave cut into the top of the enclosure ditch on the east side contained a partial human burial, but unfortunately Hawley discarded the bones; it was probably of Roman or later date (Cleal *et al* 1995, 337–8). Another possible indication of funerary activity on the site at this time is the find of a fragment of human skull from the fill of the enclosure ditch on the south-east side, dated to AD 340–510 (Parker Pearson *et al* 2009, 5), though clearly it could be post-Roman (*see* Table 5.1).

Interestingly, this evidence for ceremonial in the 4th century corresponds to a period when Roman religious activity becomes manifest at other prehistoric sites, such as the building of temples within hill forts, as at Blaise Castle and Lydney (Gloucestershire), Maiden Castle

Fig 5.3
Roman finds from
Stonehenge: (a) dupondius
(diameter 26mm) of
Antonina (AD 41–50),
the earliest coin from the
site, found near stone
56; (b and c) sestertius
(diameter 28mm – both
sides shown) of Marcus
Aurelius (AD 161–80),
the only 2nd-century coin,
found near stones 6 and
7; (d) fragment of cable
armlet (length 44mm), now
straightened, found near
stones 6 and 7.
(DP159097, DP159090,
DP159092 and DP159088;
Courtesy of The Salisbury
Museum)

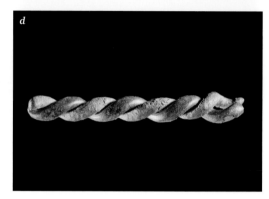

Fig 5.3
Roman finds from Stonehenge: (a) dupondius (diameter 26mm) of Antonina (AD 41–50), the earliest coin from the site, found near stone 56; (b and c) sestertius (diameter 28mm – both sides shown) of Marcus Aurelius (AD 161–80), the only 2nd-century coin, found near stones 6 and 7; (d) fragment of cable armlet (length 44mm), now straightened, found near stones 6 and 7. (DP159097, DP159090, DP159092 and DP159088; Courtesy of The Salisbury Museum)

(Dorset) and Rainsborough (Northamptonshire), for instance, especially around the 360s. This was a time of great political and religious upheaval, with competing 'mystery cults' emerging across the empire, which might form a context for this sudden religious interest in 'ancient' sites. Despite their 'structural' evidence, Darvill and Wainwright have linked this with destruction of the stones, particularly the bluestones (2009, 18), which they believe started in the late prehistoric and Roman periods and continued with increasing vigour through to the medieval and post-medieval periods. However, reuse of prehistoric sites in the Roman period usually involved adaptation rather than destruction. Darvill and Wainwright link this posited destruction in turn with supposed pseudo-medical properties of the bluestones (ibid, 16–18) though it could be that the apparently preferential destruction of the bluestones is because they are easier to break up than the notoriously hard and unyielding sarsen; alternatively it could be that the sarsens were equally attacked but that this has left no trace – according to Atkinson sarsen tends to turn to dust and fine sand rather than forming chips (1956, 119–20), though sarsen hammerstones break into recognisable pieces (Parker Pearson 2012, 248–50).

Two antiquarian finds might have thrown further light on Roman religious activity at Stonehenge and in its immediate environs had they survived. During the reign of Henry VIII a 'table of metall', apparently of tin–lead alloy and inscribed with indecipherable letters, was found 'neere' Stonehenge but then lost (Chippindale 2012, 29). Was this a Roman lead curse of the type often found at religious sites (Hassall 1980)? Later, in about 1635, a hoard of pewter was ploughed up near 'Normanton ditch' (Cunnington 1930, 208). It has been suggested that this was Roman pewter (Grinsell 1957, 123). If so it might have been a votive deposit (Lee 2009, 77–104), but the finds are lost and the precise location of 'Normanton ditch' is in doubt, though it is probably the linear ditch (*see* Chapter 4) running through Stonehenge Bottom near Luxenborough Plantation (RCHME 1979, xxi, 25–6, 32–3).

There was a substantial Roman settlement of 3rd–4th century date between Durrington Walls and the Cuckoo Stone (Farrer 1918, 101; Wainwright *et al* 1971, 83–94, 100–22). This settlement probably accounts for the Romano-British burials at Woodhenge (Cunnington 1929, 60); they need not reflect any residual significance in the henge but were placed in 'normal' fashion on the periphery of the settlement. Nevertheless, the discovery of two coin hoards of 4th-century date (Algar 1997) adjacent to the Cuckoo Stone could – like those at Stonehenge – be read as evidence of ritual activity attaching to an ancient site; more recent excavation here uncovered two Roman buildings, initially interpreted tentatively as shrines (Parker Pearson *et al* 2007, 121–6). Material found around Countess Farm suggests late Roman occupation in that area (Darvill 2006, 209). Some undated enclosures, such as the rectangular example south-west of Fargo Plantation, could be of Romano-British date (RCHME 1979, xii, 24–5); otherwise, so far as is known, habitation of this period lies outside the WHS boundary, most notably at Butterfield Down to the east of the Avon (Rawlings and Fitzpatrick 1996), at Figheldean to the north (Graham and Newman 1993, 34–6; McKinley 1999) and on Winterbourne Stoke Down to the west (Hoare 1812, opp p 170; Cunnington 1930, 209).

However, there is some evidence for cultivation during the Roman period: a buried soil in the ditch of Amesbury 42 long barrow contained quantities of Romano-British pottery (Richards 1990, 109), and three dense scatters of Roman material were found by the Stonehenge Environs Project; one coincides with the settlement near Durrington Walls mentioned above, and the others are to the west of The Diamond and at Rox Hill (ibid, fig 17). The area by The Diamond has also yielded brooches, ornaments and ironwork (Grinsell 1957, 122): this scatter suggests the remodelling and reuse, with substantial manuring, of the Bronze Age fields (*see* Chapter 4, esp Fig 4.13). These scatters are as dense as the one by the Cuckoo Stone and could represent settlement, but no structural evidence has yet been found. Romano-British settlement and farming to the north on Salisbury Plain is now known to have been widespread and intense if poverty-stricken (McOmish *et al* 2002, ch 4; Fulford *et al* 2006, 201–15), as it was to the south of Stonehenge where the major communications centre of Sorviodunum (Old Sarum) was only 9.5km from the stones. Stonehenge, however, as in the Iron Age, seems to have been central to a small pocket of higher ground avoided by normal settlement and agricultural activity, other than grazing.

Instances of Romano-British tracks or streets reusing Late Bronze Age linear ditches have been suggested on Salisbury Plain, at Old Ditch West and Knook Down West, for instance (McOmish *et al* 2002, 65, 95, fig 4.11; Sharples 2010, 46). On Lake Down the flat, wide bottoms of the linear ditches suggest the possibility of similar use; ditch **c** (*see* Figs 4.18 and 4.19) is labelled 'part of a Road supposed to be made by the ROMANS' on the Doidge brothers' 1752 map of Lake (WHC 1552/2/2/4H), which at least suggests that the ditches were flat-bottomed by the mid-18th century (Komar 2010, 21).

The medieval period

In historic times the Stonehenge WHS, like the rest of Salisbury Plain, was a sparsely inhabited landscape, settlement having retreated from the downs but remained in the valleys, with the collapse of markets following the end of Roman authority, and possibly changing environmental conditions (McOmish *et al* 2002, 109). The holdings of these valley-based settlements were carefully arranged to ensure that each settlement had a balanced share of resources – meadows (and probably woodland) on the floodplain, arable on the alluvial soils of the lower slopes and pasture on the higher downs – though the boundaries on the higher land may not have been established till much later, suggesting that the pasture was arranged through a system of intercommoning between communities until the 13th or 14th centuries. At a larger scale the administrative units known as hundreds were established in the 10th century (Fig 5.4), though they were often based on earlier institutional territories (Yorke 1995, 124–5); on Salisbury Plain these were centred on the river valleys, with their boundaries following watersheds (McOmish *et al* 2002, 112–13).

The early medieval period

The early medieval (5th–11th centuries) is the least well known of all periods studied by traditional landscape archaeology. With the exception of rare frontier works and fortifications, the people of early medieval England created few 'monuments'. However, many key components of the later landscape – open fields, nucleated hamlets and villages – had their origins in this period.

This is as true of the Stonehenge landscape as of any other. Activity within the WHS is marked only by a few human burials, some of them unusual (Table 5.1; Fig 5.5), and finds of

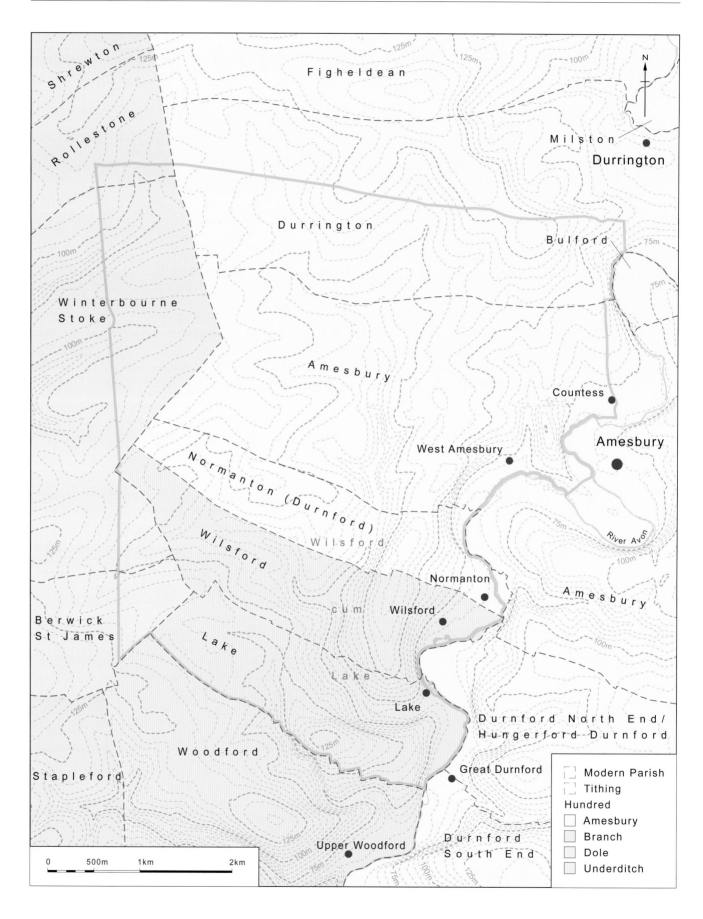

pottery and other items. These include the skull fragment from the enclosure ditch, mentioned on p 79, dating to AD 340–510 (Parker Pearson *et al* 2009, 5), which could fall very early in the post-Roman period (conventionally dated as beginning *c* 410 though perhaps actually somewhat later). There are also two human teeth, one dated AD 680–880 and the other 770–950 (ibid). A penny of Æthelred II (998–1003) and a handful of Saxon sherds have also been found at Stonehenge (Davies 1995, 432; Mepham 1995). There is not much that can be said about these isolated finds. However, more interesting is a decapitated skeleton from a grave, possibly marked by a pair of upright posts, adjacent to Y hole 9 (Fig 5.6); this has been taken by some commentators to mean that the two postholes 'can be interpreted as the remains of a gallows' (Darvill 2006, 221) and that Stonehenge might have been an execution site in the 7th to 9th centuries AD. Leaving aside the illogicality of the first suggestion – beheading does not involve a gallows – the second may be of significance: it is not unusual for 'deviant' burials of this period to be placed at prehistoric ceremonial sites or close to territorial boundaries (Pitts *et al* 2002, 139–43), and this draws attention to the fact that the boundaries of Amesbury hundred with Underditch and Dole hundreds, possibly following administrative boundaries established as early as the 7th century (Yorke 1995, 124–6; Darvill *et al* 2005, 80), lie close to the south and west of Stonehenge.

Another unusual inhumation was recovered from the west bank of the River Avon at Lake – a young woman buried under several oak planks, face down – dated to AD 450–610 (McKinley 2003). As with the decapitated burial at Stonehenge, this raises questions of extraordinary ritual, execution or sacrifice. The river, too, was a later hundred boundary. A number of intrusive burials of early medieval date were inserted into existing barrows, including one in the Lake group (though which is unknown), and probably Amesbury 44, Wilsford 16 and 30, and Winterbourne Stoke 4 and possibly 23a (Grinsell 1957, 201, 242–4). A number of other undated burials, especially from the western and northern parts of the WHS, might be of this period (RCHME 1979, 7).

Reoccupation of Vespasian's Camp in the post-Roman period has been suggested on the basis of place-name evidence (Bond 1991, 385), but limited excavation failed to recover any evidence to substantiate the idea (Hunter Mann

1999). Other finds include scatters of pottery and two brooches near Countess Farm. Traces of five sunken-floored buildings, also near Countess Farm but just outside the WHS boundary, offer rare evidence of habitation (Darvill *et al* 2005, 78–9). There are also hints of continuing activity within the late Roman settlement at Butterfield Down (Darvill 2006, 217–18).

No further archaeological evidence has yet been found within the WHS to cast light on the settlement pattern or agricultural activity of this time. Some of the undated earthworks recorded by the current project might, of course, be of this period – it could be suggested that some of the unusual platforms on the western slopes of Stonehenge Bottom (Field *et al* 2012, 23–4) represent buildings of early medieval date, but further, intrusive, research would be required to test this idea. Nevertheless, place-name evidence suggests that some of the medieval settlements to be discussed below had their origins in this period, if not earlier (Lewis 1994, 187–8; Lane 2011, 5). Amesbury, an important centre in the late Anglo-Saxon period, possibly began as the centre of a royal estate (Haslam 1984, 89, 130–2; Bond 1991, 386). Durrington, Wilsford and Lake also probably existed by this time.

The conversion of Wessex to Christianity in the middle of the 7th century marks a change, in that the early religious foundations at Wilton and Amesbury were planted in the region. It has been suggested that despoliation of the Stonehenge stones owes something to early Christian zeal for the destruction of heathen temples and this has been related directly to Amesbury, where a suspected early minster church was superseded by the abbey founded in 979 (Cleal *et al* 1995, 343–4). However, though Stonehenge lies in proximity to Amesbury, the land on which the monument stands seems never to have belonged to Amesbury Abbey, so the proximity may be irrelevant – though iconoclasts are not, of course, constrained by considerations of ownership. On the other hand, Hill (2008, 21) claims that Stonehenge was mentioned as a boundary marker of lands given to Wilton Abbey in 937 but this seems to be an error – the lands given to Wilton Abbey that year were distant from Stonehenge (Crittall 1956, 232–3). There is no clear-cut evidence for early medieval destruction at Stonehenge. Cleal *et al* note that there is nearly as much pottery of 10th and 11th century date at Stonehenge as there is later medieval pottery (1995, 344, 435), but the significance of this seems doubtful.

Fig 5.4 (opposite)
Medieval and later settlements and boundaries.

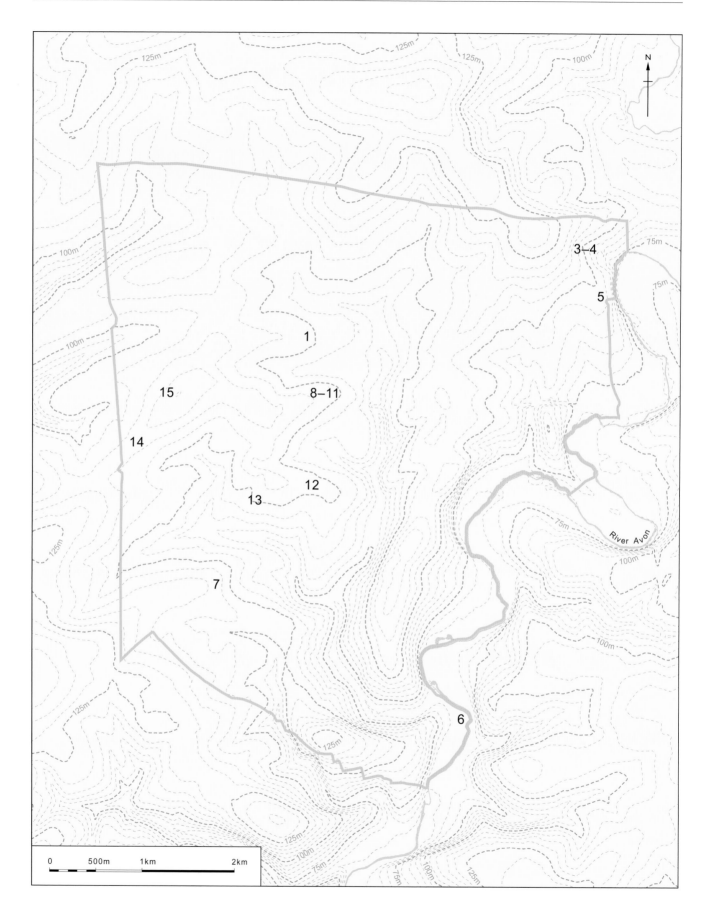

Table 5.1 Early medieval burials within the Stonehenge WHS.
This includes sites of uncertain attribution and date (see Fig 5.5).

No.	Site or parish	Location	Details	Dating
1	Amesbury 44	SU 11797 4278	Inserted inhumation	Not securely dated
2	Durrington	Near western parish boundary	30 inhumations	Undated
3	Durrington Walls	SU 1481 4365	Inhumation	Undated
4	Durrington Walls	SU 1476 4366	2 inhumations	Undated
5	Durrington 67	SU 1514 4321	11 inhumations	Undated
6	Lake	SU 1370 3880	Prone female inhumation	AD 450–610
7	Lake barrows	SU 409 102, barrow unknown	Inserted inhumation	Not securely dated
8	Stonehenge	Ditch (E side)	Skull fragment	AD 340–510
9	Stonehenge	Ditch (E side)	Tooth	AD 680–880
10	Stonehenge	Grave near Y9	Decapitated male inhumation	AD 660–890
11	Stonehenge	Stonehole 27	Tooth	AD 770–950
12	Wilsford 16	SU 1203 4123	Inserted inhumation	Not securely dated
13	Wilsford 30	SU 1141 4107	Inserted inhumation	Not securely dated
14	Winterbourne Stoke 4	SU 1012 4167	Inserted inhumation	Not securely dated
15	Winterbourne Stoke 23a	S1043 4219U	Inserted inhumation (doubtful)	Not securely dated

Fig 5.5 (opposite) Distribution of early medieval burials. The unlocated inhumations from 'near the western boundary' of Durrington parish (2 in Table 5.1) are omitted.

The high medieval period

The principal settlements of this period (12th–16th centuries) – Amesbury, West Amesbury, Countess, Wilsford, Normanton, Lake, Durrington, Winterbourne Stoke and Berwick St James – were in the valleys; of these only West Amesbury, Wilsford, Normanton and Lake are actually within the WHS. Some of these settlements represent the increasing fragmentation of large early medieval estates into smaller manors. This process may have begun before 1066 but two places, Countess and Normanton, derive their names from post-Conquest owners, while West Amesbury possibly originated in the 13th century as a planned 'colonisation' from Amesbury manor (Crowley 1995, 27).

The land of these manors, tithings and parishes was distributed, as described above, in strips from the flood plains up to the high downs; arable was largely restricted to the lower slopes, but from time to time areas of the higher downland were put under the plough. The open fields of Amesbury Countess and West Amesbury, extending to the King Barrow Ridge and Coneybury, were intensively cultivated, leaving few upstanding prehistoric monuments – even the interior of Vespasian's Camp was ploughed by the 14th century (RCHME 1979, xv–xvi). A slightly unusual arrangement obtained in the Manor of Lake, where the permanent pasture of Lake Down lay at the centre of the manor and the arable beyond it in West Field, levelling the Late Bronze Age linear ditches **a** and **c** in this area (ibid, xviii, map 3; *see* Fig 4.19). To the south, strip fields on the flanks of Rox Hill overlie prehistoric fields without obliterating them, suggesting that this episode of medieval farming was short-lived. In Durrington, however, the open field was more conventionally placed

*Fig 5.6
Imaginative reconstruction drawing of an execution at Stonehenge, c 8th century AD. A skeleton was found by Hawley in 1923 (1925, 31–2). The bones were believed to have been destroyed during the Second World War but, following some detective work, they were rediscovered (Pitts 2001, 127–8) and analysed. Radiocarbon determinations gave a mean date range of AD 660–890 (Hamilton et al 2007) and it was noted that the skeleton, which was of an adult male, had been decapitated with a sharp blade, probably a sword (Pitts et al 2002).*

adjacent to the village; cultivation has distorted the shape of the massive bank and ditch of Durrington Walls, all but flattened the earthwork of Woodhenge and in fact levelled a large number of other early features (RCHME 1979, xviii–xix; McOmish 2001, 78–9). Such levelling may have resulted from the deliberate spreading of earthworks to make use of the good soil within them (Kirkham 2012).

Evidence of medieval strip farming in the form of ridge and furrow does not survive as earthworks in the WHS but a few examples can be seen on aerial photographs – on the east side of the King Barrow Ridge, for example (RCHME 1979, pl 9). One notable group of strips lies to the south of the Winterbourne Stoke Crossroads and extends across the line of the current A366 Salisbury–Devizes road, showing that this route must have taken a different course in the medieval period (ibid, xix, 30, pl 22). Cultivation of these thin soils required, as in previous periods, heavy manuring to maintain fertility. In this case it was supplied by folding sheep on the arable at night (Bond 1991, 407; Hare 1994, 160).

The pasture of the high downs was largely given over to sheep, with no archaeological trace left but the occasional penning; a square enclosure on Winterbourne Stoke Down, known now from aerial photography though it survived as an earthwork until the Second World War, is probably one of these stock enclosures (RCHME 1979, 25). Other pennings existed in Stonehenge Bottom below Luxenborough Plantation, and other possible examples have been noted just above Normanton (ibid, xxi, 24) and, according to Darvill (2006, 247), on Wilsford Down and King Barrow Ridge. There is no evidence to suggest that these pennings contained sheephouses, as elsewhere (Hare 1994, 161); they might be of late medieval origin but were still in use in the early post-medieval period (see Chapter 6). Rabbit farming may have been established by some manors in the medieval period. The name Coneybury is first mentioned in Amesbury in 1382 (Bond 1991, 398); Darvill states that a pillow mound south-west of Druid's Lodge was excavated in the 1950s (2006, 247) but the date of the mound is not mentioned.

Manorial boundaries were established on the downs by the 14th century (McOmish et al 2002, 113) incorporating many of the prehistoric earthworks as markers and in some cases fixing the parish boundaries that have survived to the present day. Some of the Winterbourne Stoke Crossroads barrows mark the parish boundary between Winterbourne Stoke and Wilsford, with the corner of Amesbury parish falling on Winterbourne Stoke barrow 10; the 'Monarch of the Plain' (Amesbury 55) marks an angle change in the boundary between Winterbourne Stoke and Amesbury but probably also marks the boundary between two of Amesbury's manors. Part of the northern earthwork of the Greater Cursus is the parish boundary between Amesbury and Durrington, and several stretches of the later Bronze Age linear ditches mark modern parish boundaries, such as that between Wilsford and Winterbourne Stoke. The lynchets of prehistoric fields form the boundary between Wilsford cum Lake and Woodford, and hence the southern boundary of the WHS itself.

Curiously, Stonehenge itself does not appear to have been used as a boundary marker; this may be because land units established in prehistory were sufficiently robust to resist change in later times, or because of an appreciation of the importance of the site in medieval times. A perambulation of West Amesbury dated 1639 does not mention the stones (Inst Hist Res, Seymour papers).

Most of the medieval settlements survive today – Amesbury as a market town, the others as villages – but all have changed to a greater or lesser degree since their medieval foundations. Fragments of only two medieval buildings are known to survive within the WHS: Wilsford church was largely rebuilt in the Victorian period, but the tower retains 12th-century fabric (RCHME 1987, 206–7), the oldest medieval structure known to survive within the WHS (Fig 5.7); the only known medieval domestic building surviving in the WHS is West Amesbury House, which contains fabric dating to the 15th or early 16th centuries, or possibly earlier (Fig 5.8; Lane 2011, 7–8, 21–3, 61, 68). There is a tradition that West Amesbury House represents a grange of Amesbury Abbey, which had a small holding here of about 100 acres (40.5ha), the only land held by the abbey within the WHS; however, it is just as likely that this house was the manorial centre of one of the other West Amesbury manors, D'Aubeny's (ibid, 8).

The medieval villages were largely linear in plan, with houses on one or both sides of a street, while the smaller hamlets were possibly more irregularly grouped farmsteads that later diminished to single farms (Lane 2011,

Fig 5.7
Wilsford Church.
Photograph taken in 1857
before rebuilding.
(© Salisbury and South
Wiltshire Museum)

8). Change in the settlement pattern, brought about at least partly by declining populations from the 14th century onwards (Hare 1994, 167–8), can be seen archaeologically at West Amesbury and, more dramatically, at Lake.

West Amesbury today is a scatter of buildings extending from West Amesbury House along the north side of the Amesbury–Wilsford road (Lane 2011, 61–5 *et passim*). Earthworks represent medieval plots arranged along the valley floor between the river and the road. The manorial history of West Amesbury is complex (Bowden 2011, 10–11) but is of passing interest in that one of its manors included Stonehenge. The earthworks of the medieval village are fragmentary and indicate only the probable locations of abandoned properties (Fig 5.9 between **a** and **b**). The population seems, from the available documentary evidence, to have been stable for several centuries, so the abandonments probably represent settlement shift rather than shrinkage (ibid, 10, 12).

The village at Lake now lies along the Avon valley (Lane 2011, 70–3 *et passim*) but its medieval predecessor occupied a narrow combe, Lake Bottom (the lowest reach of Stonehenge Bottom); this is the feature from which the name, first recorded in 1289, probably derives – *lacu*, 'side channel of a river' (Gelling and Cole 2000, 20). The extensive earthworks (Fig 5.10) represent at least three phases of village development arranged along the combe bottom. The

remains overlie earlier – probably prehistoric – fields and have themselves been subsequently damaged by landscaping, including the creation of an ornamental pond or canal. The decline of the population may have begun as early as the 14th century, but depopulation of this area may be associated with the gentrification of the landscape and its conversion into a park in the 17th century (*see* Chapter 6). Lake had a chapel until the mid-16th century but the

Fig 5.8
West Amesbury House.
Part of the medieval roof
structure photographed
in 1979 during RCHME
architectural investigation.
(BF50119 24L/37 © Crown
copyright. HE)

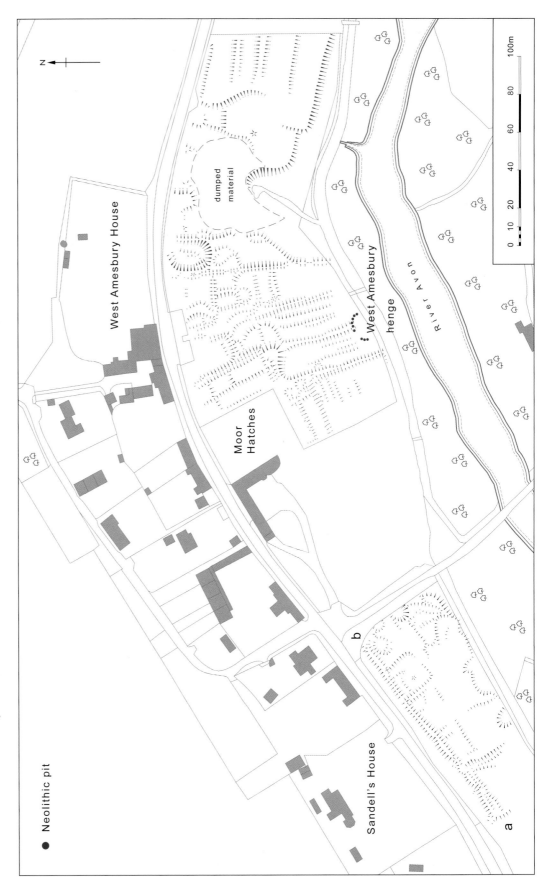

Fig 5.9
Analytical earthwork survey by the RCHME of village earthworks at West Amesbury. Moor Hatches is a substantial early 18th-century farmhouse, possibly with earlier origins; Sandell's House is one of the many buildings in the WHS where Arts and Crafts influence can be seen. Earthworks of medieval properties can be seen between **a** and **b**, with garden remains and other features in front of West Amesbury House.
(920424 © Crown copyright. HE)

Fig 5.10 (opposite)
Analytical earthwork survey by the RCHME of the village and parkland remains at Lake. The hollow way (**a**–**b**) is partly filled by a later pond (**c**) and the probable dovecot (**d**) sits on its southern bank. Wilsford barrow 87, to the south, has been heightened to form a prospect mount. The contours are at 5m intervals.
(831669 © Crown copyright. HE)

● Neolithic pit

West Amesbury House

dumped material

West Amesbury henge

River Avon

Moor Hatches

b

Sandell's House

a

Lake House

Staircase Plantation

b

c

a

d

N

80m
75m
70m
65m
65m
70m
75m
80m
85m
90m

75m

0   100   200m

89

community was always part of Wilsford parish; the site of the chapel is lost but it is said to have been within the gardens of Lake House (Watts 1962, 221). Lake Bottom is now dry but is recorded as carrying a stream, at least seasonally, in the 19th and 20th centuries (Watts 1962, 213; Richards 1990, 211), and may have been wetter in the medieval period.

The first medieval village, established by the 13th century and probably earlier, comprised a double row of plots laid out along either side of a village street which was probably, for part of the year at least, a flowing stream (*see* Fig 5.10, **a–b**). This is an arrangement seen at other chalk downland villages in medieval Wiltshire and it raises questions about how such streets were actually used, though presumably the stream was channelled. The manorial curia, including chapel and mill, was at the eastern end of the settlement by the river. At some time the morphology of the village was changed by the creation of three or more enclosed farmsteads overlying some of the earlier peasant properties. Whether this was imposed by the manor or negotiated by the villagers (*see below*), it represents a major disruption to the village's social and economic life. The farmsteads themselves were later subject to amalgamation of holdings. These horizons of change possibly mark a time, or times, when the population of the village was in decline, probably from the 14th century onwards. The construction of the ornamental pond (**c**) in the 17th century destroyed part of the village street, emphasising to the displaced villagers the permanence of the new arrangement (Bowden 2011, 2–9), though the village may already have been substantially abandoned before this time (Hare 1994, 165).

It has been suggested that these linear villages were planned settlements, their layout dictated by manorial owners, while others have noted that the layout reflects local tradition and organisation by the communities (Lewis 1994, 187). This is plausible, given the communal nature of agricultural practice at the time – the management of the common fields and grazing relied upon a strong sense of common interests which could have extended to guiding the form and layout of plots within the settlement (Lane 2011, 21).

The road pattern in the medieval period is difficult to reconstruct with certainty. The bridging point of the Avon at Amesbury was a hub; from here a road connected the settlements on the west bank of the Avon. The main route to the west passed through Vespasian's Camp on the current line of Stonehenge Road; the early date of this route is suggested by the division of the hill fort into 'Great Walls' and 'Little Walls' in a document of 1397 (RCHME 1979, 22). When this route reached the unenclosed higher ground beyond the common fields, however, travellers were free to follow numerous trackways across the open down. Traces of these are seen here and there as ruts and hollows, such as the narrow hollow ways – for pedestrians and pack animals rather than vehicles – on the eastern flank of Stonehenge Bottom. The base of a wayside cross at Winterbourne Stoke Crossroads, however, suggests that this road junction was already of significance, or at least that a route down into the valley of the Till from the open downs was worth marking (or perhaps that the settlements along the Till needed symbolic protection from the pagan Stonehenge Down – such crosses had many purposes). The Packway is recorded in the 1550s (Crowley 1995, 95) but possibly not on its current line; a hollow way parallel to the modern road but about 150m south of it can be traced through some of the fields at Larkhill. Such long-distance droveways linked principal market centres but tended to avoid settlements and steep combes, keeping to the higher ground of Salisbury Plain wherever possible; they are probably of considerable antiquity (Stevenson 1995, 95; McOmish *et al* 2002, 123).

Stonehenge itself attracted the attention of medieval writers and was accorded the status of a 'marvel' (Chippindale 2012, 20). It may be no coincidence that these early references were made at the time of the 12th-century renaissance – a period of intellectual revitalisation in western Europe – when interest in such places might be expected. On the other hand there is little evidence that Stonehenge was much visited. The physical evidence consists of: one cut halfpenny of Henry II (1158–80); a small quantity of metalwork, including six arrowheads; and some pottery, much of which dates to the 12th and 13th centuries (Davies 1995, 432; Montague 1995, 433–4; Mepham 1995). Some of the possibly early trackways converge on Stonehenge but this relative paucity of material culture might suggest that they were going past the monument – using it as a way marker – rather than to it. Nevertheless, the survival of Stonehenge when so many other monuments were dismantled or levelled is probably due to continuing respect.

6

The landscape of 'improvement'

Given that inscription of Stonehenge as a World Heritage Site is based on the unique complex of Neolithic and Bronze Age monuments, it is unsurprising that the post-medieval landscape has received little archaeological attention, other than in Darvill 2006 (chs 10 and 11) and brief summaries in management documents (Darvill *et al* 2005; Young *et al* 2009), the latter based on rapid desk-based landscape regression (Bond 1991, 384).

The current project, though also barely scratching the surface, nevertheless highlights the rich and diverse physical remains and cartographic and documentary sources that relate to changes in the Stonehenge WHS landscape from the mid-16th century onwards. These changes were bound up in the changing perceptions of the day – of enlightenment, the spirit of scientific enquiry and progress; of what constitutes beauty in the landscape and political changes incorporating the creation of a national identity – but interpreted in unique and sometimes intensely personal ways by the major landholders in quests for their own private arcadia (Whyte 2002; Tarlow 2007). However, change was also driven by the wider and equally dramatic impacts of enclosure and the drive for agricultural 'improvement' and profit. Within the Stonehenge WHS landscape the most prominent 'improvers' were the 3rd Duke and Duchess of Queensberry and the Duke family. Understanding of the Stonehenge WHS landscape requires an appreciation of these individuals (Bowden 1998, 26).

The growth and development of landed estates was a phenomenon of the post-medieval period, largely enabled by the suppression of the monasteries and the emergence of a global economy (Everson and Williamson 1998, 145; Williamson 2007, 4). Their distinguishing feature was the power, afforded by the recognition of absolute property rights, over the exploitation and physical appearance of extensive tracts of countryside. The downs provided a relatively blank canvas and yet in the Stonehenge WHS landscape, despite some expansion of arable in the 18th and 19th centuries, the wholesale transformation of the countryside was reserved for the mid-20th century conversion to arable. Instead, pockets of change are most evident in the existing fields, the expanded parks and new plantations, and along the rivers and roads. The cumulative effect of such 'improvement' altered the ways in which this landscape was experienced and yet it managed to remain the perfect setting for those in pursuit of a rural idyll; escaping to the country is nothing new (Schama 1995, 11; Johnson 2007, 5).

Landscape

As noted above, the medieval downland landscape was dominated by sheep and corn agriculture in which resources were held and worked in common, underpinned by the feudal manorial system (*see* Chapter 5), and the strong historical associations with manorial units are clearly reflected in the post-medieval tithing boundaries in both the Till and Avon valleys (Aston 1985, fig 15; McOmish *et al* 2002, fig 5.2). Across the chalk-lands there is evidence for the amalgamation of holdings in the 15th and 16th centuries and a considerable decline in the number of tenants. Landowners continued to expand and consolidate their estates, particularly in the 18th century, and into the 20th century the agricultural land within Amesbury parish was divided between a few very large farms (Crowley 1995, 33).

Small blocks of the downs were broken up from the early 18th century onwards, as short-term arable and to improve the pasture for the new Wiltshire sheep (Molland 1959, 73; RCHME 1979, xvi), although the downland soil was too thin to sustain tillage through 'burn-baking' (stripping back and burning turf in an

Durrington

Countess

Amesbury

West Amesbury

Normanton

Wilsford

Lake

Great Durnford

Upper Woodford

Land use
Arable
Arable & pasture
Meadow
Park
Pasture
Settlement/road
Wood/plantation

0   500m   1km   2km

attempt to improve fertility) alone, which produced generally poor results. Much is often made of the effects of parliamentary enclosure on the English landscape for this period (Chapman and Seeliger 2001); however, within the Stonehenge WHS landscape so much was acquired by the Duke family at Lake in the late 16th century (Watts 1962, 218) or brought 'in hand' by the 3rd Duke of Queensberry at Amesbury Abbey during the 18th century (eg WHC 1619/box 7) that few Acts were necessary. Where enclosure awards exist they provide interesting detail on provision for the repair of roads, maintenance of water meadows, rental payments due to mills for water and the continued practice of feeding flocks in common (Sandell 1971).

Despite formal enclosure, many of the downs in this area remained open pasture until the Second World War (Fig 6.1). The divisions shown on the award maps, for example the allotments in Winterbourne Stoke's Tenantry Sheep Down (WHC EA 104), were primarily to enable owners to visualise their holdings, with little or no effect on the physical landscape. As the Durrington Enclosure Act clearly specifies, allotments were 'to be delineated on a plan and shown to the proprietors' (WHC EA 144). The same may be true of the former open fields. Unfortunately, Flitcroft's maps of the Amesbury estate pre-date the acquisition of West Amesbury and Countess Court manors but still illustrate the amalgamation of open field furlongs into large regular fields (WHC 944/1, 2). Comparison with later maps suggests that these large fields were still open, divided by tracks and new plantations in the 19th century.

Settlement

Each of the small settlements at Lake, Wilsford, Normanton, West Amesbury and Countess saw some adjustment in the post-medieval period as the result of long-term cumulative changes in demographics, the relationships of owners and tenants to the land and agricultural practices (Hare 1994, 165). The overall pattern is one of gradual contraction well into the 18th century, followed by gentle small-scale rebuilding and accretion (Fig 6.2). The increasing emphasis on gentlemen tenant farmers may have helped reduce some villages to a large house and farm. By the mid-18th century Normanton, for example, had contracted to a single farm arranged around a square courtyard (WHC 1619H). This

type of shrinkage, rather than complete desertion, is especially common in the Avon and Till valleys (Hare 1981, 146, and 1994, 167; Aston 1985, fig 15).

In 1579 George Duke acquired the overlordship of the Manor of Lake and set about building a suitably imposing house (see p 95) to replace the manor (Watts 1962, 215; Lane 2011, 71). It is not clear exactly when the village of Lake was removed and emparked; however, the surviving earthworks testify to some prior consolidation of holdings (see Chapter 5). In the mid-18th century Lake comprised just the house and its park, stables, the farm and a mill (WHC 1552/2/2/4H; WANHS 1952), and the settlement remained relatively static under the Duke family, who held the estate until 1897 (Watts 1962, 215). The settlement earthworks to the south of the road at West Amesbury are similarly overlain by elements of the post-medieval formal garden (see Chapter 5; Bowden 2011, 12).

Most of the surviving buildings in the Stonehenge WHS landscape represent 18th-century investment coincident with the consolidation of holdings and improvements in agricultural practice (Lane 2011, 11). Examples with earlier elements include the west range of West Amesbury House and the 17th-century timber framing in the earliest phases of some farmhouses, including Normanton House. One of the unexpected discoveries of the project was an 18th-century aisled barn at West Amesbury, concealed by its conversion to cottages in the 1930s (ibid, 18–19, 63). On acquisition of the various manors in the 18th century the Duke of Queensberry set about alterations and improvements. At Countess he invested substantially in new timber-framed farm buildings, including three barns and a granary (ibid, 60).

The 19th century saw some small-scale growth in the settlement pattern, and farmsteads and isolated barns were introduced onto the downs. Some were located at the heads of combes: for example Down (now Springbottom) Farm, Wilsford and Westfield farms, Lake (WHC TAs Wilsford and Lake). Others, like Fargo Cottages, were inserted into former burnbake plots (WHC TA Amesbury; 1877 OS 25-inch map), and cottages were built along the valley road at Normanton and Wilsford (Watts 1962, 219; Stevenson 1995, 82). The only new public building within the Stonehenge WHS landscape was a small school built between Lake and Wilsford in 1857 (Watts 1962, 221), at the hamlet of Teasle. The general lack of development along the

Fig 6.1 (opposite)
Land use, c 1840. Based on information contained in the various tithe awards which were digitised as part of the project.

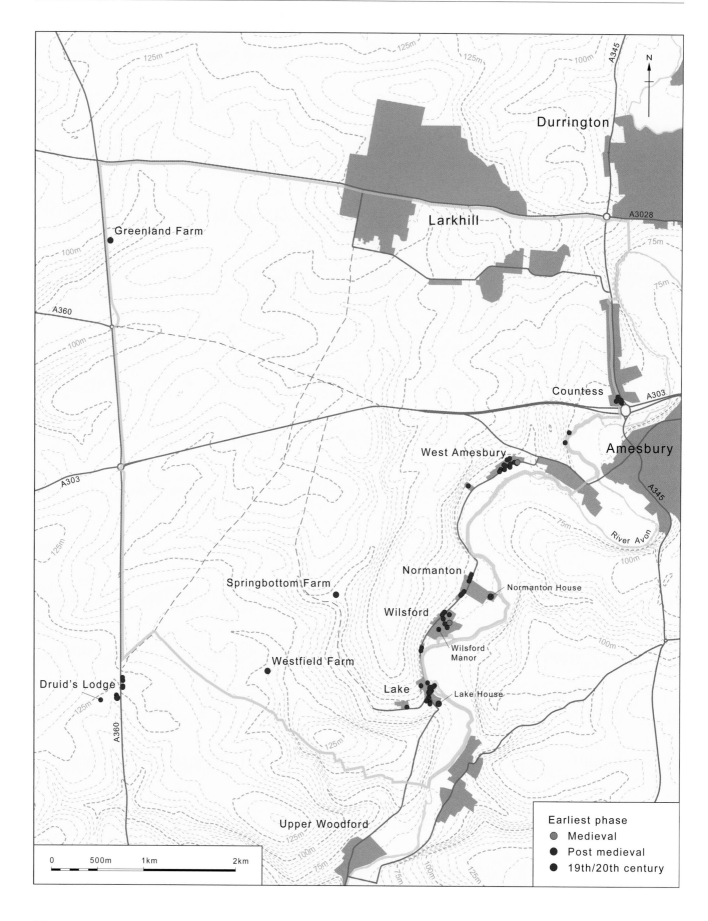

Avon valley provided the sparsely populated riverside ambience craved by members of the Arts and Crafts Movement as the 20th century began.

Houses, parks and gardens

Amesbury Abbey has seen several episodes of large-scale reconstruction. It was dismantled following the dissolution (Aston and Bettey 1998, 119) and replaced by a Palladian mansion, designed by John Webb, who was at the time deep in debate over the antiquity of Stonehenge (Field and Pearson 2010, 36–7), in the late 1650s and early 1660s. Wings were added by the Queensberrys in the mid-18th century but subsequently the house fell into decay. There is a certain irony in that the 4th Duke of Queensberry's absence and neglect contributed to the property's picturesque appeal when it came to be let in the early 19th century, benefiting from a desire for idealised beauty in the landscape without any of the effort or expense. When Sir Edmund Antrobus brought the estate in 1824 the house was so full of dry rot that it prompted rebuilding and enlargement (though some elements of Webb's seminal work were

retained) in the 1830s (Antrobus 1902, 279; Bold 1988, 110).

At the turn of the 20th century a number of houses in the Avon valley saw interventions under the direction of the Arts and Crafts architect Detmar Blow. The late 16th-century Lake House, complete with striking chequerwork of flint and limestone (Fig 6.3), was largely unaltered when Blow was asked to undertake renovation for the new owner, Joseph Lovibond, under the advice of the Society for the Protection of Ancient Buildings (SPAB). Blow's work was considered a showpiece (Watts 1962, 215; Lane 2011, 71). Blow may have done similar work at West Amesbury House and worked on the Amesbury Abbey estate, including supervising the straightening of stone 56 at Stonehenge itself (Drury 2000, 111–13; *see* Chapter 7). Lovibond's experiments with concrete in the construction of new estate buildings contrasts with the traditional materials and techniques used at Wilsford, but can still be argued to reflect a practical vernacular approach (Lane 2011, 46). The Arts and Crafts influence can be seen in several houses at Wilsford and West Amesbury, but is epitomised by Wilsford Manor.

Fig 6.2 (opposite)
The phasing of historic buildings based on rapid architectural assessment (Lane 2011). (For milestones and toll-houses see Fig 6.10.)

Fig 6.3
Lake House, photographed in 1924. (CC001309, Historic England Archive)

At Wilsford, Blow was commissioned to create the perfect retreat in which his patrons, Lord and Lady Glenconner, could protect themselves and their children from the pressures of modern life (Dakers 1993, 168). They sought 'a house in the country' rather than a grand country house (Drury 2000, 118). Wilsford Manor was unashamedly romantic – the deliberate restoration of an earlier form of the house and the embodiment of a utopian vision of the simple country life. It was built between 1904 and 1906 in local 17th-century style by local labourers, who were required to replace whole courses of flint if 'not perfectly convenient to the eye' (Tennant 1906, 454). The children had their own rustic nursery wing and adjoining two-storey playhouse – their personal fantasy kingdom safely detached from the cares of the world (Fig 6.4).

The park of Amesbury Abbey reached its greatest extent during the mid-18th century under the tenure of the 3rd Duke and Duchess of Queensberry (Fig 6.5). It is by far the best documented within the Stonehenge WHS landscape and sits comfortably within the landscape park movement of the 18th century,

which oversaw broad changes from classical calm and symmetric designs to wilder and asymmetric romanticism (Uglow 2004, 128). Garden features also survive as earthworks at West Amesbury and Lake but are relatively poorly dated (Bowden 2011). Amesbury Abbey may not have been one of the great 'political' gardens of the 18th century such as Stowe (Wickham 2012, 135), but was still an idiosyncratic mixture of loyalist fashion, Tory order and topographic practicality. It provides stark contrast to the later more sympathetic ideals described above. Expansion and landscaping of the parkland was a grand statement of wealth, an imposition of power and demonstration of man's control over nature (Everson and Williamson 1998, 151; Wickham 2012, 5).

The duchess clearly took the lead in developing Amesbury Abbey park (Fig 6.6). She was one of the most celebrated women of her day and had grown up at Petersham, Richmond, praised for its early landscaping (Batey 1988, 78). Lord Carleton, from whom the Queensberrys inherited Amesbury Abbey, was a lifelong friend and patron of Joseph Addison, author of a series of seminal articles on aesthetics and

Fig 6.4
The rustically thatched children's wing and more formal house of Wilsford Manor, from the nursery garden, photographed 1906.
(527569 © Country Life)

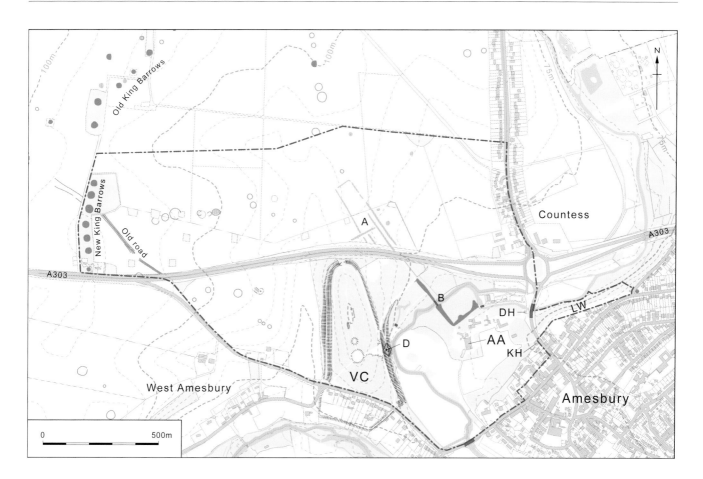

perception in *The Spectator* (1712–13), and had already begun improvements, including planting schemes (Batey 1988, 78). Together with support from their close associates John Gay and Alexander Pope, the Queensberrys were therefore well primed to consult the 'genius of the place' – the character and feel of the estate (Symes 2006, 58). Their 'retirement' to the country following the scandal over Gay's opera *Polly* gave the duchess opportunity for extensive landscaping, particularly after Gay's death in 1732 (Margetson 1985, 833), bringing together art and nature, memory and literature (Myers 2013, 5).

The duchess found the formal gardens and remaining abbey walls surrounding the house oppressive and had them removed in 1733, and replaced them with a ha-ha or sunken fence (Bold 1988, 106). A typical device of Charles Bridgeman, it implies his involvement at Amesbury several years before 1738, when he produced his exquisite plan (Bodleian Library, MS Gough Drawings a3* folio 32). The duchess told her friends she was 'planting mad' (Batey 1988, 79), and schemes throughout the 1730s and 1740s opened up the park,

softening and naturalising the earlier rigid geometric plantations mapped by Flitcroft when the Queensberrys inherited the estate (WHC 944/1&2). The landscaping incorporated the creation of romantic new garden buildings and expansion of the park as the duke acquired neighbouring manors in 1735 and 1760 (Crowley 1995, 33).

The incorporation of earlier prehistoric earthworks within a designed landscape is a widespread phenomenon; indeed many would have been hard to ignore and more difficult to remove. Given the general ubiquity of archaeological monuments in the Stonehenge WHS landscape it is unsurprising that several have been utilised within aesthetic schemes. They presented opportunities for enhancement with relative ease; barrows in particular could be heightened into prospect mounts (Batey 1988, 79; Field *et al* 2001, 197–202). Wilsford 87, a round barrow some 300m south-west of Lake House, was raised by about 2m to provide a more impressive panoramic view above the narrow framed vista along the avenue below (Symes 2006, 101; Bowden 2011, 7). In this context one does wonder exactly what John

Fig 6.5
The designed landscape of Amesbury Abbey (AA), which reached its maximum extent, approximated by the chain-and-dot green line, in the early 1760s. The Iron Age hill fort of Vespasian's Camp (VC) contains slight earthwork traces of two modified round barrows (Amesbury 24 and 25) plus elements of Bridgeman's Wilderness design above Gay's Cave and The Diamond (D). Diana's House (DH), Kent's House (KH) and the Lord's Walk (LW) already formed part of the park in 1725. In the early 1770s the Queensberrys rebuilt and refurbished the bridges (dark grey), altered the course of the river and perhaps created a new avenue (A) to the north-west, aligned on the Balluster Bridge (B) but since ploughed out. The inclusion of the New King Barrows required the diversion of the old road.

Aubrey meant by his comment on some of the barrows above Amesbury being 'raised' by the servants of Edward, Earl of Hertford, 'to keep them out of idleness' (Aubrey 1626–97, 282). Was this an early example of landscape gardening and does it perhaps explain the remarkable size and uniformity of the New King Barrows? Unfortunately the limited archaeological information about these mounds (Cleal and Allen 1994) does not afford any clues.

Vespasian's Camp was probably planted in the 1740s, once a drawn-out legal exchange of the property was completed. Although purchased in 1735 it was an arable field until at least 1741 (WHC 283/6), and landscaping of the two, or perhaps more, round barrows within is dated to 1770 (RCHME 1979, 22; Sue Haynes pers comm), suggesting a time frame covering several decades for work on the pleasure ground. Vespasian's Camp, at a distance but clearly visible from the house, formed a convenient backdrop and giant mount overlooking the sinuous River Avon (Batey 1988, 80; Haynes 2012, 35). Charles Bridgeman's design included glades, pavilions and statuary secreted within newly created blocks of wilder-

ness, quartered by a series of yew-lined allées converging on the enhanced southernmost barrow (Amesbury 24). The hill fort's ramparts defined the extent of the pleasure ground with a perimeter walk apparently within them rather than along the top, unlike the ramparts of hill forts elsewhere which have been converted for use as elevated walkways or carriage drives (Bowden 1998; Oswald 1999). Bridgeman favoured dramatic terraces and used the natural gradient of the hillside, in direct view of the house, to cut steep pathways creating a multifaceted Diamond, in plan and elevation, centred on a grotto (Fig 6.7).

Garden buildings were widely used as expressions of dissent or affiliation and their design is full of oblique references (eg Sheeran 2006, 9; Wickham 2012, 121). The grotto at the heart of The Diamond was conceived by the duchess and John Gay, who planned a cave there in which Gay could write (Batey 1988, 79). Rather than any mythical or historical figure associated with the hill fort, Gay's muses were solely of the artificial cave, which he anticipated 'peopled with nymphs'. The coveted hillside only became part of the Amesbury

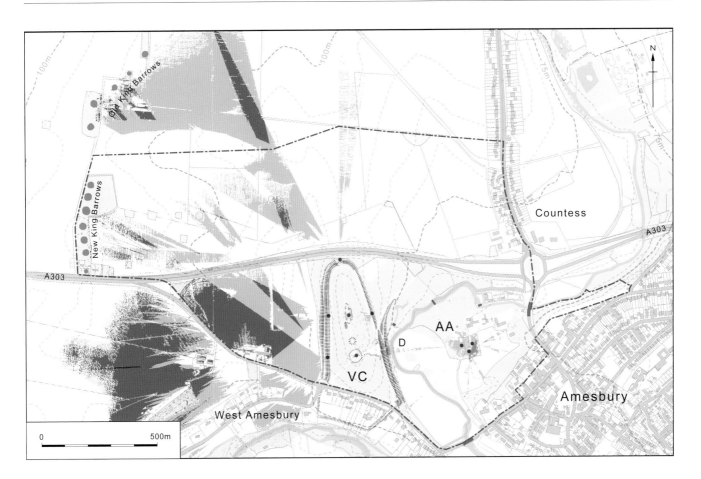

Fig 6.7

The principal views enjoyed from points within the park of Amesbury Abbey, created in GIS using an eye level of 1.6m above the modern lidar surface model. Even from the ramparts of Vespasian's Camp (VC) the views extend only as far west as Coneybury Hill. From within the park, Stonehenge could only be seen from the King Barrow Ridge, which perhaps explains the extension of the park to that point. Modern planting preserves the view west from the house (AA) towards The Diamond and Gay's Cave (D).

estate after his death. However, the new grotto became known as Gay's Cave, and perhaps provided a very suitable place for melancholy reflection and remembrance. The curious rusticated architecture does not seem to include any sarsen.

Other garden buildings at Amesbury included a highly fashionable dairy in Kent House, one of the two early-17th century lodges, and a Chinese temple summerhouse built astride a branch of the River Avon in 1747, during the heyday of garden buildings in the 'Chinese taste' (Batey 1988, 80; Bold 1988, 123). Its refurbishment in 1772 can also be seen as part of wider improvements to bridges on the Amesbury estate, a number of which were rebuilt in the 1770s. The course of the River Avon was also altered (WHC 283/188).

The ultimate romantic ruin was of course Stonehenge itself, which drew the attention of antiquaries, other scholars, artists and educated tourists in search of the picturesque (Piggott 1976; Darvill *et al* 2005, 26–27), although Gilpin rejected the idea that Stonehenge could be considered 'picturesque' (Chippindale 2012, 99–100). Among the most famous depictions

are the watercolours of Turner and Constable. When Constable exhibited his *Stonehenge* in 1836, his caption stated that 'the mysterious monument … standing remote on a bare and boundless heath, as much unconnected with the events of past ages as it is with the uses of the present, carries you back beyond all historical recall into the obscurity of a totally unknown period' (ibid, 105). By the late 19th century, as visitor numbers began to increase, the monument and its landscape differed markedly from expectations generated by printed and painted representations. It is important to acknowledge the symbiotic relationship such sites had within the Romantic movement, which allowed for the combination of intuition and scientific method and therefore the emergence of the increasingly academic discipline of archaeology (Girdwood 1986, 42; Smiles 1994, 8). It is also interesting to observe its manifestation in the parks and gardens of those associated with Stonehenge. Stukeley's survey was to enable a short-lived copy for the Earl of Pembroke at Wilton, one of the first projects for primitive monuments in British gardens (Thacker 1983, 44). Sir Richard Colt Hoare dismantled the wooden Druid's Cell or Hermitage at Stourhead in 1814 but added 'gothic' features elsewhere (Woodbridge 2002, 31). Cunnington's museum at Heytesbury, a large rustic summerhouse created of natural materials, was known as the 'Moss House' (Cunnington and Dyer 1975, 37).

Perhaps the most curious episode from this period is that of Gaffer Hunt, mentioned by both Wood in 1747 and John Smith in 1771 as having a hut among the stones. This was said to lean against one of them, apparently stone 60. Attached to the back was a lean-to where horses could be sheltered and, most intriguingly, beneath one of the stones, stone 59, was his cellar where he kept 'liquors to entertain the traveller'. The nature of this can only be imagined but it emphasises the possibility of otherwise unrecorded digging.

Woods

Until the 19th century the Stonehenge WHS landscape contained little woodland. Small woods were tucked into corners of parish boundaries or along the steepest 'cliffs' above the river and orchards among the small settlements. Lake and Amesbury Abbey parks contained avenues, plantations, wilderness and shrubberies. A number of new plantations were laid out and expanded in the 19th century as game coverts and shelter belts and for timber (Watts 1962, 219; Darvill 2006, 261). Perhaps surprisingly, an even greater area of woodland was planted in the second half of the 20th century, in rigid geometric shapes, mainly associated with the military camps at Larkhill (eg Bishop 2010, 6).

One of the earliest plantations is the formal circular clump at the summit of Rox Hill, an eye-catcher on the horizon as part of the aesthetic design for Lake, established by the mid-18th century (WHC 1552/2/2/4H). Some, like Fargo, replaced blocks of burnbake on the downs while others surrounded substantial barrows, such as Luxenborough on West Amesbury Down (RCHME 1979, xviii). The plantations are characteristically defined by wood banks emphasising their ownership and control. They typically comprise a low bank with an outer ditch, each with an elevation of around 0.5m, and are best preserved around the New King Barrows (Bishop 2011b, 23), at the oval plantation on West Amesbury Down and at Fargo (Bishop 2011a, 54). That along the eastern side of the Fargo Plantation deviated

westwards slightly to avoid the barrow mound of Amesbury 52 and probably overlies its surrounding ditch (Amadio and Bishop 2010, 35).

Livestock

Inherent within sheep and corn agriculture is the need for livestock to be moved around. By the late 18th century sheep were principally seen as mobile fertilisers; they could be fed on the thin pasture of the downs during the day and folded on next year's arable field overnight (Hare 1994, 161; Smith 2005, 193). Until the 19th-century agricultural advances (Molland 1959, 65), the fertility of the thin chalk soils could only be maintained by intensive use of the sheepfold (Bettey 2000, 43; McOmish et al 2002, 115).

Although there are several references to Cow or Sheep Downs in Cunnington's notes and the tithe awards they should not be taken at face value: livestock species and holdings were interleaved, occupying downs and arable, pasture and water meadows at various points of the day, month and year. For example, a note at the beginning of a survey in 1742 describes how West Amesbury's 'Cow Down' was traditionally used (WHC 283/6): by cows from 1 May until Martinmas (11 November), by sheep until the Sunday after Candlemas (2 February), and then it was laid up until the end of April. A number of sheepfolds, dew ponds and sheep-washes have been identified within the Stonehenge WHS landscape (Fig 6.8).

Pennings, sheepfolds and field barns

Permanent sheep enclosures were used to protect flocks during the winter from the medieval period into the 19th century (Hare 1994, 161) and were supplemented by more mobile temporary hurdle folds or pennings. Both types fulfilled a range of functions, including the gathering and sorting of sheep. Although little physical evidence for them survives, the Stonehenge WHS Landscape Project, benefiting from the better recognition and understanding of these features over the last few decades (eg Smith 2005, 194; Bishop 2009, 27), has identified two additional permanent sheepfolds.

A square sheepfold on Winterbourne Stoke Down is the only example within the Stonehenge WHS landscape known to have been defined by an earthwork bank and narrow external ditch. The boundary of two tithe allotments

Fig 6.8 (opposite) Sheepfolds (red), dew ponds (blue), plots listed in the tithe awards as sheep-wash (blue-green) and dovecots (black).

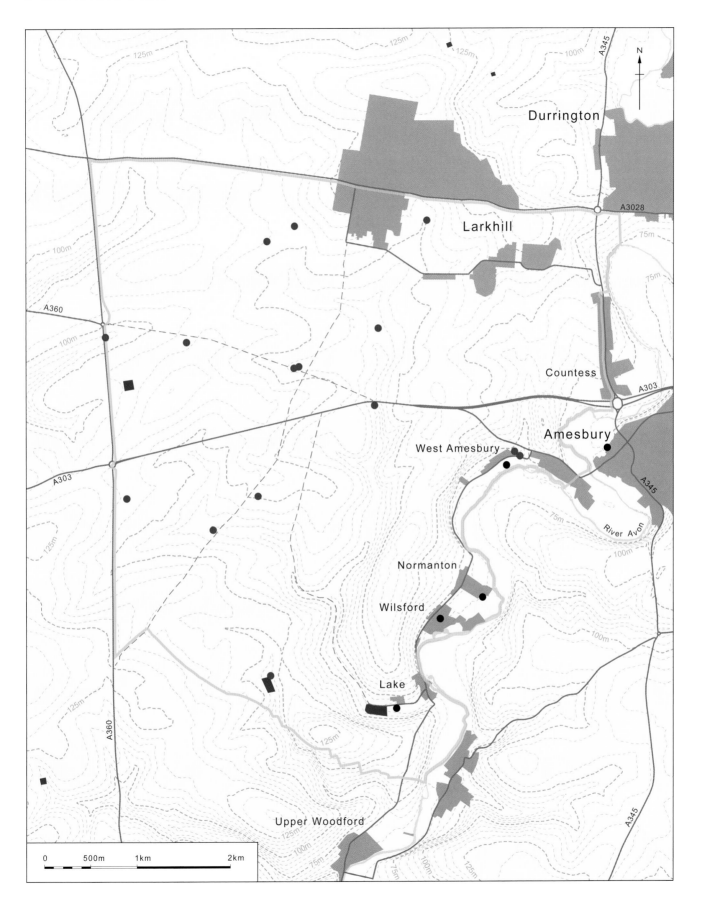

cuts across it (WHC TA Winterbourne Stoke), but the sheepfold was extant as an earthwork enclosure within open downland well into the 20th century, when it was ploughed level. Other permanent sheepfolds appear to have been defined by narrow shelter belts. Doidge's 1752 map of Lake shows neat arrangements of small trees defining two rectangular enclosures – one on Lake Down and the other, larger and apparently containing a rectangular dew pond, at the western extent of the park, in Lake Bottom (WHC 1552/2/2/4H).

The Lake Down sheepfold was in a typical location – on pasture downland with a dew pond nearby, at the bottom of the combe. The combe could also be used for shelter and to facilitate movement of the livestock (Riley and Wilson-North 2001, 141; Smith 2005, 194). An internal division, towards its north-western end, was also defined by a line of trees and may have been used to separate rams and wethers from ewes and lambs. The sheepfold appears to have gone out of use by the mid-19th century, when the trees defined a plot listed as arable (WHC TA Wilsford), which fits a pattern observed elsewhere in Wiltshire (Merewether 1851; Hare 1994, 161).

Merewether states (1851) that the term 'pennings' was not applied exclusively to

earthworks; the location of more temporary sheepfolds, defined by hurdles which were moved across the downs, is implied by the presence of dew ponds and 'pennings' place names, although the latter lie mostly beyond the WHS boundary. Stukeley's sketch of Wilsford 5 (Bush Barrow) shows a small irregular hurdle fold with the thorn bushes behind that were to provide the barrow's popular name (1740, 45; RCHME 1979, title page). Hoare mentioned that West Amesbury penning occupied 'a little vale' (1812, 198), that is Stonehenge Bottom, and had an earthwork enclosure existed Hoare would probably have described it further. Amesbury shepherds clearly made use of the natural topography for herding but used hurdles to pen the sheep, a tradition that continued into the early 20th century (Fig 6.9).

Field barns or farmsteads were established in the mid-19th century on top of the downs. One at Fargo Down Barn, Durrington, was defined on all four sides by a narrow shelter belt of trees, a circular dew pond and a tight courtyard arrangement of a barn and other buildings at its north-western corner. The dew pond and buildings were removed before the Second World War, when the enclosure was incorporated within the defensive network surrounding Larkhill, but the tree belts survive. Other barn

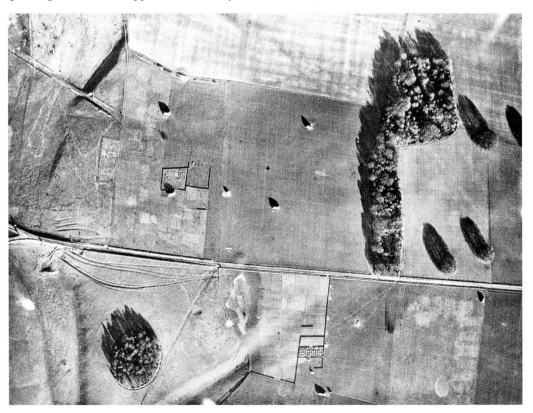

Fig 6.9

Aerial photograph, taken in the early 20th century, of King Barrow Ridge and Amesbury Down showing periodic movement of sheepfolds. Several other features can be seen, such as the braided hollow ways leading down into Stonehenge Bottom to the left.
(CCC11752/341 SU 1342/13, Historic England [Crawford Collection])

groups were established along the Stonehenge–Larkhill byway and on the King Barrow Ridge, while the more substantial Fargo (formerly 'Virgo') Cottages occupied Stonehenge Down about 600m west of Stonehenge, its occupants being engaged in both arable and pastoral tasks.

Water supply

Dew ponds (*see* Fig 6.8) are a characteristic feature of chalk downlands, where the porous rock means a general absence of surface water. Although some dew ponds may date to the medieval or even earlier periods they were a familiar sight from the 17th century onwards. Several 'sheep ponds' and 'wells' were marked in 1773 (WANHS 1952), although perhaps not all; the surviving pond on the northern side of the former A344, north-west of Stonehenge, was apparently truncated by the turnpike but was not marked. It was supplemented in the 19th and early 20th century by a square pond situated 50m to its east-north-east, slightly further down the shallow valley in which it sits. The latter has since been ploughed almost level, but its retaining bank can be observed as a parchmark (Amadio and Bishop 2010, 31).

Many new square and round dew ponds were constructed in the 19th century and lined with clay, concrete, pitch or rammed chalk (Smith 2005, 199; Hey 2010, 355). Those of square design are attributed to the Cruse family of Imber (Sawyer 2001, 58–60; McOmish *et al* 2002, 11). Within the Stonehenge WHS landscape the number of dew ponds more than doubled by 1880 and include the example at Airman's Corner (Field 2009, 8). Andrews' and Dury's map of 1773 depicts wells in Stonehenge and Wilsford Bottoms and at Springbottom Farm, and 'Stonehenge Barn and well', the latter being situated in the Bottom near where the Cursus crosses it (WANHS 1952; Field *et al* 2012, 26). A well-house was present there in 1877 and until at least 1901 (2nd edition OS 25-inch map). Remains of a cob-built well-house in the Bottom are located towards Lake, south of Springbottom Farm. This increase in water provision is undoubtedly related to 'improvements' in the breeding of the Wiltshire Horned sheep and introduction of other breeds which produced better wool and more lambs. The new Wiltshire Horn was not able to walk far and remained more permanently on the downs, requiring access to water (Molland 1959, 70; Smith 2005, 193–4).

The predominance of the Wiltshire Horn into the 19th century perhaps also explains the absence of sheepcotes – buildings in which the sheep could shelter over the winter months (Bond 2004, 143) – and the rarity of sheep-washes. The pure Wiltshire Horn was widely recognised as requiring little shelter from the elements and moulted naturally each spring, alleviating the need for shearing (Marshman 1984, 45). Nevertheless, sheep-washes are recorded along the River Avon (*see* Fig 6.8) in the tithe awards for Wilsford and Woodford (WHC).

Water meadows

Extensive floated water meadows once extended along the floor of the Avon valley. They were a necessary complement to the downland sheep walks and arable fields from the mid-17th century into the early 20th – an integral part of the intricately woven tapestry of the post-medieval chalk-land agricultural landscape of southern England. Water meadows were crucial to agricultural prosperity, the clear, fast-flowing water providing a warm blanket and nourishing sediments to encourage growth of an early bite for the 'Golden Hoof'; an agreement to float common meadow was an extension of the provision of hay for the common flock (Kerridge 1959, 54; Atwood 1963, 408).

The water meadows along the River Avon have been mapped from historic aerial photographs (Crutchley 2000; 2002) and, though some have been destroyed, several survive well as earthworks, including just north-east of the WHS boundary at Hindurrington (McOmish *et al* 2002, 136, fig 5.30), opposite Lake House, between West Amesbury and Normanton (Bowden 2011, 11) and within the loop of the river at Amesbury. There is some contrast with the Till valley, where, perhaps because of the less reliable flow of water indicated by the Winterbourne place names, water meadows were located downriver (Sandell 1971, 120, 144).

Rabbits, doves and game

Rabbits were a valuable commodity providing a useful way of increasing rents (Aston and Bettey 1998, 131), and the use of Stonehenge as a warren is recorded (Darvill *et al* 2005, 88). Other small animals have received substantially less attention, and yet, as the present survey shows, there is significant evidence for the keeping of poultry within the Stonehenge WHS landscape, associated with the higher-status properties from the medieval period onwards. Historically doves were an important food source for the rich in western Europe and were kept for their flesh, eggs and dung. Dovecots (*see* Fig 6.8) were typically sited away from but within sight of the main house, so that the pigeons were under its protection but were not disturbed unnecessarily and had a clear field of view to watch for approaching birds of prey. They were sited away from woodland and watermills for the same reasons (McCann and McCann 2011, 10).

A dovecot at West Amesbury was mentioned in documents between the late 13th and early 17th centuries (McCann and McCann 2011, 205) and the site, presumably within Pigeon House Close (WHC TA Amesbury), may have been destroyed during construction of the Moor Hatches farmhouse, as no particular earthwork feature suggests its location. Similarly, a dovecot is implied within 'Pigeons Close' at Normanton Farm (WHC EA 36), and there was a Dove Cote listed in the gardens at Amesbury Abbey in 1824 (WHC 283/202, plot 6). Some physical evidence survives. At Lake a roughly circular earthwork (*see* Fig 5.10 **d**), *c* 10m in diameter, clearly sits astride the southern bank defining the medieval street and is probably the site of a late 16th or 17th-century dovecot (Bowden 2011, 5, 9; McCann and McCann 2011, 14). The 18th-century dovecot at Wilsford, which had approximately 500 nest boxes inside, is a square rubble stone structure built against the churchyard wall, with a pyramidal roof. It now forms part of Wilsford House (Lane 2011, 27; McCann and McCann 2011, 221). Keeping pigeons was condemned by improvers as wasteful of crops during the Napoleonic Wars and became socially unacceptable, and many dovecots were demolished or converted, at least partly, to other agricultural uses (McCann and McCann 2011, 15).

Other small animals were apparently plentiful, providing a range of sporting activities (Crowley 1995, 18). In the early 19th century agents selling the Amesbury estate boasted 'the finest coursing ground in the Kingdom … with a great abundance of hares and partridges and a tolerable number of pheasants' (WHC 283/202, 3), but they were trying to tempt prospective buyers. The presence of a swannery on the River Avon, also listed in the sales particulars, would benefit from further research. Many of the plantations within the Stonehenge WHS landscape still provide pheasant coverts.

Roads

The undulating Wiltshire downs presented an inhospitable wildscape to the traveller, a place frequented by shepherds and sheep but also in the popular imagination by vagabonds, thieves and ne'er-do-wells. Major routes avoided the area.

Although parishes were obliged from 1555 to maintain the roads that passed through them they often lacked the expertise and incentive to invest. Roads on chalk needed little maintenance compared with routes on clay but the state of the roads varied considerably by location, by season and from year to year (Gerhold 2005, xvii). The London to Barnstaple route was the only main road through the WHS to be surveyed by Ogilby (1675, plate 32), and both Amesbury and Shrewton, through which it passed, derived some prosperity from it as 'thoroughfares' in the late 17th century (Chandler 1991, table 2). It passed across the open down to the north of the present A344 and was supplemented by other routes including the Amesbury–Mere road (ibid, 95), now the A303, valley roads connecting the villages alongside the rivers, and numerous unenclosed paths and tracks across the downs. One such route emerges from a gap through the King Barrows as a hollow way 15m wide and is cut by the unfinished turnpike road (*see below*), descends into Stonehenge Bottom and crosses the floor on a low causeway about 12m wide; it is difficult to trace on the western slopes but appears to use a shallow re-entrant (Field *et al* 2012, 31).

Several north-to-south tracks are shown as passing close to Stonehenge in Andrews' and Dury's 1773 Map of Wiltshire (WANHS 1952), one of them evidently the way from Wilton mentioned by Stukeley in 1740 beside which he excavated one of the Normanton barrows. None explicitly led to the stones but, as in the medieval period, used them as a waymarker in the otherwise featureless countryside. By the mid-18th century, with improvements in the breeding of horses and coach design, attitudes to overland travel were changing, with travellers preferring turnpike 'roads' over poorly maintained 'ways' (Chandler 1991, 88).

Turnpike trusts

Two main turnpike networks passed through the Stonehenge WHS landscape (Fig 6.10), the Wilton Trust, established by an Act of 1760 (Cossons 1959, 262), and the Amesbury Turnpike Trust (1761) during the period of 'Turnpike Mania' (Chandler 1979, 2; Wright 2008, 9). The latter included the London road, now the A303, and extended from near Andover in the east to Willoughby Hedge at West Knoyle, with smaller branch routes in the Avon and Wylye valleys (Cossons 1959, 257).

The Trusts utilised existing routes across the Stonehenge WHS landscape. The remarkably straight Wilton road, now the A360, probably formalised routes that cut across medieval and earlier cultivation patterns (RCHME 1979, plate 22). The extension of Amesbury Park necessitated the rerouting of the Amesbury to Market Lavington public road, the course of which can now only be traced as a cropmark (ibid, 32). In 1775 the duke built the Queensberry Bridge to carry the main London road (Chandler 1979, 2), part of his wider scheme to rebuild bridges across his estate.

Considerable effort was expended in a new route to Shrewton across Stonehenge Bottom, parts of which survive as earthworks, among the most impressive in the WHS; the road crosses Stonehenge Bottom on a substantial causeway, crosses the Avenue, and clips the mound and berm of barrow Amesbury 43 (Amadio and Bishop 2010, 30; Field et al 2012, 29). However, the route was not sanctioned by Parliament and construction was aborted (Chandler 1979, 3); the lack of traffic is demonstrated by the fact that the Stonehenge Avenue ditches still survive as slight earthworks where the roadway crosses them. The favoured route was the recently removed A344, which is not documented before 1773 (RCHME 1979, xxiii). The characteristic splaying of roads to avoid muddier, poorly drained sections is particularly evident either side of the A303, on the flanks of Stonehenge Bottom (see Fig 6.9; Field et al 2012, 31).

Associated buildings, including coaching inns (Chandler 1980), were established; in distinct linear zones along each turnpike trust's network, the different styles of surviving milestones and toll-houses can almost be said to reflect a 'brand image' (Newman et al 2001, 169; Wright 2008, 5). Toll gates and houses were located on the main London road at the edge of Amesbury and at the beginning of other turnpikes managed by the Amesbury Trust. Although the gates have long gone, two of the three toll-houses survive (see Fig 6.10). The West Amesbury toll-house was demolished in the early 20th century (Chandler 1979, 3; Haynes and Slocombe 2004, 4). The Countess toll-house, of the same design, is therefore the earliest surviving example. It controlled the southern end of the road northwards to the parish boundary and was transferred to the new Kennett and Amesbury Trust, an offshoot of the Amesbury Trust, in 1840 (Chandler 1979, 8).

The third toll-house, alongside the A345 towards the southern edge of Amesbury, was built in 1836 at the start of a new branch of the Swindon, Marlborough and Everleigh Trust turnpike network, which improved the connection between Amesbury and Salisbury (Chandler 1979, 8). Its classical design is thought to have been a deliberate evocation of the Workhouse by the same architect (Fig 6.11; Morrison 1997, 188, and 1999, 72; Haynes and Slocombe 2004, 3), which was to occupy the adjacent plot to the south-east.

Waymarking

All that remains of the medieval cross at Winterbourne Stoke Crossroads (see Chapter 5) is the hollow stone base, also known as the 'Drinking Stone'. Road signs and guideposts, a legal requirement from 1697 (Piggott 1976, 115), have been replaced as the roads throughout the WHS have become wider and busier. Tracks, and even the former turnpikes, across the open downs were still marked with picket posts late in the 19th century (OS 1878 25-inch map). The uniform carved limestone and sarsen milestones (see Fig 6.10) along the Amesbury Trust routes are assumed to date from its earliest years. Milestone 79 is considerably larger and more elaborate, standing 1.15m high and 0.7m wide. It was originally located adjacent to Amesbury Park, the home of the trust's principal creditor, the 3rd Duke of Queensberry (Chandler 1979, 2), and is the only milestone to bear a date (1764), which suggests that it was the first erected by the trust, perhaps with some ceremony.

Nearly all of the milestones in the area have been moved from their original positions, and the Wilton milestone, once located south of the Winterbourne Stoke Crossroads, is now lost. Amesbury milestone 80 is now situated on the

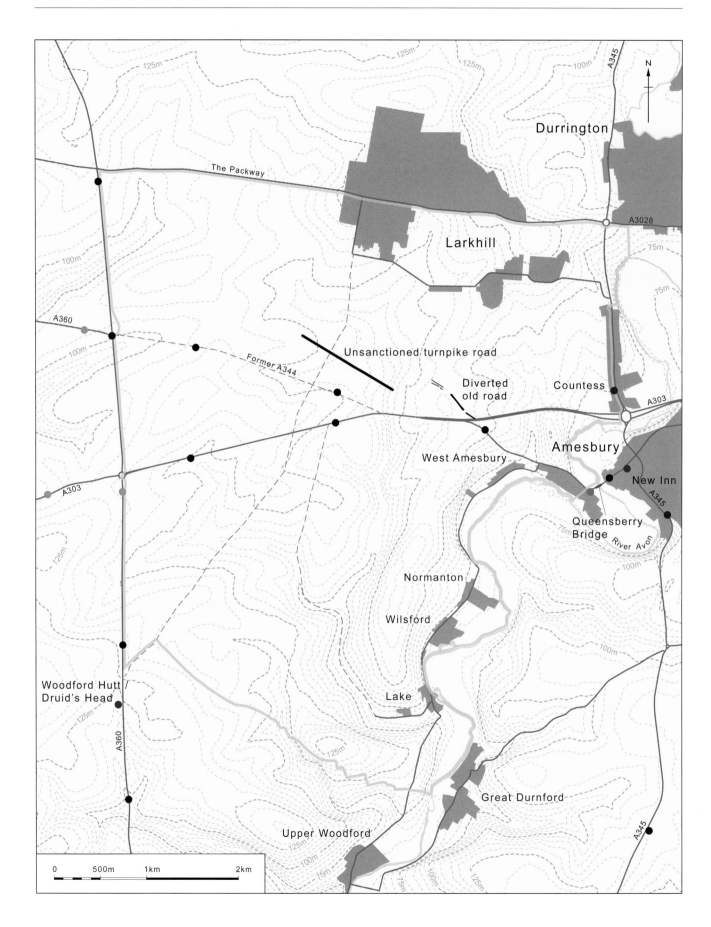

*Fig 6.11 (left)
The Swindon, Marlborough
and Everleigh toll-house,
built in 1836.
(BF050094 14B/19
© Crown copyright. HE)*

northern side of the original route of the A344, opposite Stonehenge, and rather forlornly slumping to the east. It can be seen located south of the road, close to the Heel Stone, in photographs taken in 1881 (Bishop 2011a, fig 3) and was probably moved during mid-20th-century road improvements. Its counterpart on the A303 is almost completely buried within the roadside embankment.

The Wilton Trust milestones bear distinctive cast-metal plates, are much squarer in profile and have been moved to significantly different locations (Fig 6.12). They are probably replacements erected in the early 19th century, when use of cast-metal plates became increasingly common (Darvill 2006, 261; Wright 2008, 31). Their new locations also suggest that the route was resurveyed: perhaps greater clarity and accuracy were required for tighter timetables as stagecoach travel reached its peak in the 1830s (Chandler 1979, 5). Most milestones were also removed during the Second World War and then reinstated, not always in the same position (Oliver 1993, 68), and several of the milestones have been moved for more recent road improvements, including that at Airman's Corner for the new Stonehenge visitor centre.

*Fig 6.12
A distinctive Wilton Trust
milestone standing beside
the B3086.
(Sharon Soutar)*

The later 19th century

The number of stagecoaches passing through Amesbury reached 15 a day in the 1830s, with a noticeable increase in long-distance traffic passing through (Chandler 1979, 2; 1980). This peak was short-lived as turnpike routes across the country were eclipsed by other communication networks, especially the railways (Newman *et al* 2001, 171). Throughout the 1840s usage and the number of routes dropped. By 1848 a branch of the London and South Western Railway had reached Salisbury, and the turnpike trusts were wound up between 1870 and 1877 (Cossons 1959, 265; Chandler 1979, 8; 1980). Property belonging to the Amesbury Trust, including toll-houses, gates, posts and lamps, was auctioned on the last day of trading at the George Inn, Amesbury. By the end of the 19th century all main roads were vested in the county council and some of the smaller roads, including part of the Packway, were to be adopted and improved by the military in the early 20th century (Cossons 1959, 265). Increased ease of travel by road and rail facilitated the growth of tourism at Stonehenge (Fig 6.13).

Stonehenge: enclosure and visitors

Throughout the later 19th century demands to do something about the growing numbers of visitors and, more particularly, what they were doing there became increasingly frequent. In 1895 Edgar Barclay wrote that 'Except during the inclement winter months, never a day passes without the arrival there of carriages, and often three or four parties are present at the same time' (1895, xi).

Many complaints concerned the habit of visitors hammering or chiselling off fragments of stone, although the owner, the 3rd Sir Edmund Antrobus, was adamant both that this practice was less common than was claimed and that the principal culprits were archaeologists. Indeed, in his pioneering paper on the petrology of the stones, Nevil Story Maskelyne (1878) described obtaining, without consent, 20 fresh samples of his own. There were also complaints from scholars about having to share Stonehenge with people who used it merely for leisure. In 1885 someone using the signature 'F.R.S.' complained (*The Times* 5 September) about the presence not just of tourists but of 'neighbouring rustics' with no 'intelligent interest' in the

Fig 6.13
Foreign tourists at Stonehenge in the early 1890s. Photograph, possibly by Charles Latham, from the album Baudenkmaeler in Grossbritannien [Monuments in Great Britain], edited by the German architect Constantin Uhde and published by Ernst Wasmuth, Berlin, in 1894. (YDE01/02/67, Historic England Archive)

stones. Antrobus responded to such complaints by instructing the caretaker to ensure that no picnicking occurred among the stones, but those with a more 'intelligent interest' wanted him to go further.

A deputation representing the Wiltshire Archaeological Society visited the monument in August 1886 to report on its state in the light of concerns about damage by visitors, and to make recommendations as to what should be done. The group included Henry Cunnington, who had previously been forced to publish an apology in the local press after being caught undertaking illicit excavation at the monument. The deputation expressed its concern at the increasing numbers of visitors, and the 'irreparable injury to the stones constantly going on at the hands of thoughtless and mischievous visitors' (*The Times* 17 August 1886, 4). It demanded proper protection – a fence, preferably a ha-ha, some distance beyond the earthwork enclosure, and a caretaker to regulate visitors, prevent picnicking and, above all, prevent injury to the stones. This raised the question of whether the costs incurred, including the caretaker's wages, should be met by charging an entrance fee. In an editorial the next day, it was argued, despite Antrobus's assertions to the contrary, that the main problem was indeed the 'excursionists and bean-feasters'. Insisting that 'Stonehenge is now threatened not so much by the natural processes of decay as by the destructive agency of human wantonness and vulgarity', the anonymous author complained that although rabbits were undermining the stones, they were easier to deal with than humans (*The Times* 18 August 1886).

Suggestions about what to do revolved around two main options – railings or a ha-ha – preferably with a caretaker to control admission, with the implication that some classes of visitor would be excluded. For example, the aforementioned 'F.R.S.' had suggested 'a deep ditch ... and admission thus confined to one entrance, where a janitor might be placed to admit only those who can undertake to behave themselves properly within the enclosed area' (*The Times* 5 September 1885). Support was offered by 'M' of Salisbury: once those who came to Stonehenge merely to enjoy themselves were banished to the Plain, 'then others who really care for such monuments would be able to examine the stones with some pleasure, which has now become impossible' (*The Times*, 9 September 1886, 4).

A subsequent outbreak of complaints appeared in the same newspaper in 1893, this time prompted by a visit by 'Archaeologist', who expressed his 'disgust' upon discovering schoolchildren present. This correspondence ended with the caretaker, William Judd, pointing out that 'Children have just as much right to visit there as antiquarians' (*The Standard* 25 September 1893, 2).

When the fence was erected in 1901 by the 4th Sir Edmund it was neither railings nor ditch but barbed wire, although a ha-ha remained the preferred option for many. The rationale for barbed wire was safety, but of the stones, not the visitors. The collapse of stone 22 was at least partly blamed on the lack of control on access. One of the members of the committee advising Antrobus in 1901 (*see* Chapter 7), G F Browne, Bishop of Bristol and formerly Disney Professor of Archaeology at Cambridge, later recounted that, 'We were all agreed that it was unsafe to leave this great monument open to a wandering public. It must be protected from mischief wrought by casual passers-by. Whether the mischief was wilful or merely ignorant did not matter; it must be stopped' (Browne 1915). He claimed that the use of barbed wire was his idea. Further support for the fence came from those concerned about the growing influx of military personnel to Salisbury Plain, increasing the potential for 'unintentional harm' (*The Times* 9 April 1901, 11).

Logs were used to block tracks approaching the monument. Despite talk of diverting the track that crossed the western side of the enclosure, that did not happen – Antrobus and his supporters accepted its status as a public right of way. Consequently, a substantial stretch of Stonehenge's earthworks, and one of the Station Stones, remained outside the wire, although a separate fence was erected around the latter.

The fence aroused considerable opposition, with the use of barbed wire itself a focus of complaint. Its increasing use in the British countryside was both unpopular and of uncertain legality. Moreover, its recent deployment by both sides in the Boer War had attracted much adverse coverage. Lady Florence Antrobus's assurance that the fence was 'composed of the lightest barbed wire of a neutral tint, and absolutely invisible at a distance' (Antrobus 1913) was unlikely to win over opponents, especially as she argued that its presence would prevent unwanted visitors from cluttering up views of the stones.

The enclosure prompted a legal challenge, led by the Commons and Footpaths Preservation Society, whose chairman, George Shaw Lefevre, was a former First Commissioner of Works and the man primarily responsible for the successful passage of the 1882 Ancient Monuments Act. The challenge, which was focused more on the blocking of tracks than the fence, was unsuccessful. The immediate impact of the fence on movement around the landscape is hard to gauge as there are no available pre-enclosure visitor numbers.

When Cecil Chubb bought Stonehenge at auction in 1915, the fence remained. When he handed Stonehenge over to the Office of Works in 1918, it agreed to continue with the existing admissions policy for the duration of the war, which ended 16 days later. There was no intention on the part of the Office of Works of reducing or removing the admission charge, nor were there any plans to take down the fence. Instead, one of its first actions was to seek permission to move the track that crossed the monument further to the west, thereby allowing the whole of the monument to fall within the wire. In addition, the idea of a ha-ha – a ditch lined with spiked poles and barbed wire – was resurrected. That scheme eventually foundered on grounds of cost and practicality in the 1920s.

7

Stonehenge in the 20th century

In the 20th century an increasingly professional and scientific archaeology sought to create, mainly through excavation, new understandings of Stonehenge and its surroundings, replacing antiquarian speculations. At the same time, both monument and landscape underwent considerable transformation – some of the most important episodes of excavation at Stonehenge during the 20th century were driven by a desire to interfere with the monument's physical appearance, often but not solely because of concerns about stability. The romantic ruin of previous generations – leaning monoliths, twisted trilithons and recumbent sarsens – was rationalised into a more upright, orderly design and secured for posterity with concrete, while the visibility of the earthworks was enhanced

for the paying visitor. Meanwhile, modern developments in the immediate vicinity, notably the First World War aerodrome, prompted the first calls for Stonehenge to be provided with a more appropriate backdrop, which generally meant the pastoral setting, stripped of modern intrusions, that was presumed to be the 'natural' state of the chalk downlands (eg Carrier 1936).

Stonehenge was subjected to more alteration during the 20th century than at any point since the Bronze Age (Fig 7.1). The changes are particularly evident when comparing the 1906 balloon photographs (Capper 1907; Barber 2006; 2011) with more recent aerial views (Figs 7.2 and 7.3), but much had happened even before 1906. Between 1901 and 1964,

Fig 7.1
Stonehenge prior to any 'restoration'. This photograph (before 1881), attributed to J L Lovibond, shows stones 6 and 7, directly behind the seated gentleman, sometime before the erection of J J Cole's scaffold (see Fig 7.5). (OP24751, Historic England Archive)

Fig 7.2
Stonehenge: Vertical aerial view taken by 2nd Lt Philip Sharpe from a tethered Royal Engineers' balloon in the summer of 1906 (Capper 1907). The larch poles, erected in 1902, can be seen propping the stones deemed most at risk of falling. The barbed wire fence, put up in 1901, crosses the monument on the eastern side of the track, which all parties accepted was a public right of way. The Station Stone beyond was provided with its own fence.
(© Society of Antiquaries of London)

Fig 7.3
Stonehenge: Vertical aerial view taken 3 March 2006. (NMR 24182/003)

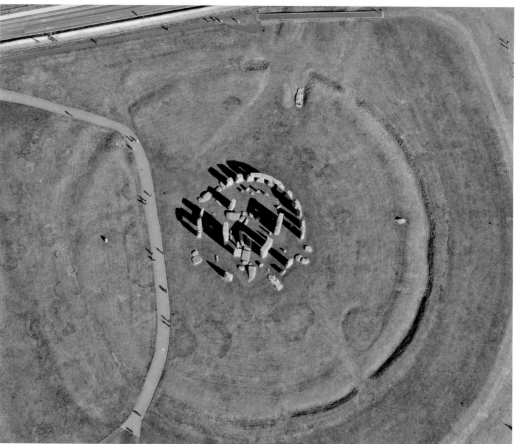

13 of the 17 sarsens in the outer circle were either straightened or re-erected, while of the 8 standing sarsens belonging to the inner horseshoe setting, 4 were straightened and 2 re-erected. In addition, 2 bluestones have received concrete support, and at least 7 others have been moved or adjusted (Cleal *et al* 1995, 188–229).

This work was accompanied by excavation – more than half of the monument has now been explored – the most obvious impact of which has been on the eastern half of the ditch. This was backfilled during the 1920s excavations with less material than had been excavated from it, in order to make it more apparent to visitors. Similar considerations lay behind the decision to mark the locations of the excavated Aubrey Holes. Surplus soil from the ditch and concreted stoneholes was used to level some of the trackways that had crossed the enclosure and was distributed elsewhere across the monument. What remains is recognisably Stonehenge, but in some respects as much a product of the 20th century as of prehistory.

A complex and shifting mosaic of land use reflecting the combined needs of agriculture, the military and in particular heritage has altered the appearance of the landscape considerably. Much that has happened to Stonehenge's surroundings arose from changing perceptions about how to achieve a setting worthy of the monument, something inextricably linked to beliefs about how it should be experienced by visitors. The need to deal with increasing visitor numbers has been of equal importance, as well as a desire to protect archaeological remains in the wider environs. The belief that Stonehenge's impact was 'lost and the spell broken unless it stands in solitary grandeur dominating the bare plain' (WORK 14/837, 19 November 1936) has been at the heart of efforts to manage this landscape since Stonehenge entered public hands in 1918. However, this desire to turn the clock back to a particular version of the past has always had to accommodate modern needs. Nonetheless, much of what has happened at Stonehenge and in the landscape around it has happened with the consent, if not always the unconditional approval, of the Office of Works and its successors.

Accounts of Stonehenge's recent history tend to be dominated by issues of visitors and access (*see* Chapter 6), how to cater for the increasing numbers of people who come to the site each year, and how to deal with those whose interests and beliefs differ from those presented in the guidebooks. The conflicts of the 1980s and 1990s and the debate over visitor facilities have been covered in considerable detail elsewhere (Chippindale *et al* 1990; Bender 1998; Worthington 2004, 2005). The free festivals of those years have left their own archaeological traces (Bishop 2011a, 61; Parker Pearson 2012, 198; Darvill *et al* 2013, 86). This chapter shows that arguments over physical and intellectual access to Stonehenge began long before the 1980s, and had considerable impact on the appearance of the monument and its landscape (Barber 2014a).

Stonehenge: repair and restoration

Restoring Stonehenge 1 – 1881: Antrobus and Cole

Accounts of Stonehenge's recent history tend to treat the various episodes of stone straightening and re-erection as essential maintenance to a monument that had suffered not just several millennia of exposure to the elements but also the neglect of private owners. Little is known about the attitudes of Stonehenge's earlier private owners towards the preservation of the monument. When a trilithon collapsed in 1797, the 4th Duke of Queensberry is said to have rejected a request to re-erect the stones because 'he thought the whole more picturesque in its present state' (Stackhouse 1833, 31). From the mid-1820s to 1915 Stonehenge was owned by the Antrobus family, passing through the hands of four successive owners called Sir Edmund. The 2nd Sir Edmund permitted at least one episode of excavation – Captain Beamish's investigation of an area in front of the Altar Stone in 1839 (Chippindale 2012, 161) – and a decade later agreed to re-erection of stones (*Archaeological Journal* **6**, 1849, 299), though the plan was never carried out. By the 1860s, however, he was rejecting requests for both excavation and re-erection on the advice of his son: 'You are the custodian of the place; whatever happens, you ... will be held responsible by the public' (*Hansard* 15 April 1874). Among the requests turned down was one from the British Association for the Advancement of Science to excavate the whole of 'the flat surface within the stone circle ... as far as the natural surface of the chalk' and possibly the ditch (Lane Fox 1870).

Caricaturing Antrobus as allowing Stonehenge to fall further into ruin through neglect, while simultaneously upholding the rights of property by opposing proposed ancient monuments legislation, overlooks the fact that his approach to the care of the monument was rooted in the widely held principles of the most radical conservation thinking of the time. His three decades of ownership (1870–99) were characterised by near inflexible adherence to three basic tenets: refusal to allow any archaeological excavation; rejection of any idea of restoration; and insistence on free and unrestricted public access. His contention that Stonehenge was safer in private hands was justified by pointing to the growing demands from archaeologists for excavation, restoration and enclosure (*see* Chapter 6).

Excavation Antrobus felt to be at the very least disfiguring. He could, and did, point to many earthworks on his land that had suffered at the hands of antiquaries. At Stonehenge he also claimed that any digging had the potential to further destabilise the stones (*Hansard* 15 April 1874). Understanding his opposition requires some appreciation of just how contentious an issue restoration was by the late 19th century. His own public utterances on the matter mainly relate to a little-discussed episode that occurred in 1881. Debate surrounding Sir John Lubbock's proposed ancient monuments legislation had prompted the voicing of concerns about the condition of Stonehenge. Consequently, stones that had been leaning for as long as anyone could recall were suddenly in danger of collapsing unless something was done. These concerns led to a visit in July 1881 by a committee of Fellows of the Society of Antiquaries (*Proceedings of the Society of Antiquaries of London* **9**, 1881–3, 9–16). There were three main areas of concern: stones 6 and 7 and their lintel, the leaning stone 56 and the trilithon that had collapsed in 1797. Antrobus's response was to ask his architect, J J Cole, to inspect the monument (Fig 7.4).

Prior to undertaking his inspection, Cole informed readers of *The Times* of Antrobus's attitude to the matter of the stones that were leaning or had fallen: 'To restoration I am distinctly opposed, but this might be considered in the light of preservation, not only of the monument, but of its observers' (*The Times* 16 August 1881, 4). In other words, no fallen stones would be re-erected. Otherwise, the need for inter-

Fig 7.4
View westwards across Stonehenge taken from the top of the sarsen circle by J J Cole, August 1881. In the distance are Virgo, or Fargo, Cottages and associated farm buildings, constructed c 1847. The proximity of arable to Stonehenge is clear.
(AL0913/010/01, Historic England Archive)

vention was dependent solely on the safety of visitors. Cole rejected the idea that stone 56 was in any danger of collapse, but both he and Antrobus had concerns about stones 6 and 7, which led to the erection of temporary timber scaffolding (Fig 7.5). Antrobus justified this intervention as being essential for safety reasons. However, he added that 'If I could have bound [the stones] to fall by night, with an engagement that no visitor should be present, so entire is my detestation of restoration of such a monument I think I should have been tempted to agree to it, and have left all alone' (quoted by T Lloyd Fowler, *The Standard* 20 September 1881).

Antrobus's aims in 1881 belonged to the more extreme non-interventionist end of the restoration spectrum, as exemplified by the ideas of John Ruskin and William Morris. Morris's SPAB had been launched four years earlier, in 1877, with a manifesto that rejected restoration, calling instead on architects and owners 'to put Protection in the place of Restoration, to stave off decay by daily care … and otherwise resist all tampering with either the fabric or ornament of the building as it stands' (Morris 1877). Cole's timber scaffolding – which would strike any visitor as an obviously modern intervention – was fully in keeping with this anti-restoration ethos.

To Ruskin, Morris and their followers, the authenticity of a building resided principally in the craftsmanship and beliefs of those who created it, and in the marks of its antiquity. For a monument such as Stonehenge, its ruinous condition was a telling indication of its great age. The straightening of leaning stones and the re-erection of fallen ones denied the passage of time and eradicated part of the monument's history, diminishing the value and authenticity of what remained. Restoration was, as Ruskin famously wrote, 'a lie' (1871, 162). Rather than returning the monument to a former state, restoration fixed a building for all time in a state in which it had never previously existed. As one contemporary writer complained, 'No sooner has Stonehenge been set on its legs again … than it ceases to be a historical monument and becomes a mere duplicate, a thing of no value, a modern antique' (*Daily News* 18 August 1881).

At the same time that Antrobus was insisting on maintaining Stonehenge as a picturesque ruin, the emerging discipline of archaeology was seeking to establish the authenticity of monuments such as Stonehenge in a very different way – through the application of scientific methods to uncover the story of Stonehenge's origins and history, to replace antiquarian speculations with an authoritative account, which would in turn inform efforts to return individual stones to their original settings. The principal targets for intervention – the leaning and fallen stones – were also the elements that contributed most to Stonehenge's status as a picturesque ruin rather than an object of scientific study.

Fig 7.5
Cole's timber support just visible for stones 6 and 7 and their lintel. Photograph probably dates from the mid-1890s.
(OP24757, Historic England Archive)

Restoring Stonehenge 2 – 1901: Antrobus and Blow

When Antrobus died in 1899, Stonehenge was more or less as it had been when he inherited it, apart from Cole's timbers and a few episodes of unauthorised excavation – Antrobus gave permission to no one, not even Charles Darwin, who obtained only the caretaker's consent for his investigations into the activities of earthworms at the monument (Litchfield 1915, 226–7). Within two years of Antrobus's death all his principles had been broken, under the guidance of an architect with impeccable anti-restoration Arts and Crafts credentials.

This turnaround began with a further fall of sarsens, though not the ones deemed most likely to drop. Despite the intense scrutiny of the monument during the 1880s and 1890s, no one had identified stone 22 as a likely candidate for collapse. It fell on 31 December 1900, bringing down lintel 122. As with the previous collapse in 1797, bad weather played its part, although many viewed (and continue to view) the event as an inevitable consequence of Antrobus's neglect.

By this time, Stonehenge was in the hands of Antrobus's son. The 4th Sir Edmund quickly made known his willingness to sell Stonehenge, albeit at an excessive price. The collapse led him to do something his father had always refused to do – take advice from archaeologists, principally the Society of Antiquaries and the Wiltshire Archaeological Society. These and other bodies, including SPAB, contributed representatives to a committee set up to advise Antrobus in 1901, and willingly consented to a list of recommendations that broadly reflected the demands that the same organisations had made repeatedly on the previous Sir Edmund: that Stonehenge needed to be enclosed and access restricted, that certain leaning stones needed to be straightened and stabilised, that some fallen stones should be re-erected and that archaeological investigation should take place anywhere that this repair work would disturb the ground (*The Times* 3 April 1901, 12). However, Antrobus's principal adviser in 1901 was the architect Detmar Blow, a personal friend of both Ruskin and Morris who had worked under the auspices of SPAB – indeed, he consulted SPAB before accepting Antrobus's invitation to work on Stonehenge. At the time, he was working on Antrobus's Amesbury home (Drury 1985; 2000, 111; *see* Chapter 6).

The committee approved not just the re-erection of stone 22 and replacement of lintel 122, but also recommended the straightening of stones 6 and 7, returning stone 56 to the upright position that it was incorrectly presumed to have slipped from as a result of the Duke of Buckingham's diggings of 1620, and the re-erection of stones 57 and 58 and their lintel 158, which had collapsed in 1797. They also approved the enclosure of Stonehenge within a fence (*The Times* 3 April 1901, 12), and the diversion of the track which crossed the western half of the earthwork enclosure. All that was achieved was the straightening of stone 56 and the erection of the fence, followed at the end of 1902 by the addition of larch poles to shore up various stones. The fuss caused by the fence and the simultaneous introduction of an admission fee probably prevented further work.

So the collapse of stone 22 led to the straightening of stone 56, while stone 22 lay where it fell until 1958. Stone 56, as noted earlier, had been causing concern since around 1880 (Petrie 1880, 33), but prior to that it had been a significant component of the romantic, picturesque ruin that Stonehenge had become, occupying a central place in many famous depictions of the monument. In 1881 Cole had denied that it was in danger of falling (*see* Fig 4.16). Subsequent inspections during the 1880s and 1890s had failed to produce any evidence that it was in danger.

The decision to straighten stone 56 in 1901 was, unsurprisingly, immediately queried – while some continued to question whether it was really in danger of falling, others argued that it could and should be secured in its leaning position (eg *The Times* 19 April 1901, 3), stating that once it was upright, 'the appearance of Stonehenge will be totally changed'. In response, it was contended that the fact that it was leaning was itself proof that its final collapse was only a matter of time, while some long-recognised cracks visible on the surface of the sarsen had now become 'grave flaws in the stone' – over time, frost action would surely cause the stone to 'snap off by its own weight' (*The Times* 23 April 1901, 3).

The work was undertaken in August and September 1901 (Fig 7.6). Blow was in overall charge, including of the engineering and concreting operations (Blow 1902). Archaeological work necessary prior to pouring in the stone's new concrete foundation was super-

vised by William Gowland, whose background in mining engineering and considerable archaeological experience (Harris and Goto 2003) made him an obvious choice to oversee this part of the operation. His excavations were restricted to the area immediately around stone 56, plus some small holes dug to take the ends of supporting wooden poles and to secure the winches (Gowland 1902).

Contemporary response to Blow's work seems to have been somewhat muted. Instead, attention focused mainly on the results of Gowland's excavations and the row over the fence – Stonehenge had for the first time been physically separated from its surroundings and efforts made to control visitors (*see* Chapter 6). At the same time, the feasibility of intervening directly in the physical appearance of the monument had been demonstrated, as had the potential for modern, 'scientific' excavation methods to provide a new basis for interpreting the site's early history.

Restoring Stonehenge 3 – 1919–1920: Peers and Hawley

When the 4th Sir Edmund died the Amesbury estate passed to his brother Cosmo, who decided to sell. In 1915 Stonehenge was bought by Cecil Chubb who, in 1918, was persuaded to hand it over to the nation in the form of the Office of Works. Charles Peers, who was both Chief Inspector of Ancient Monuments at the Office of Works and Secretary of the Society of Antiquaries, set in place a plan that effectively combined completion of the 1901 committee recommendations with the rejected 1869 excavation proposals. The leaning and fallen stones were to be dealt with by the Office of Works, and the necessary archaeological work, as well as a wider exploration of the monument, would be undertaken by Colonel William Hawley on behalf of the Society of Antiquaries (Fig 7.7). The letter from the Antiquaries to the Office of Works proposing the excavations was actually

Fig 7.6
The straightening of stone 56 in 1901. Photograph by Clarissa Miles, a friend of the Antrobus family. (AA80/06439, Historic England Archive)

Fig 7.7
An Aerofilms aerial view taken during Hawley's excavations in 1924. The excavated Aubrey Holes have been marked on the surface, and the track in the foreground is in the process of being levelled and turfed. The excavation trench to the right is exploring the complex of stakeholes identified on the south-east side of the monument. (EPW010990 © Historic England. Aerofilms Collection)

written by Peers (TNA, WORK 14/485, 24 January 1919).

A survey of the monument undertaken shortly afterwards singled out the stones already propped by wooden poles as the ones most needing attention – the twisted pair stones 6 and 7 and their lintel, plus the stones of the north-eastern façade of the circle, especially stones 30 and 1 (TNA, WORK 14/485, 29 September 1919; WORK 14/2464, 1919). The survey report recommended that the bases of all these stones should be encased in concrete. In recommending that the stones that had fallen in 1797 and 1900 be reinstated, Peers pointed to the results of the 1901 excavations, arguing that excavation of the stoneholes would reveal clear indications of the original position of each fallen stone. However, he insisted that 'the monument should show no sign of repair … [S]tones that are merely leaning, but not dangerously so, should be left as they are, & anything that could possibly be considered as "smartening up" of this remarkable monument carefully avoided' (TNA, WORK 14/485, 29 September 1919).

Peers's approach towards conservation and restoration, and the development of what has been termed the 'Ministry style', has come under considerable critical scrutiny (eg Coppack 1999; Fergusson and Harrison 1999; Emerick 2003; Turner 2007; Thurley 2013). He formalised procedures that were essentially anti-restoration in many respects, but in others were markedly at odds with the ideas of Ruskin and Morris. It was essential for the Office of Works …

to avoid, as far as possible, anything which can be considered in the nature of restoration, to do nothing which would impair the archaeological interest of the Monuments, and to confine themselves rigorously to such works as may be necessary to ensure their stability, to accentuate their interest and to perpetuate their existence in the form in which they have come down to us. (Office of Works, 1912)

The Peers approach presented the picturesque ruin as the opposite of a stable and intelligible one, but he sought to remove the remains of the centuries post-dating the key periods of the building's history, something that was of course anathema to the anti-restoration movement. At the same time, the SPAB-influenced idea of 'repair by building', in which, for example, a modern brick buttress might be inserted as a clearly modern support for stone 56 (as suggested 40 years earlier: *Proceedings of the Society of Antiquaries of London* **9**, 1881–3, 9–16), was anathema to Peers. As far as possible, the visitor should experience nothing but the authentic, original fabric. SPAB and others argued that Peers's preference for 'invisible' repairs – hidden supports, or the concealed use of modern materials – was dishonest, and undermined the authenticity of the building. Peers countered that it was 'better to risk a deception by inconspicuous additions than to proclaim them by conspicuous and unsympathetic materials' (1931, 320).

The 'Ministry style', regarded by Peers and his colleagues as essentially anonymous, inconspicuous and scientific, could be the product of considerable intervention and alteration to both the monument and its setting, resulting in a neat and orderly presentation conforming to a particular aesthetic sensibility, a style that came to characterise monuments in state guardianship and which resulted from 'an impulse to create a tended and tidied ambience within which remains would stand in an ordered and disciplined manner' (Fergusson and Harrison

1999, 210). Peers also regarded the repairs as a once-and-for-all intervention. The monuments were to be frozen, maintained and preserved in perpetuity in the state in which they emerged after clearance and repair (ibid, 210–11). Peers's approach was mainly put into practice at medieval monuments, where the aim was to clear away the 'clutter' of later centuries and stabilise what remained of the original structure. Any repair or rebuilding work should be invisible, the end result being a structure whose ground plan should be intelligible to the visitor. This was the aim at Stonehenge as well. As Peers later argued:

The recovery and demonstration of its plan adds enormous significance to an abandoned building, and though it can never recall it to life it can show all and sundry what life has been. Where much still remains the task is simpler, and while, as always, the machinery of repair, even reinstatement, must remain unobtrusive, the cumulative effect of a goodly measure of its architectural beauty, and set reverently in a simple setting of grass lawns, can hardly fail of its appeal. (Quoted in Emerick 2003, 113)

Peers's belief that the work at Stonehenge could be justified with reference to archaeological evidence was not borne out in practice. Problems arose with the first stoneholes to be examined – 6 and 7 (Fig 7.8). Hawley's

Fig 7.8
Stones 6 and 7 in 1920, their lintel removed and their stoneholes excavated. The stones are in the process of being restored to their presumed original vertical position and lowered onto a concrete foundation to a position and depth decided on by Hawley. (BB81/00859, Historic England Archive)

excavation of the stoneholes gave no clear indication of where to replace the sarsens, and it was decided to leave the matter to his judgement (TNA, WORK 14/485, 18 February 1920). The same applied to a related problem – if it was not clear where the bases of the stones should rest, then how high above the ground should the lintels sit? Similar complications were encountered later, when work began on the stones on the north-east side of the outer circle. Once stone 30 had been straightened, it was found that its lintel no longer fitted onto the adjacent stone 29, so this too had to be adjusted and set in concrete. It also proved necessary to secure stone 2 and two nearby bluestones (31 and 49) in concrete (Hawley 1922).

The reason why no further work on the stones occurred was not, as is often presumed, financial. Peers recognised that when it came to straightening and resetting stones, the desire for perpendicularity and stability was taking precedence over the limited archaeological evidence for their original positions. In the late 1930s, after his retirement, renewed requests to the Office of Works to re-erect fallen sarsens

were met with the response that to do so without any clear evidence of the original position of the stones might be construed as 'faking' (TNA, WORK 14/464, 8 August 1938). In the light of the experiences of 1919–20, it could no longer be assumed that clear evidence would be found of the fallen stones' exact original positions.

Restoring Stonehenge 4 – 1952–1964: Atkinson, Piggott and Stone

The question of 'faking' Stonehenge surfaced again two decades later, as Richard Atkinson and Stuart Piggott were preparing for their first re-erection. As late as 1952, plans or suggestions about hauling stones upright were rejected on the basis that 'we would be well advised to leave Stonehenge as it is' (TNA, WORK 14/464, 8 October 1952). Two years later the Ancient Monuments Board approved a plan put forward through the Society of Antiquaries to deal with some of the leaning and fallen stones, including those that had fallen in 1797 and 1900.

Piggott, Atkinson and Stone had begun work at Stonehenge in 1950, initially with the

Fig 7.9
An Aerofilms view taken on 31 July 1958 during Atkinson and Piggott's restorations at Stonehenge. In the centre is the re-erected trilithon of the inner horseshoe setting, which had fallen in 1797. (AFL03/a72753 © Historic England. Aerofilms Collection)

intention of undertaking some small-scale excavation to support the publication of earlier work at the site, especially Hawley's. This soon developed into something far more wide-ranging, with considerable impact on the appearance of Stonehenge (Fig 7.9).

Shortly before work commenced on the first planned re-erection, the minister of works told the House of Commons that there was 'no intention of faking Stonehenge' (*Hansard* 25 February 1958). Echoing the justifications for earlier work, he stated that only stones that had fallen in 'recent times' and whose original position was therefore known would be raised. In addition some leaning stones were, for safety reasons, to be returned to their presumed original upright positions before being set in concrete to preserve them for posterity. In approving the plans, the Ancient Monuments Board had noted that these operations would 'enhance the value of the monument for the student and make it more intelligible to the ordinary visitor' (AMB 1955, 6). After completion of the 1958 season, it added that Stonehenge had indeed been made 'more intelligible and spectacular', in the process arousing considerable public interest, and consequently boosting visitor numbers and revenue (AMB 1959, 5).

The last re-erection occurred in 1964. The collapse of stone 23 the previous year was attributed by the Ancient Monuments Board to the weather in terms that closely resembled the original accounts of the 1797 and 1900 falls, pointing to a rapid thaw, heavy rain and March gales (AMB 1964, 3). Others have suggested that the blow it received in 1958 when its neighbour stone 22 was being raised may have played a part (Chippindale 2012, 205).

The final touch to these works was the resurfacing of the central area in an attempt to counteract damage from visitors' feet (AMB 1962, 3). This was preceded by removal of 'superficial mud and soil', re-excavation of the most recent trenches within that central area, and their backfilling with clinker and gravel. The Ancient Monuments Board accepted that this work would 'alter the traditional appearance of Stonehenge, but, apart from keeping visitors outside the Circle altogether, we see no alternative' (AMB 1963, 9). In 1978, when visitors were excluded to prevent continuing damage to the stones themselves, the central area was returfed and fenced off, and has remained so.

The Stonehenge landscape

Early flight

In 1909 Larkhill became the location for some of the earliest experiments in heavier-than-air flight in Britain (Brown 2013) and became a base for the fledgling Royal Flying Corps (RFC). Several hangars of that date survive. Two fatal flying accidents are marked by memorial stones (Bishop 2011a, 33–5, 55–7).

The First World War aerodrome

For a few brief years Stonehenge had a military aerodrome as a neighbour (Fig 7.10). During its active lifetime – October 1917 to January 1921 – it was home to a range of aircraft. The planes had left by early 1921, but some of the buildings remained standing until the 1930s. Their removal followed a public appeal to buy the land on behalf of the National Trust, with the aerodrome the focus of debate about modern intrusion into the Stonehenge landscape (Barber 2014b). Attention shifted from Stonehenge itself to a matter of much wider interest during the interwar years – its setting.

Prior to the First World War, Stonehenge's immediate surroundings had been a mixture of arable and pasture. Cole's 1881 photographs graphically illustrate William Long's oft-quoted concern that Stonehenge might one day be lost in a field of turnips but, as noted above, this occurrence of arable farming almost up to the enclosure earthworks was an extension of existing arable, although this was a particularly destructive episode. It encompassed most of the barrows to the immediate west of Stonehenge, the larger mounds being levelled first. This activity coincided with the construction of Fargo Cottages (Long 1876, 186, 198). The cottages survived until 1918, when they were demolished because they had become an obstruction to activities at the aerodrome, and were rebuilt later that year at the eastern apex of the Stonehenge Triangle, almost out of sight of the monument (*The Times* 28 March 1918, 3). When the aerodrome was first established the previous October, however, they had not been in the way. Documentary sources suggest that the downland west of Stonehenge was selected as the site of an aerodrome because it comprised an open expanse with no obstructions to flying, was close to existing military facilities

Fig 7.10
The Stonehenge Aerodrome was serviced by the Larkhill Military Light Railway. On formation of the Air Ministry (AM) a series of numbered markers were placed around the perimeter (extant – blue; known from documentary sources – light blue).

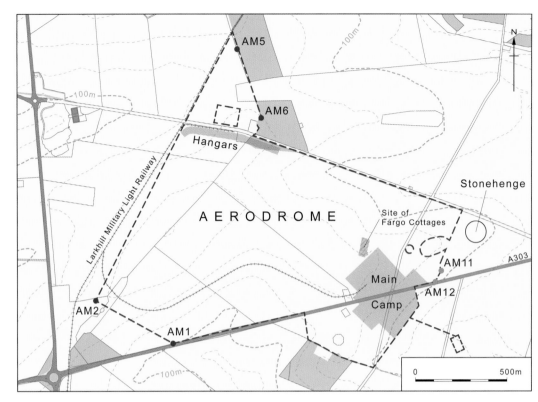

at Larkhill and was easily accessible by the Amesbury–Shrewton road (the A344). The original location for the aerodrome's buildings was behind Fargo Plantation, on the northern side of the road, with the hangars along the southern side of the road, facing onto Stonehenge Down, the take-off and landing ground (TNA, WORK 14/214, 22 January 1919).

Established as an RFC training base, with no permanent buildings, in January 1918 the aerodrome was redesignated the No. 1 School of Navigation and Bomb Dropping, and, more importantly, the RFC contingent was joined by the Royal Naval Air Service (RNAS) Handley Page Training Flight, in advance of plans for the new Royal Air Force to take over heavy bombing on its official formation in April 1918. The arrival of the RNAS appears to have been the reason for the decision to establish another camp on the other side of the landing ground, adjacent to the London–Exeter road (the A303). This was initially occupied by the RFC, with the RNAS taking over the Fargo site. Once the two services had merged, the Fargo site became known as the 'Night Camp', reflecting the fact that the Handley Pages were primarily night bombers, while the newer site became known as the 'Main Camp', where the main hangars, technical buildings, offices and accommodation blocks were located (Priddle 2003; Crawford 2012).

The Main Camp, sharing the same orientation as Stonehenge, had an awkward relationship with the main road. This arrangement was in keeping with earlier precedent at Larkhill, where a gap was left between hangars so as not to interfere with the observation of midsummer sunrise from Stonehenge (Brown 2013, 63–5). It is not so apparent why similar steps were taken at the new aerodrome – there seems to have been little contemporary interest in observing midwinter sunset from Stonehenge. A possible explanation concerns the view of Stonehenge from Normanton Gorse. George MacGregor Reid's quasi-druidical Universal Bond were allowed to camp there in the days around midsummer, and had done so since at least 1913 (Stout 2008, ch 10; Hutton 2009, ch 11); they performed rites within Normanton Gorse and at the nearby barrows Wilsford 3 and 4. The orientation of the aerodrome buildings may represent some attempt to preserve lines of sight between Stonehenge and these places. As with Larkhill, the wishes of the landowner may have played a part here. The land south of the road was owned by Lord Glenconner, whose wife, Pamela, had 'acquired a most opportune, and enduring, affection for Reid and his followers' (Hutton 2009, 357). The Glenconners were influential and well connected, and may have been able to insist on the view being preserved when the land was requisitioned.

Other ephemeral military constructions within the WHS included the Military Light Railway (James 1987, 203–6 *et passim*). Some earthworks of this survive, particularly within Fargo Plantation and near Larkhill (Bishop 2011a, 30–1, 35, 58); elsewhere it has been traced by geophysical survey (Vince Gaffney pers comm).

After the war: removal of the aerodrome

Once the war had ended, calls for the aerodrome to be removed began, particularly when it became apparent that the RAF intended to retain it permanently. Eventually the Air Ministry found an alternative – Old Sarum. Activities at Stonehenge Aerodrome ended by early 1921 (Fig 7.11) and the buildings were auctioned off, on condition that they be dismantled and removed by the purchasers within three months. Once the buildings were gone, the Disposals Board would arrange for the land to be reinstated to its pre-war condition and hand it back to its owners.

The owner of the land north of the A303, Isaac Crook, acquired several of the buildings at the auction, and subsequently obtained others (TNA, MUN 4/6054, 9 May 1923). He approached the Directorate of Lands in June 1922 and offered to 'make arrangements with the persons who had failed to remove the buildings which they had purchased', and waived any payment from the government in lieu of reinstatement of the ground if they were to return the land to him immediately (TNA, MUN 4/6054, 14 May 1923). The Directorate agreed, at which point the condition to dismantle the buildings became unenforceable. Legal advice was sought, and the various government departments concerned were told that the decision to return the land while the buildings

Fig 7.11
RAF vertical view of part of the Main Camp, taken on 24 July 1921, just after the aerodrome had closed. The name of the aerodrome was marked out in turf-cut chalk letters on the ground. Traces of the former location of Fargo Cottages can be seen towards the centre of the photograph.
(CCC8535/916 SU 1142/7, Historic England [Crawford Collection])

were still standing, and to waive responsibility for reinstatement, was effectively 'acquiescence on the Government's part to the buildings remaining in situ' (ibid).

Crook subsequently achieved a certain amount of notoriety – among archaeologists at least – by converting part of the site into a pig farm, possibly as early as 1922. Less well known is that some of the buildings were also rented out as living accommodation, mainly to people with connections to the military personnel at Larkhill. This situation persisted until 1927, when complaints from archaeologists led to action being taken, the catalyst being a claim that Crook had put the aerodrome site up for sale (Fig 7.12).

The sequence of events is complex, but ultimately led to a public appeal being launched in 1927 to raise money to buy the aerodrome site and buildings, as well as several other parcels of land around Stonehenge. For the first time the idea that Stonehenge needed to be returned to an appropriate setting was publicly aired. Readers were informed that the 'solitude of Stonehenge should be restored and precautions taken to ensure that our posterity will see it against the sky in lonely majesty before which our ancestors have stood in awe throughout all our recorded history' (*The Times* 5 August 1927). Effectively the aerodrome was the spur to a debate about what constituted acceptable or unacceptable modern intrusions in the landscape, a debate that resulted not only in the eradication of the aerodrome, but also the removal of the Stonehenge Café, built in 1927 adjacent to the cottages in Stonehenge Bottom, and the demolition of those cottages, with alternative accommodation being provided for the custodians further east, out of sight of Stonehenge. Plans in the 1930s to close part of the Amesbury–Shrewton road (the A344), however, came to nothing.

When the appeal was launched the public was told that options to buy the various par-

Fig 7.12
RAF oblique view taken in the summer of 1928. Hawley's excavations had ended, although the huts and latrine provided for him by the Office of Works still remained. Several aerodrome buildings remain standing, some still occupied as dwellings.
(CCC11796/4519, Historic England [Crawford Collection])

cels of land had been obtained, but came with time limits. If the money could not be raised, the danger was that the land would instead fall into the hands of 'the speculative builder' who would unleash all manner of modern horrors on the landscape, including a 'garish bungalow town', as well as cafés, hotels, a cinema and 'anything else that our enterprising corporals of industry might fancy to be potentially lucrative' (*The Times* 5 August 1927, 7; *London Mercury* **16**, no. 94, August 1927, editorial notes). One of the final public appeals was a letter signed by Arnold Bennett, Sybil Thorndike, Rebecca West and others, pleading for one last effort to protect Stonehenge forever from the threat of 'submergence under the rising tide of bunga-lows' (*The Times* 23 March 1929). Such threats to amenity were common spectres in the British rural landscape during the interwar years.

In the case of Stonehenge these threats were non-existent. They were raised as a means to attract attention and donations, although some at least of those involved in the appeal consid-ered them plausible threats. However, when the first discussions with Crook about purchasing the aerodrome site took place, the chief concern was not any speculative developer, but the fear that if he got wind of plans for a public appeal, he might raise his price (TNA, WORK 14/488, 8 July 1927). The public was also unaware when the first appeal was launched that not only had an option to buy the aerodrome site already been secured, but the money to pay for it had also been guaranteed (ibid). The reasons for this were straightforward: it was hoped that an influx of funds from the public would mean that the anonymous philanthropist wouldn't actu-ally have to part with any money, but mainly there was concern that publicising the fact that the main objective – the aerodrome – had been secured would jeopardise any attempt to raise money for the neighbouring, less threatened, plots.

The appeal didn't go entirely as hoped. Despite the extensive publicity and the high hopes of the organising committee, the target of £35,000 needed to secure around 1,444 acres of farmland was not reached until March 1929, which required negotiations to extend some of the options on several occasions. Removing the aerodrome buildings was a slow process, with the last hangar not coming down until 1930, while rehousing occupants of the accommodation blocks took even longer (*The Times* 4 August 1930, 7). Traces of some

of the aerodrome buildings can still be seen as earthworks and parchmarks, and some of its boundary markers survive (*see* Fig 7.10; Komar and Bishop 2010, 10–13, 21–4; Bishop 2011a, 57; Field and Pearson 2011, 12–13).

The expansive pastoral idyll envisaged in the appeal literature didn't materialise. The land purchased as a result of the fundraising was handed over to the National Trust, which leased much of it back to the farmers who had previously worked it. A considerable part of this was arable. The only part not to revert to agri-culture was an area north of the A344 on which the Office of Works was able to establish the first car park in an attempt to stop the growing numbers of visitors parking immediately adja-cent to the monument itself.

Archaeology and agriculture

The matter of arable agriculture, and especially ploughing, is one that the Office of Works and its successors took a long time to address. The destructive nature of the plough was recog-nised to a degree, but the response of bodies such as the Office of Works and the National Trust prior to the mid-20th century can today seem remarkably simplistic. Earthworks such as barrows could be restored to their former profile simply by replacing any soil and turf that had been removed. Meanwhile, despite the post-war advent of aerial archaeology, which had notable early successes in the Stonehenge landscape, recognition that archaeological features might survive beneath the modern surface remained unappreciated. In any case, to many the recognition of cropmarks seemed to demonstrate that some trace of the past would always survive to be recognised by new scientific methods of prospection, such as the airborne camera.

Concerns about plough damage to the Stonehenge Cursus (Fig 7.13) were raised in 1917 – not for the first time. The Office of Works had been informed that the whole of the Cur-sus west of the Avenue, previously pasture, had been ploughed up. It sent a representative to inspect the damage. He considered that it was the enclosing earthworks of the Cursus that were of primary concern, not the interior (TNA, WORK 14/214, 28 April 1917). Little damage, in his opinion, had occurred to the earthworks themselves, and what had happened could easily be rectified – by replacing disturbed soil and turf, the approximate contours of the

Fig 7.13
RAF vertical showing the
extent of arable within and
around the western end of
the Greater Cursus by the
early 1920s (south to top).
The trapezoidal military
grenade range can also be
seen between the Cursus and
the barrows. Only the most
visible earthworks remained
outside the ploughed area.
(CCC8535/164 SU 1143/4,
Historic England [Crawford
Collection])

Cursus could be recreated. Of greater concern
was some of the military activity, in particular
the establishment of 'a station for practising
bomb throwing about 40 yards long', which
involved some damage to the bank and ditch in
its construction, and had obvious potential for
further damage. Also of concern was the ongoing impact of the military's chosen method of
sewage disposal. The most prominent feature
of this was the cutting of a drain across the full
width of the Cursus (*see* Chapter 1), which connected with a network of drainage channels to
the south, constructed in order to disperse military effluent across Stonehenge Bottom.

The ploughing of earthworks continued to
cause alarm throughout the interwar years and
thereafter (Fig 7.14), with particular concerns
expressed about damage to the Stonehenge
Avenue and to various barrows on National
Trust land (*see* Chapter 1). In 1941 the Ministry
of Works was faced with a request to plough up

grassland within the Stonehenge Triangle 'in
the interests of food production' (TNA, WORK
14/2463, 24 December 1941). The Chief Inspector of Ancient Monuments, B H St J O'Neil, was
opposed to ploughing within the area under
state guardianship, not because of any perceived
threat to buried archaeological deposits but
because of the setting of the site (TNA, WORK
14/2463, 16 January 1942). Stonehenge should
be surrounded by grass, not crops. In justify-
ing refusal, O'Neil and his colleagues asserted
that the turf and topsoil within the triangle had
been unploughed since at least the Bronze Age,
and that it would be 'botanically impossible' to
reinstate it. Moreover, 'valuable scientific information can be obtained from such undisturbed
soil, which would be totally lost if it were to be
ploughed' (TNA, WORK 14/2463, 26 January
1942). No explanation was offered as to the
form of this information, although a later communication claimed that it could be retrieved

by 'geochronological methods' (TNA, WORK 14/2463, 3 February 1942). The Wiltshire War Agricultural Committee seems to have had no real intention of cultivating this land anyway. It simply wanted to 'forestall criticism about the potential use of the land' (ibid) and expected to be given a good reason not to go ahead, which O'Neill's response provided.

Damage to earthworks continued after the war. A letter to *The Times* (23 April 1954) reported on the ploughing up of Scheduled barrows in the Normanton Down group: 'Two of the smaller barrows have been obliterated, a miniature long barrow is half destroyed and the ditch of a large barrow is badly damaged. The plough being used is … a "prairie buster" … an implement of destruction of surface contours which is excelled only by the bulldozer.' When the matter came to court Paul Baillie Reynolds, Chief Inspector of Ancient Monuments, was asked for his assessment of the damage. He told the court that 'In my opinion no serious archaeological damage has been done to the barrows' (quoted by Grinsell 1978, 5, who had some trenchant remarks to make about this 'opinion'). According to *The Times*, 'It was

Fig 7.14
A US Air Force vertical taken on Christmas Eve 1943. The low sunlight picks out the slightest of earthworks. The mosaic of arable and pasture is evident, as is the fact that the site of the 1917–21 aerodrome buildings had yet to be 'reconstituted'. (US/7PH/GP/LOC122N/1022, Historic England [USAAF Photography])

agreed that they had been damaged but it was those that, although they could be seen, and were photographed from the air, could not be seen on the ground' (7 July 1954, 5).

The 'disenchantment' of Stonehenge

In the first edition of *Stonehenge Today and Yesterday*, the first 'official' guide to the stones, Frank Stevens offered a 'vision of rolling downs, a short, crisp, elastic turf dotted with flocks, and broken here and there by some crested earthwork or barrow, which … breaks the sky-line with its sharp outline' (1916, 8). Stevens also noted a common reaction among visitors – that the immensity of the downs could provoke a sense of disappointment with Stonehenge itself, 'dwarfed by the wide expanse of downland which surrounds it' (ibid, 12; *see also* Hudson 1911, 233).

In subsequent editions Stevens complained that Stonehenge was now dwarfed by the 'recent erections of the Great War' (1929, 9), the grandeur of the downs being obscured by the immensity of the concrete, metal and timber constructions of the military. Much was made by contemporaries of this unwanted juxtaposition of ancient and modern, as well as the apparent contrast between the endurance of Stonehenge and the transience of the aerodrome, particularly as the latter was gradually abandoned and its buildings began to decay, ironically at the same time as Stonehenge's sarsens were being shored and secured using concrete, metal and timber. The aerodrome had to go, and Stonehenge needed to be put back. There was, it seems, no place for ruins in this landscape.

The idea that Stonehenge belonged to a landscape of rolling downland pasture populated solely by sheep and barrows was not based on scientific evidence but was rooted in a long-standing acceptance of the timeless nature of that setting, 'untouched, unploughed, centuries old', solemn and silent (Jefferies 2006, 161–6). The Stonehenge Appeal of 1927 had at its core an insistence that the landscape around Stonehenge should be restored to this particular vision, one that emphasised peace and solitude, and isolation from the intrusions of modern life.

Equally, this idealised and romanticised setting had little to do with what was known of the landscape in more recent years. Particularly

during the 18th and 19th centuries the surroundings of Stonehenge were characterised as much by arable as by pasture, but the presence of arable was ignored or glossed over by many contemporary writers, or, if acknowledged, the plough was disparaged as a recent intruder. With some notable exceptions, such as William Stukeley, the plough was also generally seen as disfiguring rather than destructive, the damage caused being primarily aesthetic: 'a ploughed down is a down made ugly' (Hudson 1987, 20). This popular vision of Stonehenge occupying a romanticised natural wilderness – the extensive upland pasture that, it was argued, must have proved so attractive to the first primitive herdsmen to encounter Salisbury Plain (Stevens 1916, 9, 89) – may have been inspired as much by depictions in art and literature as by the assumptions of early 20th-century archaeology (Wickstead 2014).

Central to the powerful landscapes of Turner and Constable was the tall, leaning stone 56. The 'pedant bent on restoration' had, in 1901, ensured that no one could ever again experience the monument that they had painted – 'this heavy monster, bowed under the weight of innumerable years, was dragged up from its recumbency, bolted, concreted, and stiffened into an unnatural uprightness, and now stands rigid and awkward as an aged man stayed up into an affectation of youth. It appears out of all relation to its fellows, each of whom has some venerable stoop' (Noyes 1913, 34–5).

For many, though, the 'disenchantment of Stonehenge', as it was described by Canon Rawnsley (*Manchester Guardian* 27 December 1901, 8), co-founder of the National Trust, began not so much with the resurrection of that single stone as with the use of concrete, heavy machinery and barbed wire, the caretaker's hut, turnstile and admission charge. Just occasionally, the fence did allow some to experience the stones in silence and solitude, as when naturalist W H Hudson clambered through the fence one night in the summer of 1908 (Hudson 1911, 255–6). For many, though, Stonehenge was changed for ever. Rawnsley was particularly angered by the barbed wire, which …

with all its associations of suburban privacy and petty ownership, insults the eye and offends the heart. The cruelty of the whole thing lies in the fact that it imparts into the surroundings an alien, a disturbing, and irritating element which, quite apart from the harm to the line of vision, wounds the scene in its tenderest point, its power to impress the visitor

with the sense that the sole guardians of that lonely place are the ancient pylons of the desert shrine, and that here, if anywhere, men may still be free as the wind to wander, to wonder, and to praise. (*Manchester Guardian* 27 December 1901, 8)

The stated aim in establishing a car park on land which the public had been told would revert to pasture was to prevent people from parking along the roadside adjacent to Stonehenge, which spoiled any residual sense of isolation. The café proved a popular attraction (Fig 7.15), something that was recognised by the National Trust, which briefly considered retaining it, and also by the lessee, who built another at Winterbourne Stoke Crossroads (TNA, WORK 14/837, 23 April 1935, 9 November 1936). However, in 1938, once its lease had expired, the Stonehenge Café was demolished, having fallen prey to a renewed desire to clear away unwanted clutter from the landscape:

the whole effect of [Stonehenge] is ... lost and the spell broken unless it stands in solitary grandeur dominating the bare plains. We can't get rid of the road or the cars in transit along it, but we have made an immense improvement by getting visiting cars and everything else out of sight. To retain a cheap flashy little building like the worst type of bungaloid growth spoils the whole scene and vulgarises unspeakably this world famous and most impressive monument. (TNA, WORK 14/837, 19 November 1936)

However, removing visitor attractions didn't help with the problem of visitor numbers. In 1901 the admission charge was seen as a deterrent, a means of keeping out those deemed not to possess 'intellectual interest' in the monument. During the First World War the admission charge was a means of fundraising for the Red Cross, but once the Office of Works had taken over and the war ended, it became revenue, not just for Stonehenge but to fund the maintenance of other properties. Concerns

Fig 7.15
A 1928 oblique view showing the caretakers' cottages (right) and Stonehenge Café (left), located at Stonehenge Bottom, close to the junction of the A303 and A344. The cottages were built in 1918, the café in 1927. All were pulled down in 1938. (CCC8817/2511 SU 1242/190, Historic England [Crawford Collection])

Fig 7.16
The earthworks of the
Stonehenge Café site in
2010, visible as a sharp
rectangular cut adjacent
to the former A344. The
café's modest car park is
the small square projection
immediately in front.
Earthworks of quarrying,
other possible buildings and
one of the possible solution
holes (top right) are also
visible (see also Fig 3.10).
(NMR 26554/013)

about both the number and kind of visitors continued to be expressed. For example, in 1921 George Engleheart, Wiltshire Secretary of the Society of Antiquaries, protested to Charles Peers about the six charabancs 'crammed with Oldham mill-operatives' he had seen at the turnstile (TNA, WORK 14/2463, 25 October 1921).

Dissatisfaction with the visitor experience has always gone hand in hand with dissatisfaction with the presence of other visitors. Since the 1920s especially, the emphasis has primarily been about improving the former while managing the latter. The need to improve things for visitors has never focused solely on the provision of services and facilities, but has always been about the presentation of the monument in an appropriate setting, and continues to be so. 'The work of freeing the circle of discordant elements' (TNA, WORK 14/838, 21 December 1930) has resulted in a tidier monument and a less cluttered landscape, with some of the more undesirable developments of recent centuries now hidden beneath the turf (Fig 7.16) or concealed behind tree plantations, but arguably neither monument nor landscape can be said to be any closer to its prehistoric state than it was in 1901.

8

Review and prospect

What was Stonehenge?

It is some time since the builders of Stonehenge were seen as 'barbarians'. They were able to conceive and execute great projects but they were also prone to the very human traits of disagreeing with each other and changing their minds. Stonehenge was not built to one great master plan (Ingold 2013, 54–7); it is a series of variations on a theme.

As Richard Bradley has said of the European Neolithic megaliths, 'the correct interpretation of those monuments would have been contentious from the moment of their creation' (1993, 68). It is therefore pointless to seek one overarching 'meaning' for a monument such as Stonehenge, and any claim to have found such a meaning – to have 'decoded' or 'solved' Stonehenge – should be treated with suspicion. The diversity of Neolithic monuments shows that the search for a single Neolithic 'religion' is misguided (Barrett 1994, 49–50).

Stonehenge – like the Morbihan, Avebury, the Boyne Valley and Orkney – is probably best described as a spiritual and ceremonial complex. These sites all started with relatively modest monuments, perhaps the 'North Barrow' at Stonehenge, but they attracted and consumed physical energy to become much grander complexes. Other similar monuments, for whatever reason, failed to attract the same levels of energy and remained modest and isolated. This energy – collection of food, drink, materials – was expended through labour in a messy, Neolithic (or perhaps just a human), fashion; projects were begun and abandoned, restarted and changed, left incomplete. This has a bearing on the perceived astronomical aspects of Stonehenge: in stage 1 there may have been a concern with moonrise, though the periglacial stripes along the Avenue call this into question; there is no doubt that from stage 2 onwards it was aligned on midsummer

sunrise and midwinter sunset, but this was a general rather than a precise alignment and claims for other celestial alignments are at best questionable; the alignment, encapsulated in stone and earthwork, seems more likely to be 'ceremonial' than 'scientific', if that opposition is a useful concept (Ruggles 1999, 80–1). This alignment is not echoed at many contemporary sites. The symbolism appears to be one associated with death, in some phases at least, but what exists at and around Stonehenge is 'evidence for the ways in which the significance of a single place was reinterpreted over hundreds of years' (Bradley 1993, 102).

However, the building of these monuments also seems to imply a concern with the future. Building in stone may be associated with the ancestors, as Parker Pearson and Ramilisonina (1998) have claimed, but it can also be read as creating an inheritance for the descendants – rings of timber would last for decades, rings of stone for millennia. (On the other hand, Pryor sees Stonehenge as the end of an era, a last despairing attempt to halt the forces of political, religious and social change: 2001, 184.) This linking of past and future, if it was in the minds of the constructors of Stonehenge, finds an echo in the practice of archaeology as an intellectual discipline today. Archaeologists believe that properly understanding the past is the key to a well-informed and successful future, and that protecting what is best of the material culture of the past will be of benefit to the future (Fig 8.1). As Richard Morris observes, 'Archaeology itself … might be seen as but a late ripple in the cult of the ancestors' (2012, 378).

Stonehenge, with its insistence on midwinter and midsummer, was perhaps an attempt to impose order on unpredictable seasons in an unpredictable landscape. Those who use the land – the hunter, the gatherer, the farmer – need to understand the weather just as the

Fig 8.1
The project's initiator,
Pete Topping, Head of
Archaeological Survey
and Investigation, nearing
Stonehenge in 2009 with
a Trimble Differential
GPS rover. The approach
of archaeology in the
21st century is one that
is increasingly respectful
and non-intrusive, though
some intrusive research will
always be required to meet
the discipline's properly
inquisitive nature.
(Photograph by Andy Smith
for KOREC, 4 February
2009)

seafarer does. When to sow or reap is not a matter of a particular date (which is no more than a rough guide) but of the prevailing, and predicted, weather conditions. Stonehenge marked or celebrated the changing seasons; it did not measure passing time (Pryor 2001, 282).

Wide geographical contacts are evident from the beginning. The Mesolithic evidence has been mentioned in Chapter 2. Neolithic stone axes from a variety of origins are found in the area, and the Avon valley seems to be the conduit in this, as in subsequent phases (Field 2008, 45). A mace-head of gneiss found with one of the early cremation burials at Stonehenge itself (Montague and Gardiner 1995, 394–5) must have come from a considerable distance, perhaps from Scotland or Brittany, and recent research has revealed that many of the animals consumed at Durrington Walls were from the south-west peninsula or west Wales, while others were of Scottish origin (Viner *et al* 2010; Parker Pearson 2012, 120–1). The houses that the people of Durrington Walls lived in were similar in layout to contemporary houses in Orkney (Parker Pearson 2012, 99). The bluestones, of course, are the most obvious link with western Britain (Bevins and Ixer 2013; Bevins *et al* 2014; Fig 8.2). Famously, the 'Amesbury Archer' came from the European mainland, perhaps from the Alpine forelands of Switzerland or south-west Germany, while his 'Companion', though born in Wessex, may have travelled to the continent in childhood; the 'Boscombe Bowmen' too had travelled from some distance, probably from western Europe (Fitzpatrick 2011, 204–7, 230–4).

In a later phase the burials of the Early Bronze Age suggest numerous links. Only a few examples can be given here: a set of miniature carved bone plaques from one of the Lake barrows has a remarkable parallel in Yorkshire (Bowden *et al* 2012, 28–9, fig 15); the primary burial under Wilsford 58 was accompanied by numerous objects, including a stone battleaxe probably of Cornish origin and a small bronze axe of Armorican type – it has even been tentatively suggested that the individual might have been of Armorican origin (Woodward and Needham 2012); objects from the Normanton Down cemetery echo designs from northern Britain or Ireland and from central Germany, while the Bush Barrow copper dagger is almost certainly an Armorican import (Needham *et al* 2010).

Brittany seems to be linked to the Stonehenge area through many phases; passage graves were being constructed in the former from 4500 BC – the start of a megalithic tradition that ended there about 3500 BC but continued in Britain until 2500 BC, and which informed much British megalithic practice (Parker Pearson 2012, 20). The henge and stone-circle building traditions, however, appear to have been insular developments that may have started in northern Britain. Contact with the continent waned after 3400 BC but was re-established firmly at the start of the Beaker period.

On the other hand, Stonehenge is a monument intimately related to its locality: its position was, according to the latest evidence, fixed by reference to peculiar features of the geomorphology of this particular place (Field and Pearson 2010, 61–2; Parker Pearson 2012,

Fig 8.2
Craig Rhos-y-felin,
Pembrokeshire, one of
the original sources of the
Stonehenge bluestones,
rhyolites specifically.
(© Mark Bowden)

244–5). Some, at least, of the individuals most linked with Stonehenge, such as the Stonehenge Archer, were locals (Parker Pearson 2012, 195); alongside the 'foreign' objects interred with the dead in the Early Bronze Age were many other objects of distinctly local type, such as the bone plate and sarsen block from Wilsford 58 (Woodward and Needham 2012, 119–20, 124) or the 'grape cup' from Wilsford 7 (Fig 8.3). What our survey of the landscape has shown is how so many of the monuments are placed with regard to their immediately surrounding topography – to the broad but unspectacular ridges, to the shallow valleys which are dry now but which probably held running water, perhaps seasonally, in the past.

Stonehenge was built within a pre-existing Neolithic monument complex. It was constructed over a long period but in distinct episodes of activity. Because of the longevity of its stone settings, Stonehenge was frequently used and perhaps venerated in later periods but there was no continuity. Ironically, the one period during which there is no evidence for activity at and around the site is the Late Iron

Fig 8.3
Detail of the 'grape cup' from
Wilsford 7. Height 55mm,
diameter 90mm. This is
a distinctively local object
(Needham et al 2010, 27).
(DP158905; Wiltshire
Museum, Devizes)

Age, the very period at which the druids – who Aubrey, Stukeley and many others thought were closely involved with the monument – should have been flourishing. To make this point is not to be contrary; it has been made before (Hutton 2009, 411–12). But Stonehenge did become a focus of activity again in the late Roman period: the nature of that activity is uncertain, but it is most likely to have been religious and possibly related to a subversive form of religion – a 'mystery cult'.

Stonehenge has long been seen by antiquaries and archaeologists as part of a wider landscape (eg Stukeley 1740; Hoare 1812; RCHME 1979; Richards 1990). This has informed the views of most serious commentators. When Ros Cleal and her colleagues came to write the excavation report for the 20th century they set the monument and those excavations firmly and explicitly in a landscape context (1995; *see also* Tilley *et al* 2007). For Tim Darvill landscape is 'in a very real sense, a living, breathing creature', capable of study through biography (2006, 15, 26ff). Many of the elements that make up a landscape are, of course, living things: trees, grass, organic soil, animals and, pre-eminently, the people who created and used the landscape over countless generations. But there are also many inanimate objects – rocks, mainly, but also buildings and artefacts of stone and metal – within the landscape. The landscape itself is not just an environment but an abstraction,

something perceived by the human observer as an entity, more or less coherent. Landscape can therefore have a history but whether it can have a biography is open to question. The landscape remains elusive.

Approaching the landscape

Our method in the Stonehenge landscape has been principally one of close observation and survey of the ground surface, combined with aerial, geophysical and architectural survey, photography (*see* Davies 2013), documentary research and limited laser scanning, all integrated within a project GIS to aid analysis. The detailed observation and recording of artificial irregularities in the ground surface, commonly called 'earthworks' whether they were originally formed of earth or not, is one of the oldest of archaeological techniques. It was practised by Aubrey (the Aubrey Holes), Stukeley (the Avenue and the Cursus) and by the Cunnington and Hoare team (barrow cemeteries, settlement sites, the Lesser Cursus). Analysis of earthworks based on close observation remains at the core of our work, though survey is now made easier with modern technology such as highly accurate electronic theodolites and the Global Positioning System (GPS; Fig 8.4). The Research Reports arising from the project (*see* Appendix) explain in detail the methodology used to record each site.

Fig 8.4
Surveying slight earthworks on the King Barrow Ridge with a Differential GPS rover. Hi-tech equipment makes field survey easy in some respects, but the operator has to recognise the slight rise in ground level between left foot and right foot and know that it is of potential archaeological significance.
(© Mark Bowden)

Earthwork survey has never been the favourite occupation of many archaeologists, however, and the recent development of more 'remote' approaches, such as lidar and geophysical survey, have overshadowed it; the appeal of such techniques is their apparent scientific objectivity but in reality they also rely on skilled interpretation. In fact all archaeological survey techniques have limitations and strengths, and need to be combined to maximise their potential.

None of these non-intrusive archaeological methods has ever been as fashionable as excavation. This explains to some degree the lack of detailed surveys of upstanding monuments, including Stonehenge itself (Walker and Gardiner 1995, 21–2), in the Stonehenge WHS. They had been surveyed at scales up to 1:2 500 by the OS for various map editions since the late 19th century but had never been subjected to detailed examination by archaeologists.

But keen observation of the ground surface remains at a premium. So we are told that the Y and Z holes are not visible on the surface (Chippindale 2012, 18), that the enclosing earthworks of the Greater Cursus and Stonehenge are 'barely visible' or merely a 'dull outline' (Oliver 2011, 86–7; Lawson 2007, 79) and that barrow Amesbury 41 (Fig 8.5) is 'plough-levelled' (Darvill *et al* 2013, 79). The monument known as Amesbury 50 provides a useful case study (*see* Fig 3.7). As described in Chapter 3 analytical earthwork survey had already identified this as an unusual monument, a diminutive oval barrow or a small henge with a later mound over it. Subsequently, geophysical surveys (Gaffney *et al* 2012; Linford *et al* 2012, 15–17, figs 17–22 and 26–7; Darvill *et al* 2013, 76–7, fig 11) revealed rings of postholes beneath the mound and pits in the ditch, confirming the possibility that this monument belonged to the henge tradition (though not all parties agree as to the interpretation).

Where the evidence of surviving earthworks, aerial photographic interpretation and geophysical survey is brought together – as has been attempted here – and matched with the results of fieldwalking and excavation, the picture of ancient times should be as complete as we can make it. Uncertainties persist, nevertheless.

So far in this book we have accepted that the 'Aubrey Holes' are indeed the 'cavities' seen by John Aubrey in the 17th century. This idea has been questioned, by Mike Pitts for exam-

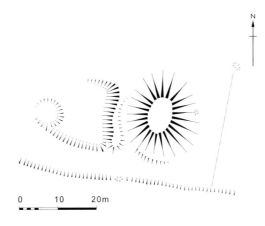

Fig 8.5
Amesbury 41: earthwork survey of the barrow mound and a subrectangular hollowed platform downslope to the west. The barrow has been protected from ploughing by the adjacent 19th-century field boundary to the south, by a surrounding fence (traces of which are visible to the east) and the hollow: this hollow, which is more than 0.5m deep, is probably the site of agricultural activity or even an agricultural building, rather than the 'truncated mound' suggested (Darvill et al 2013, 79) on the basis of geophysical survey.

ple (1981a; 2000, 148), who was troubled by the paradox that 5,000-year-old pits had survived to be seen by Aubrey in 1666 but were not visible to other antiquaries only a few years later. To anyone practised in earthwork survey this is not necessarily a great problem; it is well known that many factors – direction of approach, light conditions, the state of vegetation – affect the visibility of slight earthworks. Nevertheless, the fact that the Aubrey Holes have never since (and the unexcavated ones have not yet) been recorded as visible surface features is curious. Pitts favoured the idea that Aubrey's 'cavities' represented part of an outer stone circle incorporating the Slaughter Stone and its companions (1981a). Alternatively, perhaps it was some of the Y or Z holes, still visible today, which Aubrey saw. The difficulty with the latter explanation is that the 'cavities' marked by Aubrey on his plan (1626–97, pl VII) are around the periphery of the enclosure, in the position of the 'Aubrey Holes'. On the other hand the proportions of this sketch survey are so inaccurate that this is hardly conclusive. It might seem unlikely that this issue will ever be resolved but new evidence is constantly coming to light; the features newly revealed as parchmarks (*see* p 137) may have a bearing on this question.

Human observation is not an exact science; it is not constant; it is contingent. We see what we can conceive of seeing and what interests us (Bowden and McOmish forthcoming; *see also* Morris 2012, 56–9, 256). This is not to restate the cynical old argument that 'we see what we believe and then believe what we see'. It is more demanding than that. We can train ourselves to see things that we would not have believed, and we can be critical enough not to believe what we see, necessarily. When we are dealing with anything that is difficult to see – such as slight

Fig 8.6

The slight roughly circular hollow (shaded grey), 0.3–0.4m deep, to the north of Amesbury barrow 34 on the King Barrow Ridge. To the north-west of Amesbury 34 is a small penannular ring ditch discovered by geophysical survey in 2011 (SHL 2012, 15).

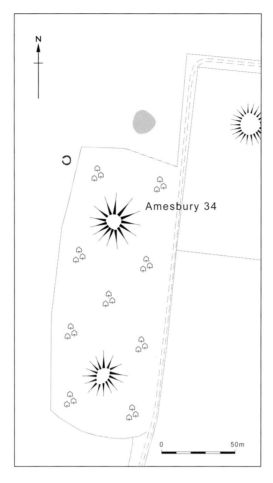

Amesbury 34

0   50m

Fig 8.7 (opposite)

Survey of some of the significant parchmarks which appeared at Stonehenge in July 2013 (Banton et al 2014) between stones 16 and 21. Stoneholes 17 and 18 have never been detected before by any means; stonehole 20 has reacted differently because it was partly excavated in the 20th century; A, B and C are three of Gowland's trenches; the four Z holes are among those that are not visible as earthworks.

earthworks, indistinct marks on an aerial photograph or a faint trace on a geophysical survey plot – we can be uncertain. Hence the exchange between William Stukeley and Roger Gale about the possibility of stoneholes surviving in the Avenue. Gale was sure that he had seen them; he knew that Stukeley had seen them (Burl 2006, 35–6), yet Stukeley had not mentioned them in his book. Although Stukeley's reply to Gale is lost, Burl and Mortimer attribute his 'forgetfulness' to religious self-delusion (2005, 16); it seems just as likely that he was prey to genuine doubts about what he had actually seen – it is a feeling familiar to all honest field archaeologists.

Slight earthworks are difficult to see, difficult to measure and often difficult to interpret. As noted above, conditions of vegetation, light and direction have to be right to make the initial observation. We have walked the King Barrow Ridge countless times and yet it was not until one of us was leading an EH members' tour in February 2012 that the hollow to the north of Amesbury barrow 34 (Fig 8.6) was seen. In a sense the archaeological significance of this

feature is unimportant: it could be the position of a relatively recent livestock drinking trough or a chalk pit (very likely), military disturbance (quite likely), a pond barrow (unlikely) or a natural solution hollow which is also the place of origin of one of the Stonehenge sarsens (just possible). Until we had seen it we could not even ask these questions. This feature has never been seen on an aerial photograph or detected by geophysical survey, but geophysical survey does show a subrectangular anomaly at the centre of it (Gaffney *et al* 2012, fig 2) – hence the suggestion about the sarsen.

Prospect

One thing is clear: the story of Stonehenge is by no means complete. The recent university-led research projects have revealed stunning new information. Our own project has added more and provided a record of the monuments as they are now, recording change and informing their management. Inevitably, the surveys have raised many new questions regarding Stonehenge itself, the Cursus, the long history of the barrow groups and their antecedents, and the emerging 'Palisade Ditch complex'; this gives a whole new aspect to the Early–Middle Bronze Age treatment of Stonehenge, but much further research is needed here, not least to refine the dating. Landscape change and development as a whole must also be considered. This landscape has not seen an enormous amount of development, but both river valleys were cultivated in Romano-British, medieval and later times: how much of the earlier landscape is obscured? Given the number of features revealed as parchmarks around Durrington Walls and Woodhenge, could we expect similar results further south around Countess, Amesbury and West Amesbury? Do the major periods of change correspond to the current chronological template, or does the template need adjusting? The modern landscape also has to be considered. To what extent has the area become a museum, stuck in time? The airfield and other buildings were razed to the ground to preserve the setting of the stones. Now the A344 has been closed and the visitor facilities removed to return the monument to a supposed prehistoric landscape, but are we preserving a 1960s landscape? Should the First World War military sewage works be preserved? One (to the south of Stonehenge) has already gone. Much uncertainty remains and much is yet to be discovered.

After a very wet spring in 2013 a sudden hot, dry spell in July caused parchmarks to form in the turf at Stonehenge (Fig 8.7). These ephemeral features were recorded before they disappeared again after just a few days of heavy showers (Banton *et al* 2014). Parching elsewhere in the Stonehenge landscape was also apparent (Fig 8.8). The question then is what these parchmarks at Stonehenge represent. One of them is almost certainly the hole for stone 17 of the sarsen circle, which has never been seen before and has not been detected by any geophysical survey. Others are Z holes or Gowland's excavation trenches; some may be previously unrecognised prehistoric features. Caution, however, is necessary: there has been a great deal of unrecorded, or inadequately recorded, disturbance in historic times (*see* Chapter 7) – so some of the parchmarks are caused by the larch poles which were put up to support leaning stones in 1902; others may be due to the scaffolding around stones 6 and 7 from 1881, the posts and machinery associated with the straightening and re-erection of stones in 1901, 1919–20 and 1958–64, or the numerous excavations in the past, particularly the 'unofficial' digging in the later 19th century. A further complication is the 'fire garden', a pyrotechnic installation at the site during the Cultural Olympiad of 2012, which is known to have created some local burning of the ground surface of the monument (Linford 2013). Despite these reservations there is a very real possibility that some of these new discoveries indicate the presence of ancient features and will have a bearing on the prehistoric story of Stonehenge itself and of Neolithic and Bronze Age Europe.

One aspect of the EH project has been the development of a GIS for the WHS landscape. Some preliminary results of this have been presented here (eg Figs 4.11, 4.12 and 6.7) but, due to diminishing resources and time, it has not been possible to exploit this as fully as had been hoped. It is, nevertheless, possible to suggest some future directions for research using this data. It would be possible to look at barrow forms, for instance: much of the accepted round barrow typology was developed in the Stonehenge landscape, so it would be appropriate to undertake some analysis with the GIS, for instance, comparing sizes and types of barrow by landscape position. This might usefully address questions such as: 'is there such a thing as a Bell Barrow?' (Field 2008, 83–4). We could also explore territoriality further, using the

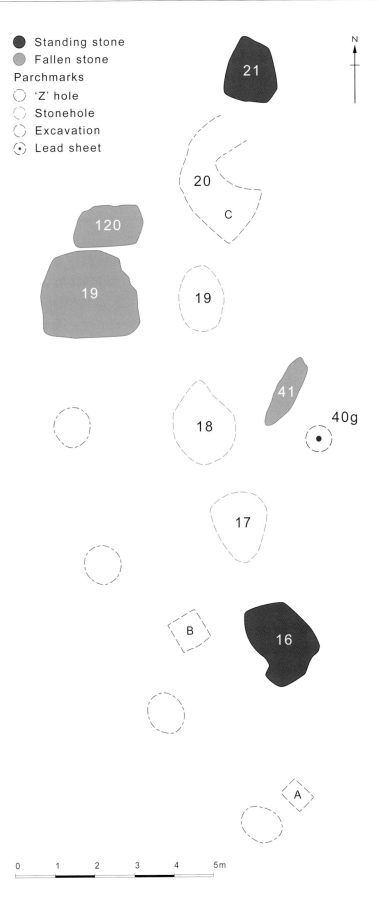

Standing stone
Fallen stone
Parchmarks
‘Z’ hole
Stonehole
Excavation
Lead sheet

Fig 8.8
Parchmarks on the King
Barrow Ridge, July 2013,
looking south. In the
extreme bottom left are
barrows Amesbury 131
(under tree clump), 132
and 133 (an oval). The
narrow parallel ditches of
the Stonehenge Avenue can
be seen heading towards the
top left corner; further right
the old Amesbury to Market
Lavington road can be seen,
apparently crossed by a
linear feature parallel to the
modern road (the A303),
which has further lines
extending from it near the
centre of the photograph.
The broad yellowish streak
running from right to left
below the modern road
indicates the damp area at
the bottom of a slight dry
valley.
(NMR 27746/007)

pattern of wider riverine activity as a basis to ask questions such as whether Spring Bottom is a territorial unit with barrows on the periphery; the King Barrows might be on the periphery of a unit based on the Avon. Are the barrow groups on ridges accumulations of monuments on the borders between settlement units? We could also use the GIS to look at aspects of hydrology and flooding, to examine the effects of fluctuating water tables and to identify hollows where water might have collected seasonally (*see* Tilley *et al* 2007, 187). Similarly, the laser scan of the stones (Fig 8.9) is open for further analysis (*see* Field *et al* forthcoming b), which might allow reconsideration of the development of the monument and the processes involved, and its later treatment.

There have been very few modern barrow excavations. Reanalysis of antiquarian finds has yielded excellent results but the time will come when fresh data is required. However, before any new barrow excavation it would be worth exploiting to the full the newest geophysical techniques. GPR may afford a means of exploring the size, position and shape of anti-

quarian trenches – antiquarian digging could be responsible for a radar anomaly detected in Amesbury 50 (Linford *et al* 2012, 16–17, fig 27), for instance. This could provide a very accurate guide for targeted excavation, minimising damage while maximising returns. Other targets for precise dating, which can only come from excavation, include the henge-like features and pit structures revealed by the recent geophysical surveys. Similarly, many questions remain concerning the extensive spread of cropmarks recorded near Woodhenge (*see* Fig 4.14; McOmish 2001) – what, for instance, should we make of the small square features that look like Iron Age barrows, in view of the recent identification of rectangular Neolithic structures in the area?

With the closure of the A344 and the opening of the new visitor centre (Fig 8.10) the Stonehenge landscape is entering a new phase in its management and its appreciation by the public. The landscape should not (and cannot) be set in aspic but neither should our knowledge and understanding of it. Research must continue.

Fig 8.9 (left)
Laser scan image of the stones.

Fig 8.10 (below)
The new Stonehenge visitor centre at Airman's Corner. The gap in the centre of the building fortuitously preserves what may have been a significant prehistoric route from the west end of the Greater Cursus down the centre of the dry valley to the River Till.
(DP163153)

APPENDIX

English Heritage Research Reports arising from the Stonehenge WHS Landscape Project

Readers requiring more information on the details recorded during the course of the project are referred to the following English Heritage Research Reports, which are available as PDFs to download, free of charge, from the Historic England website.

Note: in 2012 the Research Department Report Series became the Research Report Series.

RDRS 40-2009	D Field *Airman's Corner, Winterbourne Stoke, Wiltshire: Investigation of Earthworks*
RRS 32-2012	M Abbott and H Anderson-Whymark *Stonehenge Laser Scan: Archaeological Analysis Report: EH Project 6457*
RRS 34-2012	N Linford, P Linford and A Payne *Stonehenge Monument Field and Barrows, Wiltshire: Report on Geophysical Surveys, September 2010, April and July 2011*
RRS 6-2014	M Barber *'Restoring' Stonehenge, 1881–1939*
RRS 7-2014	M Barber *Stonehenge Aerodrome and the Stonehenge Landscape*

All the following titles are prefaced by *Stonehenge World Heritage Site Landscape Project*.

RDRS 85-2010	L Amadio and S Bishop *The Cursus Barrows and Surrounding Area*
RDRS 86-2010	S Bishop *Durrington Firs*
RDRS 90-2010	K Barrett and M Bowden *Normanton Down*
RDRS 95-2010	A Komar *Lake Down, Wilsford-cum-Lake*
RDRS 96-2010	A Komar and S Bishop *Fargo South*
RDRS 107-2010	S Bax, M Bowden, A Komar and S Newsome *Winterbourne Stoke Crossroads*
RDRS 108-2010	M Bowden *Wilsford Barrows*
RDRS 109-2010	D Field and T Pearson *Stonehenge, Amesbury, Wiltshire*
RDRS 42-2011	R Lane *Stonehenge, Amesbury, Wiltshire: Architectural Assessment*
RDRS 82-2011	S Bishop *Level 1 Field Investigations*
RDRS 83-2011	S Bishop *King Barrow Ridge*
RDRS 92-2011	M Bowden *Earthworks at Lake and West Amesbury*
RDRS 103-2011	T Pearson and D Field *Stonehenge Cursus, Amesbury, Wiltshire*
RDRS 105-2011	D Field and T Pearson *Stonehenge Down and The Triangle*
RRS 3-2012	S Soutar *Larkhill Barrows, Durrington*
RRS 29-2012	M Bowden, D Field and S Soutar *Lake Barrows, The Diamond and Normanton Gorse*
RRS 31-2012	D Field, M Bowden and S Soutar *The Avenue and Stonehenge Bottom*
RRS 35-2012	A Komar and D Field *A344 Corridor: Level 1 Survey*

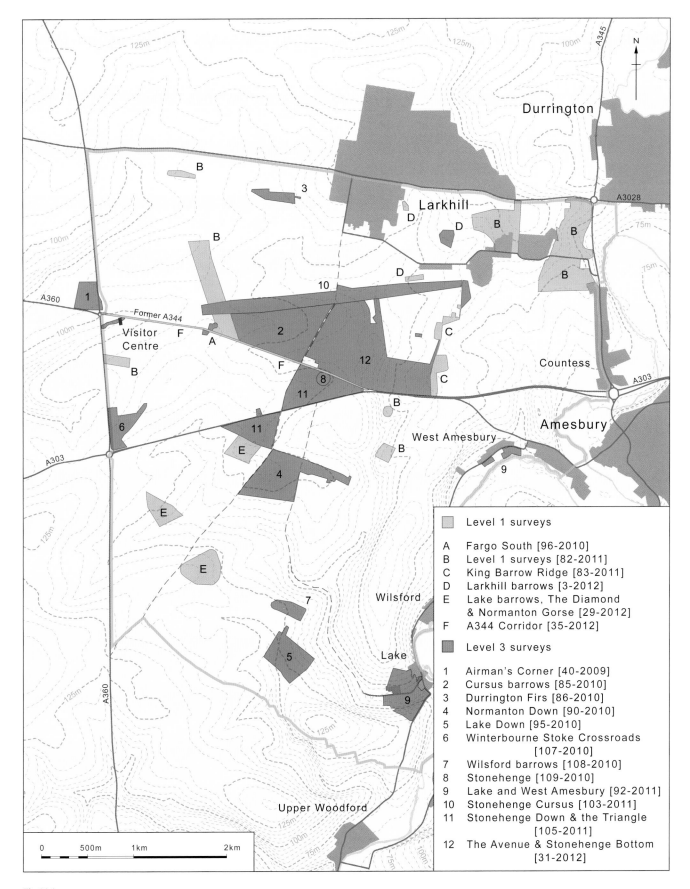

Fig A1.1
Areas surveyed by the EH Stonehenge WHS Landscape Project with their Research Report numbers.

Level 1 surveys

A Fargo South [96-2010]
B Level 1 surveys [82-2011]
C King Barrow Ridge [83-2011]
D Larkhill barrows [3-2012]
E Lake barrows, The Diamond & Normanton Gorse [29-2012]
F A344 Corridor [35-2012]

Level 3 surveys

1 Airman's Corner [40-2009]
2 Cursus barrows [85-2010]
3 Durrington Firs [86-2010]
4 Normanton Down [90-2010]
5 Lake Down [95-2010]
6 Winterbourne Stoke Crossroads [107-2010]
7 Wilsford barrows [108-2010]
8 Stonehenge [109-2010]
9 Lake and West Amesbury [92-2011]
10 Stonehenge Cursus [103-2011]
11 Stonehenge Down & the Triangle [105-2011]
12 The Avenue & Stonehenge Bottom [31-2012]

REFERENCES AND FURTHER READING

Abbott, M and Anderson-Whymark, H 2012 *Stonehenge Laser Scan: Archaeological Analysis Report* EH Project 6457 Research Report Series **32-2012**. Portsmouth: English Heritage

Ainsworth, S, Bowden, M C B, McOmish, D S and Pearson, T 2007 *Understanding the Archaeology of Landscapes: A Guide to Good Recording Practice*. Swindon: English Heritage

Aldsworth, F G 1974 'Towards a pre-Domesday geography of Hampshire: a review of the evidence'. Unpublished BA dissertation, University of Southampton

Algar, D 1997 'Durrington, Wiltshire: 1,426 and 2,536 nummi to AD328' *in* Bland, R and Orna-Ornstein, J (eds) *Coin Hoards from Roman Britain* **10**. London: British Museum, 296–338

Allen, M J 1995a 'Before Stonehenge: Mesolithic human activity in a wildwood landscape' *in* Cleal *et al* 1995, 470–3

Allen, M J 1995b 'Mesolithic features in the car park' *in* Cleal *et al* 1995, 43–7

Allen, M J and Gardiner, J 2002 'A sense of time: cultural markers in the Mesolithic of southern England' *in* Bruno, D and Wilson, M (eds) *Inscribed Landscapes: Marking and Making Place*. Honolulu: University of Hawai'i Press, 139–53

Allen, M J and Scaife, R 2007 'A new downland prehistory: long term environmental change on the southern English chalklands' *in* Fleming, A and Hingley, R (eds) *Prehistoric and Roman Landscapes* Landscape History after Hoskins **1**. Macclesfield: Windgather

Amadio, L and Bishop, S 2010 *Stonehenge WHS Landscape Project: The Cursus Barrows and Surrounding Area: Archaeological Survey Report* Research Department Report Series **85-2010**. Portsmouth: English Heritage

AMB 1955 *Ancient Monuments Boards for England, Scotland and Wales: First Annual Reports 1954*. London: HMSO

AMB 1959 *Ancient Monuments Boards for England, Scotland and Wales: Fifth Annual Reports 1958*. London: HMSO

AMB 1962 *Ancient Monuments Boards for England, Scotland and Wales: Eighth Annual Reports 1961*. London: HMSO

AMB 1963 *Ancient Monuments Boards for England, Scotland and Wales: Ninth Annual Reports 1962*. London: HMSO

AMB 1964 *Ancient Monuments Boards for England, Scotland and Wales: Tenth Annual Reports 1963*. London: HMSO

Antrobus, F C M 1902 'Amesbury Abbey, Amesbury, Wiltshire: the seat of Edmund Antrobus, Bart.' *Country Life* **11.269**, 1 March 1902, 272–9

Antrobus, F C M 1913 *A Sentimental and Practical Guide to Amesbury and Stonehenge*. Amesbury: Estate Office

Apprentice Jockey 2012 *Druids Lodge* http://theapprenticejockey. blogspot.co.uk/2011/12/druids-lodge.html [accessed 23 April 2013]

Ashbee, P 1960 *The Bronze Age Round Barrow in Britain*. London: Phoenix House

Ashbee, P 1978 'Amesbury barrow 51: excavations, 1960'. *Wiltshire Archaeol Natur Hist Mag* **70/71** (1975–6), 1–60

Ashbee, P 1981 'Amesbury barrow 39: excavations, 1960'. *Wiltshire Archaeol Natur Hist Mag* **74/75** (1979–80), 3–34

Ashbee, P 1998 'Stonehenge, its possible non-completion, slighting and dilapidation'. *Wiltshire Archaeol Natur Hist Mag* **91**, 139–43

Ashbee, P, Bell, M and Proudfoot, E 1989 *Wilsford Shaft: Excavations, 1960–2* Engl Heritage Archaeol Rep **11**. London: Historic Buildings and Monuments Commission for England

Aston, M 1985 *Interpreting the Landscape: Landscape Archaeology in Local Studies*. London: Routledge

Aston, M and Bettey, J 1998 'The post-medieval rural landscape, *c* 1540–1700: the drive for profit and the desire for status' *in* Everson, P and Williamson, T (eds) *The Archaeology of Landscape*. Manchester: Manchester University Press, 117–38

Atkinson, R J C 1956 *Stonehenge*. London: Hamish Hamilton

Atkinson, R J C 1957 'Worms and weathering'. *Antiquity* **31**, 219–33

Atkinson, R J C 1985 'Barrows excavated by William Stukeley near Stonehenge, 1723–1724'. *Wiltshire Archaeol Natur Hist Mag* **79**, 244–6

Atwood, G 1963 'A study of the Wiltshire water meadows'. *Wiltshire Archaeol Natur Hist Mag* **58**, 403–13

Aubrey, J 1626–97 *Monumenta Britannica* (facsim edn Dorset Publishing 1980)

Aubrey, J and Ponting, K G 1967 *Aubrey's Natural History of Wiltshire: A Reprint of 'The Natural History of Wiltshire'*. Newton Abbot: David & Charles

Banton, S, Bowden, M C B, Daw, T, Grady, D and Soutar, S 2014 'Parchmarks at Stonehenge, July 2013'. *Antiquity* **88**, 733-9

Barber, M 2006 'Palaeolithic contrivance over Stonehenge'. *Brit Archaeol* (Jul/Aug), 18–23

Barber, M 2011 *A History of Aerial Photography and Archaeology: Mata Hari's Glass Eye and Other Stories*. Swindon: English Heritage

Barber, M 2014a *'Restoring' Stonehenge, 1881–1939* Research Report Series **6-2014**. Portsmouth: English Heritage

Barber, M 2014b *Stonehenge Aerodrome and the Stonehenge Landscape* Research Report Series **7-2014**. Portsmouth: English Heritage

Barber, M, Grady, D and Winton, H 2003 'From pit circles to propellers: recent results from aerial survey in Wiltshire'. *Wiltshire Archaeol Natur Hist Mag* **96**, 148–60

Barclay, A and Harding, J (eds) 1999 *Pathways and Ceremonies: The Cursus Monuments of Britain and Ireland* Neolithic Studies Group Seminar Papers **4**. Oxford: Oxbow

Barclay, E 1895 *Stonehenge and Its Earthworks*. London: Nutt

Barfoot, P and Wilkes, J 1993 *The Universal British Directory, 1793–1798* **2**, pt 1, A–B. Facsim edn. King's Lynn: M Winton

Barrett, J C 1994 *Fragments from Antiquity: An Archaeology of Social Life in Britain, 2900–1200 BC*. Oxford: Blackwell

Barrett, J C and Ko, I 2009 'A phenomenology of landscape: a crisis in British landscape archaeology?' *J Social Archaeol* **9.3**, 275–94

Barrett, J C, Bowden, M C B and McOmish, D S 2011 'The problem of continuity: reassessing the shape of the British Iron Age sequence' *in* Moore, T and Armada, X-L (eds) *Atlantic Europe in the First Millennium BC: Crossing the Divide*. Oxford: Oxford University Press, 439–48

Barrett, K and Bowden, M C B 2010 *Stonehenge World Heritage Site Landscape Project: Normanton Down: Archaeological Survey Report* Research Department Report Series **90-2010**. Portsmouth: English Heritage

Barton, R N E 1992 *Hengistbury Head, Dorset* **2**: *The Late Palaeolithic and Early Mesolithic Sites* Oxford Univ Comm Archaeol Monogr **34**. Oxford: Oxford University Committee for Archaeology, Institute of Archaeology

Batey, M 1988 'Practical poetry: the landscaping of Amesbury Abbey'. *Country Life* **182.5**, 4 February, 78–80.

Bax, S, Bowden, M C B, Komar, A and Newsome, S 2010 *Stonehenge World Heritage Site Landscape Project: Winterbourne Stoke Crossroads: Archaeological Survey Report* Research Department Report Series **107-2010**. Portsmouth: English Heritage

Bayliss, A and Whittle, A (eds) 2007 'Histories of the dead: building chronologies for five southern British long barrows'. *Cambridge Archaeol J* **17.1** (Supplement)

Bender, B 1998 *Stonehenge: Making Space*. Oxford: Berg

Bettey, J 2000 'Downlands' *in* Thirsk, J (ed) *The English Rural Landscape*. Oxford: Oxford University Press, 27–49

Bevins, R E and Ixer, R A 2013 'Carn Alw as a source of the rhyolitic component of the Stonehenge bluestones: a critical re-appraisal of the petrographical account of H.H.Thomas'. *J Archaeol Sci* **40**, 3293–301

Bevins, R E, Ixer, R A and Pearce, N J G 2014 'Carn Goedog is the likely major source of Stonehenge doleritic bluestones: evidence based on compatible element geochemistry and principle component analysis'. *J Archaeol Sci* **42**, 179–93

Bishop, S 2009 *Tarrant Launceston 15 and Environs: Aerial Photograph Survey and Analysis: Special Project Report*. Research Department Report Series **31-2009**. Portsmouth: English Heritage

Bishop, S 2010 *Stonehenge World Heritage Site Landscape Project: Durrington Firs, Durrington: Archaeological Survey Report* Research Department Report Series **86-2010**. Portsmouth: English Heritage

Bishop, S 2011a *Stonehenge World Heritage Site Landscape Project: Level 1 Field Investigations: Archaeological Survey Report* Research Department Report Series **82-2011**. Portsmouth: English Heritage

Bishop, S 2011b *Stonehenge World Heritage Site Landscape Project: King Barrow Ridge: Archaeological Survey Report* Research Department Report Series **83-2011**. Portsmouth: English Heritage

Blore, F, Hitchen, M, Vallender, J and Canham, R 1995 *Archaeological Assessment of the Stonehenge World Heritage Site and Its Surrounding Landscape* London: English Heritage

Blow, D 1902 'The architectural discoveries of 1901 at Stonehenge'. *J Roy Inst Brit Architects* 3rd ser **9**, 121–42

Bold, J (with Reeves, J) 1988 *Wilton House and English Palladianism: Some Wiltshire Houses*. London: HMSO

Bond, C J 1991 'Appendix H: Landscape regression analysis', *in* Darvill, T C (ed) *Stonehenge Conservation and Management Project: Environmental Statement* **3**: *Technical Appendices*. London: Debenham, Tewson and Chinnocks, 383–444

Bond, C J 2004 *Monastic Landscapes*. Stroud: Tempus

Bowden, M C B 1998 'The conscious conversion of earlier earthworks in the design of parks and gardens' *in* Pattison, P (ed) *There by Design: Field Archaeology in Parks and Gardens* RCHME (Brit Archaeol Rep **267**). Oxford: Archaeopress, 23–6

Bowden, M C B 2004 *Oldbury Castle Hillfort, Wiltshire*. EH Archaeol Investigation Rep AI/31/2004. Swindon: English Heritage

Bowden, M C B 2005 'The Middle Iron Age on the Marlborough Downs' *in* Brown, G, Field, D J and McOmish, D S (eds) *The Avebury Landscape: Aspects of the Field Archaeology of the Marlborough Downs*. Oxford: Oxbow, 156–63

Bowden, M C B 2010 *Stonehenge World Heritage Site Landscape Project: Wilsford Barrows: Archaeological Survey Report* Research Department Report Series **108-2010**. Portsmouth: English Heritage

Bowden, M C B 2011 *Stonehenge World Heritage Site Landscape Project: Earthworks at Lake and West Amesbury: Archaeological Survey Report* Research Department Report Series **92-2011**. Portsmouth: English Heritage

Bowden, M C B and McOmish, D S forthcoming '"To make you see" – archaeological cartography: a view from Britain'

Bowden, M C B, Field, D and Soutar, S 2012 *Stonehenge World Heritage Site Landscape Project: Lake Barrows, The Diamond and Normanton Gorse: Archaeological Survey Report* Research Report Series **29-2012**. Portsmouth: English Heritage

Bowen, H C and Smith, I F 1977 'Sarsen stones in Wessex: the Society's first investigations in the Evolution of the Landscape Project'. *Antiq J* **57.2**, 186–96

Bradley, R 1993 *Altering the Earth: The Origins of Monuments in Britain and Continental Europe* Soc Antiq Scotl Monogr **8**. Edinburgh: Society of Antiquaries of Scotland

Bradley, R 2000 *The Good Stones: A New Investigation of the Clava Cairns* Soc Antiq Scotl Monogr **17**. Edinburgh: Society of Antiquaries of Scotland

Bradley, R 2007 *The Prehistory of Britain and Ireland* Cambridge World Archaeology. Cambridge: Cambridge University Press

Bradley, R, Entwistle, R and Raymond, F 1994 *Prehistoric Land Divisions on Salisbury Plain: The Work of the Wessex Linear Ditches Project*. London: English Heritage

Bronk Ramsey, C 2009 'Bayesian analysis of radiocarbon dates'. *Radiocarbon* **51.1**, 337–60

Brophy, K 2000 'Water coincidence: cursus monuments and rivers' *in* Ritchie, A (ed) *Neolithic Orkney in Its European Context*. Cambridge: McDonald Institute, 59–70

Brown, T C 2013 *Flying with the Larks: The Early Aviation Pioneers of Larkhill*. Stroud: The History Press

Browne, G F 1915 *The Recollections of a Bishop*. London: Smith, Elder

Burl, A 1979 *Prehistoric Avebury*. London: Yale University Press

Burl, A 1991 'Megalithic myth or man the mover?' *Antiquity* **65**, 297–8

Burl, A 1997 'The sarsen horseshoe in Stonehenge: a rider'. *Wiltshire Archaeol Natur Hist Mag* **90**, 1–12

Burl, A 2006 *Stonehenge: A History of the World's Greatest Stone Circle*. Constable: London

Burl, A and Mortimer, N 2005 *Stukeley's Stonehenge: An Unpublished Manuscript, 1721–1724*. New Haven: Yale University Press

Burrow, S 2010 'The formative henge: speculations drawn from the circular traditions of Wales and adjacent counties' *in* Leary, J, Field, D J and Darvill, T (eds) *Round Mounds and Monumentality in the British Neolithic and Beyond* Neolithic Studies Group Seminar Papers **10**. Oxford: Oxbow

Camden, W 1610 *Britannia*. London: George Bishop and John Norton

Campbell, G 2013 *The Hermit in the Garden: From Imperial Rome to Garden Gnome*. Oxford: Oxford University Press

Campbell Smith, W 1963 'Jade axes from sites in the British Isles'. *Proc Prehist Soc* **29**, 133–72

Capper, J E 1907 'Photographs of Stonehenge as seen from a war balloon'. *Archaeologia* **60**, 571 and plates 69 and 70

Carpenter, E and Winton, H 2011 *Marden Henge and Environs, Vale of Pewsey, Wiltshire: A Report for the National Mapping Programme* Research Department Report Series **76-2011**. Portsmouth: English Heritage

Carrier, E H 1936 *The Pastoral Heritage of Britain: A Geographical Study*. London: Christophers

Chandler, J H 1979 *The Amesbury Turnpike Trust* S Wiltshire Ind Archaeol Soc Monogr **4**. Salisbury: South Wiltshire Industrial Archaeology Society

Chandler, J H 1980 *Stagecoach Operation through Wiltshire* S Wiltshire Ind Archaeol Soc Monogr **8**. Salisbury: South Wilts Industrial Archaeology Society

Chandler, J H 1991 'Accommodation and travel in pre-turnpike Wiltshire'. *Wiltshire Archaeol Natur Hist Mag* **84**, 83–95

Chandler, J H 1998 *Printed Maps of Wiltshire, 1787–1844: A Selection of Topographical, Road and Canal Maps in Facsimile* Wiltshire Record Society **52** (for 1996). Trowbridge: Wiltshire Record Society

Chapman, J and Seeliger, S 2001 *Enclosure, Environment and Landscape in Southern England*. Stroud: Tempus

Chippindale, C 2012 *Stonehenge Complete,* 4th edn. London: Thames & Hudson

Chippindale, C, Devereux, P, Fowler, P, Jones, R and Sebastian, T 1990 *Who Owns Stonehenge?* London: Batsford

Christie, P M 1963 'The Stonehenge Cursus'. *Wiltshire Archaeol Natur Hist Mag* **58**, 370–82

Cleal, R M J 2005 '"The small compass of a grave": Early Bronze Age burial in and around Avebury and the Marlborough Downs' *in* Brown, G, Field, D and McOmish, D (eds) *The Avebury Landscape: Aspects of the Field Archaeology of the Marlborough* Downs. Oxford: Oxbow

Cleal, R M J and Allen, M J 1994 'Investigation of tree-damaged barrows on the King Barrow Ridge, Amesbury'. *Wiltshire Archaeol Natur Hist Mag* **87**, 54–83

Cleal, R M J and Pollard, J 2012 'The revenge of the native: monuments, material culture, burial and other practices in the third quarter of the 3rd millennium BC in Wessex' *in* Allen, M J, Gardiner, J and Sheridan, A (eds) *Is There a British Chalcolithic? People, Place and Polity in the Later 3rd Millennium*. Oxford: Prehist Soc/Oxbow, 317–32

Cleal, R M J, Walker, K E and Montague, R 1995 *Stonehenge in Its Landscape: Twentieth-Century Excavations*. London: English Heritage

Coles, J and Coles, B 1986 *Sweet Track to Glastonbury: The Somerset Levels in Prehistory*. London: Thames & Hudson

Coppack, G 1999 'Setting and structure: the conservation of Wigmore Castle' *in* Chitty, G and Baker, D (eds) *Managing Historic Sites and Buildings: Reconciling Presentation and Preservation*. London: Routledge, 61–70

Cossons, A 1959 'Roads' *in* Crittall, E (ed) *A History of Wiltshire* **4**. Victoria History of the Counties of England. London: Institute of Historical Research/Oxford University Press, 254–71

Crawford, O G S 1924a 'The Stonehenge Avenue' *Antiq J* **4**, 57–9

Crawford, O G S 1924b *Air Survey and Archaeology* Ordnance Survey Professional Papers **7**. Southampton: OS/HMSO

Crawford, O G S and Keiller, A 1928 *Wessex from the Air*. Oxford: Clarendon

Crawford, T S 2012 *Wiltshire and the Great War: Training the Empire's Soldiers*. Ramsbury: Crowood

Crittall, E 1956 'Abbey of Wilton' *in* Pugh, R B and Crittall, E (eds) *A History of Wiltshire* **3**. VCH. London: Institute of Historical Research/Oxford University Press

Croker, J W 1824 *Letters to and from Henrietta, Countess of Suffolk*. London: Murray

Crowley, D A 1995 'Amesbury' *in* Crowley, D (ed) *A History of Wiltshire* **15**: *Amesbury Hundred, Branch and Dole Hundred*. VCH. Oxford: Oxford University Press/Institute of Historical Research, 13–55

Crutchley, S 2000 *Salisbury Plain Training Area: A Report for the National Mapping Programme* Aerial Survey Report Series. Swindon: English Heritage

Crutchley, S 2002 *Stonehenge World Heritage Site Mapping Project: Management Report* Aerial Survey Report Series AER/14/2002. Swindon: English Heritage

Cunliffe, B W and Renfrew C (eds) 1997 *Science and Stonehenge* Proc Brit Acad **92**. Oxford: Oxford University Press/British Academy

Cunnington, M E 1914 'List of the long barrows of Wiltshire'. *Wiltshire Archaeol Natur Hist Mag* **38**, 379–414

Cunnington, M E 1929 *Woodhenge: A Description of the Site as Revealed by Excavations Carried Out There by Mr and Mrs B H Cunnington, 1926–7–8, also of Four Circles and an Earthwork Enclosure South of Woodhenge*. Devizes: Simpson

Cunnington, M E 1930 'Romano-British Wiltshire'. *Wiltshire Archaeol Natur Hist Mag* **45**, 166–216

Cunnington, R H and Dyer, J (ed) 1975 *From Antiquary to Archaeologist: A Biography of William Cunnington, 1754–1810*. Princes Risborough: Shire

Dakers, C 1993 *Clouds: The Biography of a Country House*. London: Yale University Press

Darvill, T 1997 'Ever increasing circles: the sacred geographies of Stonehenge in its landscape' *in* Cunliffe and Renfrew 1997, 167–202

Darvill, T 2006 *Stonehenge: The Biography of a Landscape*. Stroud: Tempus

Darvill, T and Wainwright, J G 2009 'Stonehenge excavations, 2008'. *Antiq J* **89**, 1–19

Darvill, T with Constant, V and Milner, E 2005 *Stonehenge World Heritage Site: An Archaeological Research Framework*. London and Bournemouth: English Heritage/Bournemouth University

Darvill, T, Marshall, P, Parker Pearson, M and Wainwright, G 2012 'Stonehenge remodelled'. *Antiquity* **86**, 1021–40

Darvill, T, Lüth, F, Rassmann, K, Fischer, A and Winkelmann, K 2013 'Stonehenge, Wiltshire, UK: high resolution geophysical surveys in the surrounding landscape, 2011'. *European J Archaeol* **16.1**, 63–93

David, A and Payne, A 1997 'Geophysical Surveys within the Stonehenge landscape: a review of past endeavour and future potential' *in* Cunliffe and Renfrew 1997, 73–113

Davies, J G 1995 'Coins' *in* Cleal *et al* 1995, 431–2

Davies, J O 2013 *A Year at Stonehenge*. London: Frances Lincoln

Drury, M 1985 'The fall and rise of Stonehenge'. *SPAB News* **6.4**, Autumn, 8–9

Drury, M 2000 *Wandering Architects: In Pursuit of an Arts and Crafts Ideal*. Stamford: Shaun Tyas

Eagles, B N and Field, D J 2004 'William Cunnington and the long barrows of the River Wylye' *in* Cleal, R M J and Pollard, J (eds) *Monuments and Material Culture: Papers in Honour of an Avebury Archaeologist: Isobel Smith*. Salisbury: Hobnob, 47–69

Elrington, C R 1962 'Woodford', *in* Crittall, E (ed) *A History of the County of Wiltshire* **6**. VCH. London: Oxford University Press/*Institute of Historical Research,* 221–7

Emerick, K 2003 'From frozen monuments to fluid landscapes: the conservation and presentation of ancient monuments from 1882 to the present'. Unpublished PhD thesis, Dept of Archaeology, University of York

Evans, J 1897 *The Ancient Stone Implements, Weapons and Ornaments of Great Britain*, 2 edn, rev. London: Longmans Green

Evans, J G 1968 'Periglacial deposits on the chalk of Wiltshire'. *Wiltshire Archaeol Natur Hist Mag* **63**, 12–26

Evans, J G, Atkinson, R G J, O'Connor, T and Green, H S 1984 'The environment in the late Neolithic and Early Bronze Age and a Beaker-age burial'. *Wiltshire Archaeol Natur Hist Mag* **78**, 7–30

Everson, P and Williamson, T 1998 'Gardens and Designed Landscapes' *in* Everson, P and Williamson, T (eds) *The Archaeology of Landscape*. Manchester: Manchester University Press, 139–65

Exon, S, Gaffney, V, Woodward, A and Yorston, R 2000 *Stonehenge Landscapes*. Oxford: Archaeopress

Farrer, P 1918 'Durrington Walls or Long Walls'. *Wiltshire Archaeol Natur Hist Mag* **40**, 95–103

Fergusson, P and Harrison, S 1999 *Rievaulx Abbey: Community, Architecture, Memory*. New Haven: Yale University Press

Field, D J 1998 'Round barrows and the harmonious landscape: placing Early Bronze Age monuments in south-east England'. *Oxford J Archaeol* **17**, 309–26

Field, D J 2001 'Place and memory in Bronze Age Wessex' *in* Brück, J (ed) *Bronze Age Landscapes: Tradition and Transformation*. Oxford: Oxbow

Field, D J 2006 *Earthen Long Barrows*. Stroud: Tempus

Field, D J 2008 *Use of Land in Central Southern England during the Neolithic and Early Bronze Age* Brit Archaeol Rep **458**. Oxford: Archaeopress

Field, D J 2009 *Airman's Corner, Winterbourne Stoke, Wiltshire: Investigation of Earthworks: Archaeological Survey Report* Research Department Report Series **40-2009**. Portsmouth: English Heritage

Field, D J and Pearson, T 2010 *Stonehenge World Heritage Site Landscape Project: Stonehenge, Amesbury, Wiltshire* Research Department Report Series **109-2010**. Portsmouth: English Heritage

Field, D J and Pearson, T 2011 *Stonehenge World Heritage Site Landscape Project: Stonehenge Down and the Triangle: Archaeological Survey Report* Research Department Report Series **105-2011**. Portsmouth: English Heritage

Field, D J, Bowden, M C B and Soutar, S 2012 *Stonehenge World Heritage Site Landscape Project: The Avenue and Stonehenge Bottom* Research

Report Series **31-2012**. Portsmouth: English Heritage

Field, D J, Brown, G and Crockett, A 2001 'The Marlborough Mount revisited'. *Wiltshire Archaeol Natur Hist Mag* **94**, 195–204

Field, D J, Linford, N, Barber, M, Anderson-Whymark, H *et al* forthcoming a 'Analytical surveys of Stonehenge and its environs, 2009–2013: part 1, the landscape and earthworks'. *Proc Prehist Soc*

Field, D J, Linford, N, Barber, M, Anderson-Whymark, H *et al* forthcoming b 'Analytical surveys of Stonehenge and its environs, 2009–2013: part 2, the stones'. *Proc Prehist Soc*

Finch, J and Giles, K (eds) 2007 *Estate Landscapes: Design, Improvement and Power in the Post-Medieval Landscape: Papers Given at the Estates Landscapes Conference, April 2003, Hosted by the Society for Post-Medieval Archaeology* Society for Post-Medieval Archaeology Monograph **4**. Woodbridge: Boydell

Fitzpatrick, A P 2011 *The Amesbury Archer and the Boscombe Bowmen: Bell Beaker Burials at Boscombe Down, Amesbury, Wiltshire* Wessex Archaeol Rep **27**. Salisbury: Wessex Archaeology

Fleming, A 1971 'Territorial patterns in Bronze Age Wessex'. *Proc Prehist Soc* **37.1**, 138–66

Forestry Commission 2013 'Scots pine – pinus sylvestris' www.forestry. gov.uk/forestry/infd-5nlfap [accessed 12 April 2013]

Freeman, J 1995 'Shrewton' *in* Crowley, D (ed) *A History of the County of Wiltshire* **15**: *Amesbury Hundred, Branch and Dole Hundred*. Victoria History of the Counties of England. Oxford: Oxford University Press/Institute of Historical Research, 242–52

Freeman, J 1995 'Winterbourne Stoke' *in* Crowley, D (ed) *A History of the County of Wiltshire* **15**: *Amesbury Hundred, Branch and Dole Hundred*. VCH. Oxford: Oxford University Press/Institute of Historical Research, 275–84

French, C, Lewis, H, Allen, M J, Green, M *et al* 2007 *Prehistoric Landscape Development and Human Impact in the Upper Allen Valley, Cranborne Chase, Dorset*. Cambridge: McDonald Institute

French, C, Scaife, R and Allen, M J with Parker Pearson, M *et al* 2012 'Durrington Walls to West Amesbury by way of Stonehenge: a major transformation of the Holocene landscape'. *Antiq J* **92**, 1–36

Fulford, M G, Powell, A B, Entwistle, R and Raymond, F 2006 *Iron Age and Romano-British Landscapes of Salisbury Plain* Wessex Archaeol Rep **20**. Salisbury: Wessex Archaeology/University of Reading

Gaffney, C, Gaffney, V, Neubauer, W, Baldwin, E *et al* 2012 'The Stonehenge Hidden Landscapes Project'. *Archaeol Prospection* **19.2**, 147–55

Gardiner, J 1995 'The assimilation of the monument and post-Bronze Age use and abuse' *in* Cleal *et al* 1995, 332–47

Garrett, J V and Hodgkins, T 1995 'Stone built sheepwashes in Gloucestershire'. *Gloucestershire History* **8**, 11–14

Garwood, P 2007 'Before the hills in order stood: chronology, time and history in the interpretation of Early Bronze Age round barrows' *in* Last 2007, 30–52

Garwood, P 2012 'The present dead: the making of past and future landscapes in the British chalcolithic' *in* Allen, M J, Gardiner, J and Sheridan, A (eds) *Is There a British Chalcolithic? People, Place and Polity in the Later 3rd Millennium*. Oxford: Prehist Soc/Oxbow, 298–316

Geddes, I 2000 *Hidden Depths: Wiltshire's Geology and Landscapes*. Bradford on Avon: Libris

Gelling, M and Cole, A 2000 *Landscape of Place Names*. Stamford: Shaun Tyas

Gerhold, D 2005 *Carriers and Coachmasters: Trade and Travel before the Turnpikes* Chichester: Phillimore

Gibson, A 1998 *Stonehenge and Timber Circles*. Stroud: Tempus

Gibson, A 2002 *Prehistoric Pottery in Britain & Ireland*. Stroud: Tempus

Gibson, A 2012 'An introduction to the study of henges: time for a change?' in Gibson, A (ed) *Enclosing the Neolithic: Recent Studies in Britain and Europe* BAR Int Ser **2440**. Oxford: Archaeopress, 1–20

Gifford, J 1957 'The physique of Wiltshire' in Pugh, R B (ed) *A History of Wiltshire* **1.1**. VCH. London: Oxford University Press, 1–20

Gingell, C 1988 'Twelve Wiltshire round barrows: excavations in 1959 and 1961 by F de M and H L Vatcher'. *Wiltshire Archaeol Natur Hist Mag* **82**, 19–76

Girdwood, A 1986 'Archaeology, the historical movement and the idea of progress'. *Scott Archaeol Rev* **4.1**, 35–43

Goddard, E H 1908 'Notes on the barrows at Lake'. *Wiltshire Archaeol Natur Hist Mag* **35**, 582–6

Goddard, E H 1914 'A list of prehistoric, Roman and pagan Saxon antiquities in the county of Wiltshire'. *Wiltshire Archaeol Natur Hist Mag* **58** (1913–14), 150–378

Gowland, W 1902 'Recent excavations at Stonehenge'. *Archaeologia* **58.1**, 37–118

Graham, A and Newman, C 1993 'Recent excavations of Iron Age and Romano-British enclosures in the Avon valley, Wiltshire'. *Wiltshire Archaeol Natur Hist Mag* **86**, 8–57

Green, C and Rollo-Smith, S 1984 'The excavation of eighteen round barrows near Shrewton, Wiltshire'. *Proc Prehist Soc* **50**, 255–318

Green, M 2000 *A Landscape Revealed: 10,000 Years on a Chalkland Farm*. Stroud: Tempus

Greenfield, E 1959 'Wilsford Down and Normanton Down, Amesbury'. *Wiltshire Archaeol Natur Hist Mag* **57**, 228–9

Grimes, W F 1964 'Excavations in the Lake group of barrows, Wilsford, Wiltshire, in 1959'. *Bull Inst Arch* **4**, 89–121

Grinsell, L V 1941 'The Bronze Age round barrows of Wessex'. *Proc Prehist Soc* **7**, 73–113

Grinsell, L V 1957 'Archaeological gazetteer' in Pugh, R B (ed) *A History of Wiltshire* **1.1**. VCH. London: Oxford University Press, 21–279

Grinsell, L V 1978 *The Stonehenge Barrow Groups*. Salisbury: Salisbury and South Wiltshire Museum

Groube, L M and Bowden, M C B 1982 *The Archaeology of Rural Dorset: Past, Present and Future*. Dorchester: Dorset Natur Hist Archaeol Soc

Hamilton, D, Pitts, M and Reynolds, A 2007 'A revised date for the early medieval execution at Stonehenge'. *Wiltshire Archaeol and Natur Hist Mag* **100**, 202–3

Harding, J 1999 'Pathways to new realms: cursus monuments and symbolic territories' in Barclay and Harding 1999, 30–8

Harding, J 2003 *Henge Monuments of the British Isles*. Tempus: Stroud

Harding, P 1988 'The chalk plaque pit, Amesbury'. *Proc Prehist Soc* **54**, 320–7

Hare, J N 1981 'Durrington: a chalkland village in the later Middle Ages'. *Wiltshire Archaeol Natur Hist Mag* **74/5**, 137–47

Hare, J N 1994 'Agriculture and rural settlement in the chalklands of Wiltshire and Hampshire from *c*1200–*c*1500' in Aston, M and Lewis, C (eds) *The Medieval Landscape of Wessex* Oxbow Monograph **46**. Oxford: Oxbow

Harris, V and Goto, K 2003 *William Gowland: The Father of Japanese Archaeology*. London: British Museum Press

Haslam, J 1984 *Anglo-Saxon Towns in Southern England*. Chichester: Phillimore

Hassall, M W C 1980 'Altars, curses and other epigraphic evidence' in Rodwell, W (ed) *Temples, Churches and Religion: Recent Research in Roman Britain*. Brit Archaeol Rep **77**. Oxford: BAR Brit Ser, 79–90

Hawley, W 1921 'Stonehenge: interim report on the exploration'. *Antiq J* **1**, 19–41

Hawley, W 1922 'Second report on the excavations at Stonehenge'. *Antiq J* **2**, 36–51

Hawley, W 1923 'Third report on the excavations at Stonehenge'. *Antiq J* **3**, 13–20

Hawley, W 1925 'Report on the excavations at Stonehenge during the season of 1923'. *Antiq J* **5**, 21–50

Hawley, W 1926 'Report on the excavations at Stonehenge during the season of 1924'. *Antiq J* **6**, 1–25

Hawley, W 1928 'Report on the excavations at Stonehenge during 1925 and 1926'. *Antiq J* **8**, 149–76

Haynes, R and Slocombe, I 2004 *Wiltshire Toll Houses*. East Knoyle: Hobnob

Haynes, S 2012 'The reinterpretation of a prehistoric landscape in the eighteenth century: how far did the presence of prehistoric earthworks at Amesbury Abbey, and in the surrounding landscape, influence the 1738 design of Charles Bridgeman?'. Unpublished dissertation, University of East Anglia

Hey, D (ed) 2010 *The Oxford Companion to Family and Local History*. Oxford: Oxford University Press

Higgs, E S 1959 'The excavation of a late Mesolithic site at Downton, near Salisbury, Wilts'. *Proc Prehist Soc* **25**, 209–32

Hill, R 2008 *Stonehenge*. London: Profile

Hoare, R C 1812 *The Ancient History of Wiltshire* **1**. London: William Miller. (facsim edn EP Publishing 1975)

Hornsey, R 1987 'The Grand Menhir Brisé: megalithic success or failure?' *Oxford J Archaeol* **6.2**, 185–217

Hudson, W R 1911 *Afoot in England*, 2nd edn. London: Hutchinson

Hudson, W R 1987 *The Illustrated Shepherd's Life*. London: Bracken (originally published 1910)

Hunter Mann, K 1999 'Excavations at Vespasian's Camp Iron Age hillfort, 1987'. *Wiltshire Archaeol Natur Hist Mag* **92**, 39–52

Hutton, R 2009 *Blood and Mistletoe: The History of the Druids in Britain*. London: Yale University Press

Ingold, T 2013 *Making: Anthropology, Archaeology, Art and Architecture*. Abingdon: Routledge

Jacques, D, Phillips, T and Lyons, T 2012 'Vespasian's Camp: cradle of Stonehenge?' *Curr Archaeol* **271**, 28–33

James, N D G 1987 *Plain Soldiering: A History of the Armed Forces on Salisbury Plain*. Salisbury: Hobnob

Jefferies, R 2006 *The Open Air*. Stroud: Nonsuch (originally published 1885)

Johnson, A 2008 *Solving Stonehenge: The New Key to an Ancient Enigma*. London: Thames & Hudson

Johnson, M 2007 *Ideas of Landscape*. Oxford: Blackwells

Jones, A M 2005 *Cornish Bronze Age Ceremonial Landscapes, c 2500–1500 BC* Brit Archaeol Rep **394**. Oxford: Archaeopress

Jones, I 1655 *The Most Notable Antiquity of Great Britain, Vulgarly Called Stone-Heng, on Salisbury Plain, Restored*. London: Pakeman and Chapman (facsim edn Scolar Press 1972)

Kerridge, E 1959 'Agriculture, *c* 1500 – *c* 1793' in Crittall, E (ed) *A History of Wiltshire* **4**. VCH. London: Institute of Historical

Research/Oxford University Press, 43–64

Kinnes, I 1979 *Round Barrows and Ring-Ditches in the British Neolithic* Brit Mus Occas Pap **7**. London: British Museum

Kirkham, G 2012 '"Rip it up, and spread it over the field": post-medieval agriculture and the destruction of monuments: a case study from Cornwall'. *Landscapes* **13**.2, 1–20

Komar, A 2010 *Stonehenge World Heritage Site Landscape Project: Lake Down, Wilsford-cum-Lake: Archaeological Survey Report* Research Department Report Series **95-2010**. Portsmouth: English Heritage

Komar, A and Bishop, S 2010 *Stonehenge World Heritage Site Landscape Project: Fargo South, Amesbury: Archaeological Survey Report*. Research Department Report Series **96-2010**. Portsmouth: English Heritage

Lambrick, G 1988 *The Rollright Stones: Megaliths, Monuments and Settlement in the Prehistoric Landscape*. London: Historic Buildings and Monuments Commission for England

Lambrick, G and Allen, T G 2004 *Gravelly Guy, Stanton Harcourt, Oxfordshire: The Development of a Prehistoric and Romano-British Community*. Oxford: Oxford Archaeology

Land Classification Survey 1947 *Land Classification of Gloucestershire, Somerset and Wiltshire*. University of Bristol/Arrowsmith

Lane, R 2011 *Stonehenge World Heritage Site Landscape Project: Stonehenge, Amesbury, Wiltshire: Architectural Assessment* Research Department Report Series **42-2011**. Portsmouth: English Heritage

Lane Fox, A H 1870 'On the proposed exploration of Stonehenge by a committee of the British Association'. *J Ethnol Soc London* new ser. **1** (1869–70), 1–5

Last, J (ed) 2007 *Beyond the Grave: New Perspectives on Barrows*. Oxford: Oxbow

Lawson, A J 2007 *Chalkland: An Archaeology of Stonehenge and Its Region*. Salisbury: Hobnob

Leary, J 2011 'It's official – the Marlborough Mount is prehistoric'. *Past* **68**, 4–5

Lee, R 2009 *The Production, Use and Disposal of Romano-British Pewter Tableware* Brit Archaeol Rep **478**. Oxford: Archaeopress

Leivers, M and Moore, C 2008 *Archaeology on the A303 Stonehenge Improvement*. Salisbury: Wessex Archaeology

Lewis, C A 1994 'Patterns and processes in the medieval settlement of Wiltshire' *in* Aston, M and Lewis, C A (eds) *The Medieval Landscape of Wessex*. Oxford: Oxbow, 171–93

Lewis, J and Mullin, D 2012 'West of Wessex but only just: round barrow construction on the Mendip Hills, Somerset' *in* Britnell, W J and Silvester, R J (eds) *Reflections on the Past: Essays in Honour of Frances Lynch*. Welshpool: Cambrian Archaeological Association, 194–209

Linford, N 2013 *Stonehenge, Wiltshire, Report on Magnetic Susceptibility Survey, January 2013* Research Report Series **49-2013**. Portsmouth: English Heritage

Linford, N, Linford, P and Payne, A 2012 *Stonehenge Monument Field and Barrows, Wiltshire: Report On Geophysical Surveys, September 2010, April and July 2011* Research Report Series **34-2012**. Portsmouth: English Heritage

Litchfield, H 1915 *Emma Darwin: A Century of Family Letters, 1792–1896*. London: John Murray

Long, W 1876 'Stonehenge and its barrows'. *Wiltshire Archaeol Natur Hist Mag* **16**, 1–244

Loveday, R 2006 *Inscribed across the Landscape: The Cursus Enigma*. Stroud: Tempus

Lynch, F and Musson, C 2001 'A prehistoric and early medieval complex at Llandegai, near Bangor, North Wales: excavations directed by C. H. Houlder, 1966–1967'. *Archaeol Cambrensis* **150**, 17–142

Margetson, S 1985 'Sweet tempered satirist: John Gay and the Beggar's Opera'. *Country Life* **178**.4596, 19 September, 832–3

Marshall, P, Bronk Ramsey, C and Cook, G forthcoming 'Radiocarbon dating' *in* Parker Pearson, M (ed) *The Stonehenge Riverside Project*

Marshall, P, Darvill, T, Parker Pearson, M and Wainwright, G J 2012 *Stonehenge, Amesbury, Wiltshire: Chronological Modelling: Scientific Dating Report*. Research Report Series **1-2012**. Portsmouth: English Heritage

Marshman, M 1984 *A Wiltshire Landscape: Scenes from the Countryside, 1920 – 1940*. Newbury: Countryside Books/CPRE, Wiltshire Branch

Maskelyne, N S 1878 'Stonehenge: the petrology of its stones'. *Wiltshire Archaeol Natur Hist Mag* **17**, 147–60

Maton, W G 1800 'Account of the fall of some of the stones of Stonehenge in a letter from William George Maton MBFAS to Aylmer Bourke Lambert FRS and FAS, read 29 June 1797'. *Archaeologia* **13**, 103–6

McCann, J and McCann, P 2011 *The Dovecotes and Pigeon Lofts of Wiltshire*. Salisbury: Hobnob for the Wiltshire Buildings Record

McFadyen, L 2007 'Making architecture' *in* Benson, D and Whittle, A (eds) *Building Memories: The Neolithic Cotswold Long Barrow at Ascott-under-Wychwood, Oxfordshire*. Oxbow: Oxford, 348–54

McKinley, J I 1999 'Further excavation of an Iron Age and Romano-British enclosed settlement at Figheldean, near Netheravon'. *Wiltshire Archaeol Natur Hist Mag* **92**, 7–32

McKinley, J I 2003 'A Wiltshire "bog body"? Discussion of a fifth/sixth century AD burial in the Woodford valley'. *Wiltshire Archaeol Natur Hist Mag* **96**, 7–18

McOmish, D S 2001 'Settlement in western Wessex' *in* Collis, J (ed) *Society and Settlement in Iron Age Europe: L'Habitat et l'Occupation du Sol en Europe – Actes du XVIIIe Colloque de l'AFEAF, Winchester, April 1994*. Sheffield: J R Collis, 73–81

McOmish, D S 2003 'Cursus: solving a 6,000 year-old puzzle'. *Brit Archaeol* **69**, 9–13

McOmish, D S, Field, D J and Brown, G 2002 *The Field Archaeology of the Salisbury Plain Training Area*. Swindon: English Heritage

McOmish, D S, Field, D J and Brown, G 2010 'The Late Bronze Age and Early Iron Age midden site at East Chisenbury, Wiltshire'. *Wiltshire Archaeol Natur Hist Mag* **103**, 35–101

Mepham, L N 1995 'Post-Roman pottery' *in* Cleal *et al* 1995, 435

Merewether, J 1851 'Diary of the examination of barrows and other earthworks in the neighbourhood of Silbury Hill and Avebury, Wilts, in July and August 1849' *Memoirs Illustrative of the History and Antiquities of Wiltshire and the City of Salisbury Communicated to the Annual Meeting of the Archaeological Institute of Great Britain and Ireland, Held at Salisbury, July 1849*. London: George Bell

Miles, W A 1826 *A Description of the Deverel Barrow, opened AD 1825*. London: Nichols

Molland, R 1959 'Agriculture *c*1793 – *c*1870' *in* Crittall, E (ed) *A History of Wiltshire* **4**. VCH. London: Institute of Historical Research/Oxford University Press, 65–91

Montague, R 1995 'Metalwork' *in* Cleal *et al* 1995, 432–4

Montague, R and Gardiner, J 1995 'Other stone' *in* Cleal *et al* 1995, 390–9

Morris, E L 1995 'Later prehistoric pottery' *in* Cleal *et al* 1995, 434–5

Morris, R 2012 *Time's Anvil: England, Archaeology and the Imagination*. London: Weidenfeld and Nicolson

Morris, W 1877 *Manifesto of the Society for the Protection of Ancient Buildings* www.spab.org.uk/what-is-spab/the-manifesto/ [accessed 5 December 2013]

Morrison, K A 1997 'The New-Poor-Law workhouses of George Gilbert Scott and William Bonython Moffatt'. *Architect Hist* **40**, 184–203

Morrison, K A 1999 *The Workhouse: A Study of Poor Law Buildings in England*. Swindon: RCHME

Murray, H K, Murray, J C and Fraser, S M 2009 *A Tale of the Unknown Unknowns: A Mesolithic Pit Alignment and a Neolithic Timber Hall at Warren Field, Crathes, Aberdeenshire*. Oxford: Oxbow

Myers, K 2013 'Ways of seeing: Joseph Addison, enchantment and the early landscape garden'. *Garden Hist* **41.1**, 3–20

Needham, S, Lawson, A and Woodward, A 2009 'Rethinking Bush Barrow'. *Brit Archaeol* **104**, 12–17

Needham, S, Lawson, A J and Woodward, A 2010 '"A noble group of barrows": Bush Barrow and the Normanton Down Early Bronze Age cemetery two centuries on'. *Antiq J* **90**, 1–39

Newman, R, Cranstone, D and Howard-Davis, C 2001 *The Historical Archaeology of Britain c.1540–1900*. Stroud: Sutton

Noyes, E 1913 *Salisbury Plain: Its Stones, Cathedral, City, Valleys and Folk*. London: Dent

Office of Works 1912 *Ancient Monuments and Historic Buildings: Report of the Inspector of Ancient Monuments for the Year Ending 31st March 1912*. London: HMSO

Ogilby, J 1675 *Britannia Volume the First, or, An Illustration of the Kingdom of England*. (facsim edn Duckham 1939) (Published in 1971 as *Road Maps of England and Wales from Ogilby's Britannia*. Reading: Osprey)

O'Kelly, M 1982 *Newgrange: Archaeology, Art and Legend*. London: Thames & Hudson

Oliver, N 2011 *A History of Ancient Britain*. London: Weidenfeld and Nicolson

Oliver, R 1993 *Ordnance Survey Maps: A Concise Guide for Historians*. London: Charles Close Society

Oswald, A W P 1999 'A hillfort on Ring Hill, Littlebury, Essex' *in* Pattison, P, Field, D and Ainsworth, S (eds) 1999 *Patterns of the Past: Essays in Landscape Archaeology for Chris Taylor*. Oxford: Oxbow, 23–8

Oswald, A W P, Barber, M and Dyer, C 2001 *Creation of Monuments: Neolithic Causewayed Enclosures in the British Isles*. Swindon: English Heritage

Parfitt, K and Needham, S 2012 'Ringlemere: a pit/post horseshoe and henge monument in East Kent' *in* Gibson, A (ed) *Enclosing the Neolithic: Recent Studies in Britain and Europe* BAR Inter Ser **2440**. Oxford: Archaeopress, 81–92

Parker Pearson, M 2012 *Stonehenge: Exploring the Greatest Stone Age Mystery*. Simon & Schuster: London

Parker Pearson, M and Ramilisonina 1998 'Stonehenge for the ancestors'. *Antiquity* **72**, 308–26 and 855–6

Parker Pearson, M, Allen, M, Baver, O, Casswell, C *et al* 2008 'Stonehenge Riverside Project 2008 Interim Report'. Unpublished report, University of Sheffield

Parker Pearson, M, Allen, M, Pollard, J, Richards, C *et al* 2007 'The Stonehenge Riverside Project 2007: Full Interim Report'. Unpublished report, University of Sheffield

Parker Pearson, M, Chamberlain, A, Jay, M, Marshall, P *et al* 2009 'Who was buried at Stonehenge?' *Antiquity* **83**, 23–39

Passmore, A D 1924 'Notes: barrow 25 (Goddard's list) Winterbourne Stoke'. *Wiltshire Archaeol Natur Hist Mag* **42**, 248

Payne, A 1995 'Geophysical surveys at Stonehenge, 1993–4' *in* Cleal *et al* 1995, 495–510

Pearson, T and Field, D J 2011 *Stonehenge WHS Landscape Project: Stonehenge Cursus, Amesbury, Wiltshire: Archaeological Survey Report* Research Department Report Series **103-2011**. Portsmouth: English Heritage

Peers, C 1931 'The treatment of old buildings'. *Architect J* **38** 3rd ser. 311–20

Peters, F 2000 'Two traditions of Bronze Age burial in the Stonehenge landscape'. *Oxford J Archaeol* **19.4**, 343–58

Petrie, W M F 1880 *Stonehenge: Plans, Description and Theories*. Repr 1989: London: Histories & Mysteries of Man

Piggott, S 1939 'Timber circles: a re-examination'. *Archaeol J* **96**, 193–222

Piggott, S 1951 'Stonehenge reviewed' *in* Grimes, W F (ed) *Aspects of Archaeology in Britain and Beyond: Essays Presented to OGS Crawford*. London: Edwards, 274–92

Piggott, S 1968 *The Druids*. London: Thames & Hudson

Piggott, S 1973 'The final phase of bronze technology' *in* Crittall, E (ed) *History of Wiltshire* **1.2**. VCH. London: Institute of Historical Research/Oxford University Press, 376–407

Piggott, S 1976 *Ruins in a Landscape: Essays in Antiquarianism*. Edinburgh: Edinburgh University Press

Piggott, S 1978 *Antiquity Depicted: Aspects of Archaeological Illustration*. London: Thames & Hudson

Pitts, M W 1981a 'Notes on two barrows near Stonehenge'. *Wiltshire Archaeol Natur Hist Mag* **74/5** (for 1979/1980), 181–4

Pitts, M W 1981b 'Stones, pits and Stonehenge'. *Nature* **290**, 46–7

Pitts, M W 1982 'On the road to Stonehenge: report on investigations beside the A344 in 1968, 1979 and 1980'. *Proc Prehist Soc* **48**, 75–132

Pitts, M W 2000 *Hengeworld*. London: Century

Pitts, M W 2001 'Excavating the Sanctuary: new investigations on Overton Hill, Avebury'. *Wiltshire Archaeol Natur Hist Mag* **94**, 1–23

Pitts, M W 2008 'Stonehenge'. *Brit Archaeol* **102**, 13–17

Pitts, M W, Bayliss, A, McKinley, J I, Boylston, A *et al* 2002 'An Anglo-Saxon decapitation and burial at Stonehenge'. *Wiltshire Archaeol Natur Hist Mag* **95**, 131–46

Pollard, J 1995a 'Structured deposition at Woodhenge'. *Proc Prehist Soc* **61**, 137–56

Pollard, J 1995b 'The Durrington 68 timber circle: a forgotten late Neolithic monument'. *Wiltshire Archaeol Natur Hist Mag* **88**, 122–5

Pollard, J and Reynolds, A 2002 *Avebury: The Biography of a Landscape*. Tempus: Stroud

Pollard, J and Robinson, D 2007 'A return to Woodhenge: the results and implications of the 2006 excavations' *in* Larsson, M and Parker Pearson, M (eds) *From Stonehenge to the Baltic: Living with Cultural Diversity in the Third Millennium BC* BAR Inter Ser **1692**. Oxford: Archaeopress, 159–68

Pollard, J and Ruggles, C L N 2001 'Shifting perceptions: spatial order, cosmology and patterns of deposition at Stonehenge'. *Cambridge Archaeol J* **11.1**, 69–90

Priddle, R 2003 *Wings over Wiltshire*. Sheffield: ALD

Pryor, F 1991 *Flag Fen*. London: English Heritage/Batsford

Pryor, F 2001 *Seahenge*. London: HarperCollins

Pryor, F, French, C, Crowther, D, Gurney, D *et al* 1985 *The Fenland Project, Number 1: Archaeology and Environment in the Lower Welland Valley* East Anglian Archaeology 27 (2 vols). Cambridge: Cambridgeshire Archaeological Committee

Rackham, O 1986 *The History of the Countryside*. London: Dent

Rawlings, M and Fitzpatrick, A 1996 'Prehistoric sites and a Romano-British settlement at Butterfield Down, Amesbury'. *Wiltshire Archaeol Natur Hist Mag* **89**, 1–43

RCHME 1979 *Stonehenge and Its Environs: Monuments and Land Use* Royal Commission on the Historical Monuments of England. Edinburgh: Edinburgh University Press

RCHME 1987 *The Churches of South-East Wiltshire*. London: HMSO

Richards, C 2013 'Interpreting stone circles' in Richards, C (ed) *Building the Great Stone Circles of the North*. Oxford: Windgather, 2–30

Richards, C and Thomas, J 2012 'The Stonehenge landscape before Stonehenge' in Jones, A M, Pollard, J, Allen, M J and Gardiner, J (eds) *Image, Memory and Monumentality: Archaeological Engagements with the Material World: A Celebration of the Academic Achievements of Professor Richard Bradley*. Prehist Soc Res Rep **5**. London: Prehistoric Society; Oxford: Oxbow, 29–42

Richards, J 1990 *The Stonehenge Environs Project* Engl Heritage Archaeol Rep **16**. London: Historic Buildings and Monuments Commission for England

Richards, J 2007 *Stonehenge: The Story So Far*. Swindon: English Heritage

Richards, J 2013 *Stonehenge* English Heritage Guidebooks. London: English Heritage

Richards, J and Whitby, P 1997 'The engineering of Stonehenge' in Cunliffe and Renfrew 1997, 231–56

Riley, H and Wilson-North, R 2001 *The Field Archaeology of Exmoor*. Swindon: English Heritage

Robinson, P 1991 'A Durotrigian coin from Stonehenge'. *Wiltshire Archaeol Natur Hist Mag* **84**, 119–20

Roe, D 1969 'An archaeological survey and policy for Wiltshire, part 1: Palaeolithic'. *Wiltshire Archaeol Natur Hist Mag* **64** 1–18

Ruggles, C L N 1997 'Astronomy and Stonehenge' in Cunliffe and Renfrew 1997, 203–30

Ruggles, C L N 1999 *Astronomy in Prehistoric Britain and Ireland*. London: Yale University Press

Ruggles, C L N and Saunders, N J (eds) 1993 *Astronomies and Cultures*. Niwot: University Press of Colorado

Ruskin, J 1871 *The Seven Lamps of Architecture*. New York: John Wiley (first published 1849)

Sandell, R E 1971 *Abstracts of Wiltshire Inclosure Awards and Agreements* Wiltshire Record Society **25**. Devizes: Wiltshire Record Society

Sawyer, R 2001 *Little Imber on the Down: Salisbury Plain's Ghost Village*. East Knoyle: Hobnob

Schama, S 1995 *Landscape and Memory*. London: Fontana

Seager Smith, R 1995 'Romano-British pottery' in Cleal *et al* 1995, 435

Sheeran, G 2006 'Patriotic views: aristocratic ideology and the 18th-century landscape'. *Landscapes* **7.2**, 1–23

SHL 2012 *Interim Geophysical Survey Report: Field Season 2 (2011–2012)* for the National Trust and English Heritage

Simpson, D D A 1975 'Introduction' to reprint of R C Hoare 1812 *Ancient Wiltshire*. Wakefield: EP Publishing for Wiltshire County Council

Slocombe, P M 1989 *Wiltshire Farm Buildings, 1500–1900* Wiltshire Buildings Record Monograph **2**. Devizes: Devizes Books

Smiles, S 1994 *The Image of Antiquity: Ancient Britain and the Romantic Imagination*. New Haven and London: Yale University Press

Smith, I F 1991 'Round barrows, Wilsford cum Lake G51–G54: excavations by Ernest Greenfield in 1958'. *Wiltshire Archaeol Natur Hist Mag* **84**, 11–39

Smith, J 1771 *Choir Gaur: The Grand Orrery of the Ancient Druids Commonly Called Stonehenge, on Salisbury Plain*. Salisbury

Smith, N A 2005 'Medieval and later sheep farming on the Marlborough Downs' in Brown, G, Field, D and McOmish, D (eds) *The Avebury Landscape: Aspects of the Field Archaeology of the Marlborough Downs*. Oxford: Oxbow, 191–201

Smith, R J C, Healy, F, Allen, M J, Morris, E L *et al* 1997 *Excavations along the Route of the Dorchester By-pass, Dorset, 1986–8* Wessex Archaeol Rep **11**. Salisbury: Wessex Archaeology

Soutar, S 2012 *Stonehenge World Heritage Site Landscape Project: Larkhill Barrows, Durrington: Archaeological Survey Report* Research Report Series **3-2012**. Swindon: English Heritage

Sparks, W W and Lewis, W V 1958 'Escarpment dry valleys near Pegsdon, Hertfordshire'. *Proc Geol Ass* **69**, 26–38

SSEW 1983 *Legend for the 1:250,000 Soil Map of England and Wales: A Brief Explanation of the Constituent Soil Associations*. Harpenden: Soil Survey of England and Wales

Stackhouse, T 1833 *Two Lectures on the Remains of Ancient Pagan Britain*. London: privately published

Stead, I M 1991 *Iron Age Cemeteries in East Yorkshire: Excavations at Burton Fleming, Rudston, Garton-on-the-Wolds and Kirkburn*. London: English Heritage in association with British Museum Press

Stevens, E T 1870 *Flint Chips: A Guide to Prehistoric Archaeology*. London: Bell and Daldy

Stevens, F 1916 *Stonehenge Today and Yesterday*. London: HMSO

Stevens, F 1929 *Stonehenge Today and Yesterday* rev edn. London: HMSO

Stevenson, J H 1995 'Durrington' in Crowley, D A (ed) *A History of the County of Wiltshire* **15**: *Amesbury Hundred, Branch and Dole Hundred*. VCH. Oxford: Oxford University Press/Institute of Historical Research, 93–105

Stone, J F S 1939 'An Early Bronze Age grave in Fargo Plantation near Stonehenge'. *Wiltshire Archaeol Natur Hist Mag* **48**, 357–70

Stone, J F S 1947 'The Stonehenge Cursus and its affinities'. *Archaeol J* **104**, 7–19

Stone, J F S and Young, W E V 1948 'Two pits of Grooved Ware date near Woodhenge'. *Wiltshire Archaeol Natur Hist Mag* **52**, 287–306

Stout, A 2008 *Creating Prehistory: Druids, Ley Hunters and Archaeologists in Pre-war Britain* Oxford: Blackwell

Stukeley, W 1740 *Stonehenge: A Temple Restor'd to the British Druids*. London: Innes and Manby

Sumner, H 1913 *The Ancient Earthworks of Cranborne Chase*. London: Chiswick

Symes, M 2006 *A Glossary of Garden History*, 3 edn. Princes Risborough: Shire

Tankins, C M 1975 'Farming changes in two Wiltshire villages: Durrington and Shrewton (1760–1860)'. Individual study for BEd degree, College of Sarum St Michael, WHC DUR630

Tarlow, S 2007 *The Archaeology of Improvement in Britain, 1750–1850*. Cambridge: Cambridge University Press

Tennant, P 1906 'Wilsford Manor: a seat of Sir Edward Tennant, Bart'. *Country Life* **20.508**, 450–7

Thacker, C 1983 *The Wildness Pleases: The Origins of Romanticism*. London: Croom Helm

Thomas, J S, Parker Pearson, M, Pollard, J, Richards, C *et al* 2009 'The date of the Stonehenge Cursus'. *Antiquity* **83**, 40–53

Thomas, N 2005 *Snail Down, Wiltshire: The Bronze Age Barrow Cemetery and Related Earthworks, in the Parishes of Collingbourne Ducis and Collingbourne Kingston: Excavations 1953, 1955 and 1957* Wiltshire Archaeol Natur Hist Soc Monogr **3**. Devizes: WANHS

Thurley, S 2013 *Men from the Ministry: How Britain Saved Its Heritage*. London: Yale University Press

Thurnam, J 1865 'On the two principal forms of ancient British and Gaulish skulls'. *Memoir Anthrop Soc* **1**, 120–68

Thurnam, J 1868 'On ancient British barrows, especially those of Wiltshire and adjacent counties, part 1: long barrows'. *Archaeologia* **42.1**, 161–244

Thurnam, J 1871 'On ancient British barrows, especially those of Wiltshire and adjacent counties, part 2: round barrows'. *Archaeologia* **43.2**, 285–544

Tilley, C, Richards, C, Bennett, W and Field, D J 2007 'Stonehenge – its landscape and its architecture: a reanalysis' *in* Larsson, M and Parker Pearson, M (eds) *From Stonehenge to the Baltic: Living with Cultural Diversity in the 3rd Millennium BC* BAR Inter Ser **1692**. Oxford: Archaeopress, 183–204

Turner, R 2007 'Fabric, form and function: the Society and "the restoration question"' *in* Pearce, S (ed) *Visions of Antiquity: The Society of Antiquaries of London 1707–2007*. London: Society of Antiquaries of London, 307–27

Uglow, J 2004 *A Little History of British Gardening*. London: Chatto & Windus

Vatcher, F de M 1961 'The excavation of the long mortuary enclosure on Normanton Down, Wilts'. *Proc Prehist Soc* **27**, 160–73

Vatcher, F de M and Vatcher, H L 1969 'Amesbury: King Barrow Wood to Stonehenge (SU 123423 – SU 134421)'. *Wiltshire Archaeol Natur Hist Mag* **64**, 123

Viner, S, Evans, J, Albarella, U and Parker Pearson, M 2010 'Cattle mobility in prehistoric Britain: strontium isotope analysis of cattle teeth from Durrington Walls (Wiltshire, Britain)'. *J Archaeol Sci* **37**, 2812–20

Wade-Martins, S 1995 *Farms and Fields*. London: Batsford

Wainwright, G J and Longworth, I H 1971 *Durrington Walls: Excavations, 1966–1968* Soc of Antiq London Res Rep **29**

Wainwright, G J, Donaldson, P, Longworth, I H and Swan, V G 1971 'The excavation of prehistoric and Romano-British settlements near Durrington Walls, Wiltshire, 1970'. *Wiltshire Archaeol Natur Hist Mag* **66**, 76–128

Walker, K E and Gardiner, J 1995 'Post-excavation rationale' *in* Cleal *et al* 1995, 20–2

WANHS 1952 *Andrews' and Dury's Map of Wiltshire, 1773: A Reduced Facsimile* Wiltshire Record Society **8**. Devizes: Wiltshire Archaeological and Natural History Society

Watts, D G 1962 'Wilsford' *in* Crittall, E (ed) *A History of the County of Wiltshire* **6**: *Old and New Salisbury, Wilton and Underditch Hundred*. London: Oxford University Press/Institute of Historical Research, 213–21

Welfare, H G 1989 'John Aubrey: the first archaeological surveyor?' *in* Bowden, M C B, Mackay, D A and Topping, P (eds) *From Cornwall to Caithness: Aspects of British Field Archaeology* BAR **209**. Oxford: BAR, 17–28

Whitaker, W and Edmonds, F H 1925 *The Water Supply of Wiltshire* Memoir of the Geological Survey of the UK. London: HMSO

Whitehead, P and Edmunds, M 2012 *Silbury Hill, Wiltshire: Palaeohydrology of the Kennet, Swallowhead Springs and the Siting of Silbury Hill* Research Report Series **12-2012**. Portsmouth: English Heritage

Whittle, A, Healy, F and Bayliss, A 2011 *Gathering Time: Dating the Early Neolithic Enclosures of Southern Britain and Ireland*. Oxford: Oxbow

Whyte, I D 2002 *Landscape and History since 1500*. London: Reaktion

Wickham, L 2012 *Gardens in History: A Political Perspective*. Oxford: Windgather

Wickstead, H 2014 'Another proof of the preceding theory: film, materialities and Stonehenge' *in* Russell, I A and Cochrane, A (eds) *Art and Archaeology: Collaborations, Conversations, Criticisms* One World Archaeology **11**. New York: Springer, 99–114

Williamson, T 2007 'Archaeological perspectives on landed estates: research agendas' *in* Finch and Giles 2007, 1–16

Wood, J 1747 *Choir Gaure, Vulgarly Called Stonehenge, on Salisbury Plain, Described, Restored and Explained*. Oxford: printed at the Theatre

Woodbridge, K 2002 *The Stourhead Landscape, Wiltshire*. London: National Trust

Woodward, A B and Needham, S 2012 'Diversity and distinction: characterising the individual buried at Wilsford G58, Wiltshire' *in* Jones, A M, Pollard, J, Allen, M J and Gardiner, J (eds) *Image, Memory and Monumentality: Archaeological Engagements with the Material World: A Celebration of the Academic Achievements of Professor Richard Bradley* Prehist Soc Res Rep **5**. London: Prehistoric Society; Oxford: Oxbow, 116–26

Woodward, A B and Woodward, P J 1996 'The topography of some barrow cemeteries in Bronze Age Wessex'. *Proc Prehist Soc* **62**, 275–91

Worley, F 2013 'Animal resources' *in* Canti, M, Campbell, G and Greaney, S (eds) *Stonehenge World Heritage Site Synthesis: Prehistoric Landscape, Environment and Economy* Research Report Series **45-2013**. Portsmouth: English Heritage, 55–87

Worthington, A 2004 *Stonehenge: Celebration and Subversion*. Loughborough: Alternative Albion

Worthington, A (ed) 2005 *The Battle of the Beanfield*. Teignmouth: Enabler

Wright, G N 2008 *Turnpike Roads*. Oxford: Shire

Wymer, J J 1977 *Gazetteer of Mesolithic Sites in England and Wales* CBA Res Rep **20**. London: Geo Abstracts and the Council for British Archaeology

Wymer, J J 1999 *The Lower Palaeolithic Occupation of Britain*. Salisbury: English Heritage/Trust for Wessex Archaeology

Yates, D T 2007 *Land, Power and Prestige: Bronze Age Field Systems in Southern England*. Oxford: Oxbow

Yorke, B 1995 *Wessex in the Early Middle Ages*. London: Leicester University Press

Young, C, Chadburn, A and Bedu, I 2009 *Stonehenge World Heritage Site: Management Plan, 2009*. London: English Heritage

Documents

Bodleian Library, Oxford

MS Gough Drawings a3*, folio 32, Charles Bridgeman's plan of Amesbury Abbey
MS Gough Maps 229, various folios, William Stukeley's sketches and plates

English Heritage Archives, Swindon

MP/STO0035   Ministry of Works plan of Stonehenge showing the area enclosed in March 1920, surveyed August 1920

Institute of Historical Research, London

Seymour papers, microfilm vol 12, folios 247–56 (originals at Longleat House, Warminster)

The National Archives (TNA), Kew

MUN 4/6054	9 May 1923, memo
	14 May 1923, memo
WORK 14/214	28 April 1917, report by Harry Sirr
	22 January 1919, memo, Charles Peers
WORK 14/464	8 August 1938, memo
	8 October 1952, memo
WORK 14/485	24 January 1919, memo
	29 September 1919, memo, Charles Peers
	18 February 1920, report by Arthur Heasman
WORK 14/488	8 July 1927, letter
WORK 14/837	23 April 1935, memo
	9 November 1936, letter, Matheson, NT
	19 November 1936, memo
WORK 14/838	21 December 1930, memo
WORK 14/2463	25 October 1921, letter, Engleheart to Peers
	24 December 1941, letter
	16 January 1942, memo
	26 January 1942, letter
	3 February 1942, note
WORK 14/2464	1919, report on condition of the stones

Wiltshire Heritage Museum (WHM), Devizes

Cunnington, W 1801–9, books 1–13, bound in three volumes, Devizes Museum, DZSWS: MSS 2594–6

Wiltshire and Swindon History Centre (WHC), Chippenham

283/6	Amesbury Abbey Survey, 1741: Walls Field, etc
283/188	Expence of New Bridge on Turnpike Road and altering course of river, 1775
283/202	Amesbury Estate sales particulars, 1823
944/1, 2	Amesbury Estate: Flitcroft's survey and key, 1726
944/3	Field book, 1771
1552/2/2/4H	Henry Doidge's map of the Manor of Lake, 1752
1619H	Map of Normanton, 1768
1619/box 7	3rd Duke of Queensberry, assorted deeds
EA 36	Enclosure award, Durnford North End/Hungerford Durnford
EA 104	Enclosure award, Winterbourne Stoke
EA 144	Durrington Enclosure Act
H2/110/1	Minutes of Amesbury Union Board, January 1836
Tithe awards (TAs)	Amesbury, 1846; Lake, 1848; Wilsford, near Amesbury, 1846; Winterbourne Stoke, 1841; Woodford, 1842